WHY ANIMAL SUFFERING MATTERS

WHY ANIMAL SUFFERING MATTERS

Philosophy, Theology, and Practical Ethics

ANDREW LINZEY

UNIVERSITY PRESS

2009

OXFORD
UNIVERSITY PRESS

Oxford University Press, Inc., publishes works that further
Oxford University's objective of excellence
in research, scholarship, and education.

Oxford   New York
Auckland   Cape Town   Dar es Salaam   Hong Kong   Karachi
Kuala Lumpur   Madrid   Melbourne   Mexico City   Nairobi
New Delhi   Shanghai   Taipei   Toronto

With offices in
Argentina   Austria   Brazil   Chile   Czech Republic   France   Greece
Guatemala   Hungary   Italy   Japan   Poland   Portugal   Singapore
South Korea   Switzerland   Thailand   Turkey   Ukraine   Vietnam

Copyright © 2009 by Oxford University Press, Inc.

Published by Oxford University Press, Inc.
198 Madison Avenue, New York, New York 10016

www.oup.com

Oxford is a registered trademark of Oxford University Press

Library of Congress Cataloging-in-Publication Data
Linzey, Andrew.
Why animal suffering matters : philosophy, theology, and practical ethics /
Andrew Linzey.
   p.   cm.
Includes index.
ISBN 978-0-19-537977-8
1. Animal welfare—Moral and ethical aspects.   I. Title.
HV4708.L5644 2009
179'.3—dc22   2008046491

9 8 7 6 5 4 3 2 1

Printed in the United States of America
on acid-free paper

For my daughter
REBECCA
whose sensitivity to animals
is rivalled only by
St Francis of Assisi.

ACKNOWLEDGMENTS

This book has had a long intellectual gestation. It has emerged intermittently over many years as I have wrestled with the basic moral case for animals. The chapters finally published here are the result of my reworking of previous papers and lectures, some published, some partly so. I would like to thank all those who have had a hand in this book's making, through either encouragement or criticism.

Chapter 1, "Why Animal Suffering Matters Morally," was tried on many students and colleagues when I taught ethics at Mansfield College, Oxford. It was presented in earlier forms to the Scripture and Society Group at Harris Manchester College, Oxford; at a day course in animal theology arranged by the Oxford University Department of Continuing Education; and as a guest lecture at the Free University of Amsterdam. It was also presented at the Second International Conference on Animal Sentience, organised by Compassion in World Farming in London in 2005. A shortened version of the chapter was published in *Colloquium: The Australian and New Zealand Theological Review* 39, no. 2, November 2007. I am grateful to Professor Mark Bernstein of Purdue University for his helpful comments on an earlier version of the chapter.

Chapter 2, "How We Minimise Animal Suffering and How We Can Change," was presented at the First International Conference on Animal Sentience organised by Compassion in World Farming in London in 2004. Parts of the chapter have appeared in truncated versions: in Jacky Turner and Joyce D'Silva (eds.), *Animals, Ethics and Trade* (London: Earthscan, 2005), and in *Essays in Philosophy: A Biannual Journal* 5, no. 2, June 2004. I am grateful to two anonymous reviewers who critiqued an earlier version. Dr. Jacky Turner gave me permission to use some paragraphs from our jointly authored article, "Making Animals Matter," which appeared in *Biologist* 45, no. 5, November 1988.

Chapter 3, "First Case: Hunting with Dogs," comprises some material presented to the Public Hearings on Hunting in London, 9–11 September 2002, arranged by the Department for Environment, Food and Rural Affairs (DEFRA) of the UK government. The hearings were intended to consider the evidence for and against hunting prior to the government's own bill on this subject, and I am grateful for the opportunity to contribute and to critique the Burns Report. The chapter also contains some material in my *Christian Theology and the Ethics of Hunting with Dogs*, which was published by the Christian Socialist Movement as a pamphlet in 2003.

Chapter 4, "Second Case: Fur Farming," began its life as a statement published by Respect for Animals in 2002. Special thanks are due to Mark Glover and Nicki Brooks of Respect for Animals in the United Kingdom for commissioning the work and for their and Richard Deville's generous assistance with research. Also thanks to Pierre Grzybowski of the Humane Society of the United States (HSUS) for information about U.S. fur farming practices and to Dr. Joanna Swabe of Bont voor Dieren of The Netherlands for her assistance in researching the current situation in the European Union. An earlier version was also published in *Animal Law Review* 13, no. 1, December 2006, and I am grateful to Jessica Minifie, Geoff Evans, and Kim McCoy for their conscientious work on the chapter.

Chapter 5, "Third Case: Commercial Sealing," also began its life as a statement for Respect for Animals (published in 2005) and, once again, my thanks are due to Nicki Brooks and Mark Glover. I am grateful to Rebecca Aldworth, director of Canadian Wildlife Issues of the HSUS for her outstanding help, including painstaking and detailed research; to Dr. David Lavigne, science adviser to the International Fund for Animal Welfare (IFAW) and formerly professor of zoology at the University of Guelph, Canada, for his invaluable assistance in research and in clarifying a range of issues; and to Ken Jones, senior fisheries management officer in the Department of Fisheries and Oceans of the government of Canada, for helping me with my enquiries. An earlier version of the chapter was published in the *Journal of Animal Law* 2, 2006, and my thanks are due to Professor David Favre from Michigan State University's College of Law for making that publication possible.

I am indebted most of all to Professor Priscilla Cohn of Abington College, Penn State University, who generously read all the manuscript at one stage or another and who provided me with indispensable advice and a searching critique. Without her outstanding support and encouragement, especially when times got tough, the book would never have been completed. Professor Mark Rowlands of the University of Miami also generously read the entire manuscript and provided me with a range of insightful comments and criticisms, which enabled me to improve the work. Responsibility for the views expressed of course remains my own.

My wife, Jo, edited and proofed the various versions of the book and saved me from many errors. Kate Kirkpatrick kindly copy-edited the manuscript with skill and patience. Cynthia Read of Oxford University Press was the most forbearing of editors, keeping faith with the project despite lengthy delays. The manuscript has benefited enormously from her professional skill and those of her colleagues.

CONTENTS

Introduction: Reason, Ethics, and Animals   1

Part I: Making the Rational Case   7

1. Why Animal Suffering Matters Morally   9
  1.1 Differences and morally relevant differences   10
  1.2 Examining the differences   11
  1.3 A test case: human infants   30
  1.4 Reconfiguring the differences and their relevance   34
  1.5 Children and animals as special cases   36
  1.6 A theological justification   37
  1.7 Christ-like suffering   39
  1.8 Summary of main points   40

2. How We Minimise Animal Suffering and How We Can Change   43
  2.1 Confronting the powers   43
  2.2 Moral change and resistance to change   57
  2.3 Cultivating and institutionalising critical awareness   60
  2.4 Vision and practicalities   68
  2.5 Summary of main points   70

Part II: Three Practical Critiques   73

3. First Case: Hunting with Dogs   75
  3.1 The drawn-out debate   77
  3.2 The oddness of the Burns Report   78
  3.3 Flawed methodology   79
  3.4 Suffering? what suffering?   81
  3.5 Addressing the moral issue   83
  3.6 Pleasure in suffering   84
  3.7 Hunting as anti-social behaviour   87
  3.8 The "no control" control   88
  3.9 Licensing versus abolition   92

3.10 Conclusion   94
3.11 Summary of main points   95

4. Second Case: Fur Farming   97
   4.1 Increasing legislation against fur farming   99
   4.2 Fur farming, harm, and suffering   100
   4.3 Animals as a special moral case   103
   4.4 Law and the protection of the weak   105
   4.5 Absence of moral justification   106
   4.6 Answers to objections   107
   4.7 Conclusion: no alternative to abolition   112
   4.8 Summary of main points   113

5. Third Case: Commercial Sealing   115
   5.1 First claim: the hunt is humane   117
   5.2 Second claim: seal pups are not killed   127
   5.3 Third claim: the hunt is tightly regulated   129
   5.4 Fourth claim: hunting is for survival   134
   5.5 Seals as economic commodities   136
   5.6 The problem of partisan governments   139
   5.7 Trade embargoes on seal products   141
   5.8 Concluding assessment   144
   5.9 Summary of main points   147

6. Conclusion: Re-Establishing Animals and Children
   as a Common Cause, and Six Objections Considered   151
   6.1 Singer, infants, and animals   152
   6.2 Rejecting institutionalised suffering   155
   6.3 Killing, rights, and suffering   158
   6.4 Common vulnerabilities   165
   6.5 Summary of main points   166

Notes   169
Index   199

WHY ANIMAL SUFFERING MATTERS

Introduction

Reason, Ethics, and Animals

The inspiration for this book came from a colleague at Oxford. Whenever an issue relating to animals was raised in conversation, he invariably remarked, "This is an emotional subject." The statement is, in one sense, obviously true. The way we treat animals does arouse strong emotions. People feel passionately about—for example—how we make animals suffer for food, science, and sport. Many people find photographs of cruelty to children or animals especially distressing. And there is nothing unusual or abnormal about that.

But that was not the intended meaning of my colleague's oft-repeated remark. What he was suggesting was that the topic was wholly a matter of emotion rather than reason—and that, by implication, there could be no rational grounds for concerning oneself with this subject, nor for objecting to our current treatment of animals. My aim is to show that the boot is on the other foot; when analysed impartially (or as impartially as we can manage), the rational case for extending moral solicitude to animals is much stronger than many suppose.

FORCES OF UNREASON

I do not deny that those who believe that reason has any part to play appear to be in short supply. On one hand, there are those, like my academic colleague, who will not admit that the case for animals has any rational foundation at all. This view is not just confined to the usual suspects, such as those who profit from the commercial exploitation of animals, but includes government officials, large sections of the media, and, most regrettably of all, parts of the academic community. The result is that, whenever issues of animal suffering are raised, especially in the media, they most usually receive a two-second put-down ("humans are more important") or are treated with a kind of intellectual disdain.

In more than thirty years of broadcasting on ethics and animals, I cannot recall a time when there was such a dearth of rational engagement. Increasingly, *any kind* of argument, however inchoate or flimsy, is tolerated in debates about the morality of inflicting suffering on animals. Philosophers and ethicists who, in a previous generation, were in the forefront of promoting enlightened public attitudes seem to have retreated in the face of increasingly fierce public controversy.

On the other hand, there are animal advocates who have so despaired of reason altogether that they have resorted to campaigns of violence and intimidation: letter bombs, harassment, and personal abuse. Of course, they are (thankfully) a tiny minority, and their actions should not be allowed to obscure the sterling work done by mainstream animal protection organisations. But that they exist at all is wholly lamentable. They rob the animal movement of the moral high ground (which is its only platform) and provide almost weekly excuses for the media to label everyone who cares for animals as extremists and fanatics. Moreover, so far has reason assumed a second (or non-existent) place that violent activists seem utterly unaware of their own moral contradiction: a movement that seeks the benevolent treatment of all sentient beings must logically include human subjects within that same category. Violence isn't just bad tactics; it is a betrayal of the cause.

This book, then, is born of a frustration that well-reasoned, logical argumentation is all but lost in the current emotional, and increasingly acrimonious, debate about animals. Such discussions often involve unfounded assumptions and straw-man arguments. That this has happened is sad for rational (intellectual) debate and ethical deliberation, but especially tragic for the welfare of millions of other species (as well as our own). For I believe—and I want to show—that there are few moral issues being canvassed at the present time that have better intellectual credentials than the recognition that animals deserve to be treated as the sentient beings that they are instead of being considered as things we can use and dispose of as we see fit for any reason or even for no reason.

"Reason" and "rationality" are words that have a long history, and their meanings have often changed over time. By "rational" here, I mean the attempt to locate a connected and consistent series of considerations in favour of one point of view rather than another. While not decrying the importance of emotional reactions, I judge them insufficient to determine the rightness or wrongness of a given action. Feelings are often good in themselves and much to be emulated in some regards, but the assumption that mere feeling ("love of animals") does the case for animals justice must be jettisoned absolutely.

AIM AND SHAPE OF THIS BOOK

This book aims to show that a strong rational case can be made for the extension of moral solicitude to all sentient beings. It shows how that case provides the basis for a formidable critique of existing practices, especially our use of animals in sport, farming, and commerce. I invite the reader to examine the arguments that are made and then see how they can be applied to three selected issues: hunting with dogs, fur farming, and commercial sealing. These subjects have already provoked considerable media commentary, but very little of it, I believe, actually goes to the heart of the ethical case against these practices. The argument of this book proceeds from a general statement of the case to applying that ethical stance to three contentious issues. In the process, a range of considerations—economic, legal, and political—is given its due while retaining the ethical focus throughout. Some account of the shape of this book may help.

Chapter 1, "Why Animal Suffering Matters Morally," examines six of the most frequently cited justifications for exploiting animals based on an appeal to "differences": animals are naturally slaves, non-rational beings, linguistically deficient, not moral agents, soulless beings, and devoid of the divine image. My concern is not to dispute the accuracy of the putative differences, but rather to show that the moral conclusions drawn from these differences are almost entirely mistaken and that another, completely opposed, conclusion follows. The differences so often regarded as the basis for discriminating *against* animals are, I propose, the grounds for discriminating *in favour* of them. When reconfigured, these considerations include the inability of animals to give or withhold consent, their inability to verbalise or represent their interests, their inability to comprehend us, their moral innocence or blamelessness, and, not least of all, their relative defenceless-ness and vulnerability. When these considerations are properly taken into account, it will be seen that it is as difficult to justify the infliction of suffering on animals as it is to do so in the case of human infants. Animals, like young children, should be accorded a special moral status. These considerations constitute the core of the rational case that is expounded and applied in the following parts of this book.

Chapter 2, "How We Minimise Animal Suffering and How We Can Change," tries to answer the question: why, if the case for animals is so strong and rationally well grounded, has it so often been overlooked? I identify and illustrate what might be described as "the powers that be," which are intellectual mechanisms that prevent us from recognising sentience in animals or help to limit its significance: the powers of misdescription, misrepresentation, misdirection, and misperception. We shall not be able to think straight or see straight unless we are aware of these avoidance mechanisms, which prevent us from grasping the seriousness of animal suffering. I then consider ways in which animal abuse is socially perpetuated through the process called "institutionalisation." What is significant about animal abuse is not just that it happens, but that, unlike most other forms of abuse, it is tolerated *institutionally*. With the help of some Chomskian analysis, I suggest ways in which moral perceptions about animals can become embodied in new institutions.

Chapter 3, "First Case: Hunting with Dogs," is the first of three chapters that translate the general case developed in chapters 1 and 2 into practical critiques. In this chapter, I interrogate the British government's own report on hunting—the Burns Report—and show why it fails as an impartial analysis. Although (remarkably) ethical issues were excluded from its remit, the committee did not of course avoid making a range of value judgments, some of which are astonishingly inept, such as the notion that only *scientifically proved* injury can constitute "cruelty." Since, for all its manifest inadequacies, the report is likely to remain a focal point and reference for continuing debates on the subject, it is vital that Burns should be exposed as an example of how *not* to deal with a moral issue, nothing less than a textbook case of how a moral issue can be obfuscated by a government report. Despite some successful prosecutions, hunting continues in the United Kingdom (and, with slight variations, in Europe and the United States), and a future government may yet reintroduce the system of licensing that Burns proposed. It is vital that the moral issue regains the centre ground.

Chapter 4, "Second Case: Fur Farming," defends the decision of some European governments, including the British government, to legislate against fur farming on the grounds of "public morality." It aims to show *why* there is a legitimate public interest in reducing suffering to animals. The ban on fur farming was the first time that the British government advanced any animal protection legislation on specifically ethical grounds. Although the major thrust of the argument relates to European legislation, it also has relevance to non-European countries, not least the United States and Russia, which still allow fur farming. Moreover, there is no reason to suppose that the veterinary objections to this practice do not also apply to fur farming in other countries, since the practices described are similar, if not uniform.

Chapter 5, "Third Case: Commercial Sealing," interrogates the claims made by the Canadian government in defence of seal hunting: that the hunt is "humane"; that seal pups are not killed; that the hunt is "tightly regulated"; and that coastal communities rely on the hunt "for their survival." Extensive analysis shows that none of these justifications can be sustained. Indeed, I show how one veterinary group seeking to establish tighter regulation actually showed *by its own admission* that regulations could not—and do not—prevent seals from being skinned alive. The Canadian government is unreasonably partisan in its defence of seal hunting and shows very little cognisance of the value of seals as sentient beings, but only as economic commodities: its official statements still liken sealing to a "fishery." The case against commercial sealing is so strong that consideration is given to the ways in which European countries can act within WTO (World Trade Organization) and EU (European Union) rules to ban seal imports, as the United States has already done.

My conclusion, "Re-Establishing Animals and Children as a Common Cause, and Six Objections Considered," takes issue with Peter Singer's neglect of considerations, such as innocence and vulnerability, that lead him to postulate that only infants who are at least one month old should be included within the moral community. Such a utilitarian position flies in the face of the historic trajectory of concern for animals and children as constituting a common cause and mistakenly places them in juxtaposition. Animals and infants constitute paradigmatic cases of innocence and vulnerability. The issue of animals cannot be divorced from a wider rediscovery of those considerations that should equally apply to vulnerable human subjects.

INTENDED READERSHIP

This book attempts to provide a clear, introductory text accessible for high school and university students. Indeed, I have planned it with the undergraduates I have taught at Oxford and Birmingham specifically in mind. I bring together the various arguments—philosophical, theological, and ethical—in order to create a text that helps to provoke students beyond conventional thinking. As I am always saying to my ethics students: "It is so much easier to have a sense of right and wrong than it is to be able to give a rational account of *why* something is right or wrong." Providing an account of why an action is right or wrong is one of the key tasks of ethics. And when it comes to animal issues, providing that account is doubly important since the subject is everywhere laden with emotionally charged rhetoric.

This volume is also intended to meet the specific needs occasioned by the increasing number of university courses in animal welfare, animal rights, human-animal studies, animal ethics, animals and philosophy, animals and religion, animal law, and even animal theology at the university level in both Europe and the United States. This is in addition to the many pre-university, advanced-level, and high school courses in the United Kingdom and the United States in liberal arts, humanities, philosophy, religious studies, and ethics that now increasingly include normative questions about our treatment of animals within their fields of study.

All of the six chapters are lengthy, but to help clarity, I have provided a summary of the main points at the end of each chapter and have signposted each chapter with sub-headings. I have also provided generous, sometimes extensive notes to help guide students in locating source materials and further readings.

TOWARD IMPARTIALITY

I am the director of the Oxford Centre for Animal Ethics (www.oxfordani-malethics.com). The aim of the centre is to enhance the ethical status of animals through academic research, teaching, and publication. It does this by inviting academics worldwide, from both the sciences and the human-ities, to become fellows of the centre and contribute to multidisciplinary research. "Putting animals on the intellectual agenda" is the centre's motto.

The process of founding the centre, and experiencing first hand the spirited support and also opposition it has received, has underlined for me how immensely difficult it is for humans to exercise impartiality in their treatment of other species. Huge vested interests are at stake, and (in one sense) humans obviously benefit from exploitation. So entrenched and powerful are these interests that one must wonder whether humans really have enough moral resourcefulness to recognise their own tyranny over other creatures. But, unless we are to abandon rational enquiry altogether, we have to be brave enough to recognise the interests even of those beings from whose discomfort we so obviously profit. We have to aim, however psychologically problematic, at an impartial (or, at least, less partial) view of animals that is not simply informed by human selfishness. To that end, this book is dedicated.

Part I

MAKING THE RATIONAL CASE

1

Why Animal Suffering Matters Morally

Traditional ethics in almost all its forms privileges human suffering over all other kinds of suffering. It seems self-evident to many people that human suffering is virtually in a class of its own, and that animal suffering, while sometimes objectionable, isn't really as important or as morally significant. There are, it is supposed, two kinds of suffering: human and animal. Human suffering always matters because it somehow represents the worst kind of suffering in the world, whereas the suffering of animals is judged to be "second class," significant (perhaps) but wholly secondary in moral importance.

Controversially, I am no longer convinced that this position is wholly rational, nor that it can be supported by the most rational considerations available. This chapter documents my wrestling. Whether readers agree with me or not, I hope they will at least accept that the case for extending moral solicitude to animals is much greater than they might have previously supposed.

A couple of basic definitions—of "suffering" and "animal"—are required. Although often used interchangeably, "pain" and "suffering" should be distinguished. Pain usually refers to the reaction following an adverse physical stimuli, what is typically taken, at least by philosophers, to be an unpleasant sensation or the result of what scientists call "noxious stimuli." Suffering is sometimes taken to be pain of a certain sort—for example, sufficiently unwarranted, prolonged, and outside the control of the subject. However, while pain usually accompanies suffering, it is not always identical with it. Suffering thus refers to more than physical pain, including what has been termed the *mental experience* of pain, including such sensations as shock, fear, foreboding, anxiety, trauma, anticipation, stress, distress, and terror.[1] In general, suffering may be defined as harm that an animal experiences characterised as a deficiency in (or negative aspect of) that animal's well-being. What is important is the recognition (informed by scientific evidence) that mammals, at least, experience both pain and suffering. "Animal" refers to mammals and birds where such suffering may be reasonably supposed. Whether suffering extends wider than the class of beings here envisaged is an important question, but its resolution in no way affects my argument.

1.1. DIFFERENCES AND MORALLY RELEVANT DIFFERENCES

Those who wish to justify or minimise animal suffering rarely argue that animals do not suffer. Rather, they argue that animal suffering matters less, if at all, because animals are *different* from human beings. There are obviously differences, sometimes important ones, both within species and between them. The ethical issue is not about *difference per se*, but whether any of the proposed differences are *morally relevant*, that is, whether any should reasonably form the basis for differential treatment of one species over another. Some differences, I conclude, do have moral relevance but in an entirely contrary way to that supposed by their proponents.

The issue of relevant differences was well aired by the Anglican divine Humphry Primatt, who wrote in 1776:

> It has pleased God the Father of all men, to cover some men with white skins, and others with black skins; but as there is neither merit or demerit in complexion, the white man, notwithstanding the barbarity of custom and prejudice, can have no right, by virtue of his colour, to enslave and tyrannize over a black man; nor has a fair man any right to despise, abuse, and insult a brown man. Nor do I believe that a tall man, by virtue of his stature, has any legal right to trample a dwarf under his foot. For, whether a man is wise or foolish, white or black, fair or brown, tall or short, and I might add, rich nor poor, for it is no more a man's choice to be poor, than he is to be a fool, or a dwarf, or black or tawny—such he is by God's appointment; and, abstractedly considered, is neither a subject for pride, nor an object of contempt.[2]

In other words, these differences should have nothing to do with differences in moral treatment because God has originated them, or, in non-religious terms, we have not chosen them. Primatt goes on to make a similar case in relation to animals:

> Now, if amongst men, the differences of their powers of the mind, and of their complexion, stature, and accidents of fortune, do not give any one man a right to abuse or insult any other man on account of these differences; for the same reason, a man can have no natural right to abuse or torment a beast, namely because a beast has not the mental powers of a man. For, such as the man is, he is as but God made him; and the very same is true of the beast. Neither of them can lay claim to any intrinsic merit . . . at their creation, their shapes, perfections, or defects were invariably fixed, and their bounds set which they cannot pass. And being such, neither more or less than God made them, there is no more demerit in a beast being a beast, than there is merit in [a] man being a man; that is, there is neither merit nor demerit in either of them.[3]

The argument is that "shapes, perfections, or defects" cannot be counted morally for or against any being. They are simply the accidents of birth or, as Primatt suggests, what is given by their Creator. None, strictly speaking, are matters of *moral* merit or demerit. That is just the way humans are, and animals also.

That said, Primatt does make one exception, namely, sentience. The capacity to feel pain and suffering *is* morally relevant. He writes of how "the differences amongst men in the above particulars are no bars to their feelings, so neither does the difference of shape of a brute from that of a man exempt the brute from feeling; *at least, we have no ground to suppose it.*"[4] That, then, is the central question: are there any grounds—other than the existence of sentience—for supposing that what Primatt calls "the particulars" provide any ground that human suffering has a greater moral claim upon us?

1.2. EXAMINING THE DIFFERENCES

Six of the most often cited "particulars," or differences, will be considered. It has been claimed that animals are

(i) naturally slaves;
(ii) non-rational beings;
(iii) linguistically deficient;
(iv) not moral agents;

  (v) soulless; and
  (vi) devoid of the divine image.

The first four differences are mainly philosophical, and the remaining two, theological. It is important that my methodology is clear: *my concern is not to dispute the accuracy of the differences, but rather to show that the moral conclusions drawn from these differences are almost entirely mistaken and that another, completely opposed, conclusion follows.* Since humans have excelled themselves at what may be called the "uniqueness-spotting tendency,"[5] my list can only comprise some fairly typical arguments. Clearly, those who maintain that animals do not suffer will find my arguments irrelevant, as I find theirs unconvincing, but it is worth remembering that, *pace* Descartes (probably), almost all mainstream philosophers and theologians have not doubted that animals are sentient, even if they have accorded various meanings to the term.

(i) Naturally slaves

The first argument is what may be termed the "functionalist teleology" of Aristotle and Aquinas. Aristotle in his well-known defence of human slavery held that animals too are slaves—indeed, slaves "by nature." They are, it was thought, made subservient to us by the order of nature, the way things are:

> [S]o it is naturally with the male and the female; the one is superior, the other inferior; the one governs, the other is governed; and the same rule must necessarily hold good with respect to all mankind. . . . It is evident then that we may conclude of those things that are, that plants are created for the sake of animals, and animals for the sake of men. . . . As nature therefore makes nothing either imperfect or in vain, it necessarily follows that she has made all things for men.[6]

The world, then, consists of a hierarchy in which the inferior exist for the superior, which extends both within as well as between species. Men are at the pinnacle, followed by women, slaves, animals, and, last, plants. Since nothing is without a purpose, it follows that the existence of one being is to serve another.

Aristotle's position was largely taken over by St. Thomas Aquinas, whose influence within the Catholic tradition has been immense. St. Thomas similarly maintained that "all animals are naturally subject to man."[7] We "perceive a certain order of procession of the perfect from the imperfect . . . thus the imperfect are for the use of the perfect." Humans, therefore, rightly make use of both plants and animals, and it is therefore "in keeping with the order of nature, that man should be the master of animals."[8] And he cited here in support the view of Aristotle that the hunting of wild animals is "natural and just."[9]

Elsewhere, St. Thomas presented the issue more starkly. After quoting a line from Psalm 8:8, "Thou has subjected all things under his feet, all sheep and oxen; moreover, the beasts also of the field," he asserted:

> Hereby is refuted the error of those who say it is sinful for a man to kill brute animals, for by divine providence they are intended for man's use according to the order of nature. Hence it is not wrong for man to make use of them, *either by killing or in any other way whatever.*[10]

Let us suppose that Aristotle is right, that there is an intellectual hierarchy in the world, and that reason is bound to rule. Does it necessarily follow that animals should be denied solicitude? Perhaps it is true that the "imperfect" are there to serve the "perfect" or the "more perfect," and perhaps there is a "natural" dominance that arises between different kinds of people, such as between slaves and "free," and between men and women. The question remains: how precisely is that *relevant?* It seems there is a gap in Aristotle's thinking—a missing link in the argument; he simply does not provide the crucial intellectual elaboration that demonstrates that those who are *naturally* inferior should be treated as *morally* inferior as well.

In other words, Aristotle confuses *natural* hierarchy with *moral* hierarchy. The argument is based on his perception of how nature is, but even if he is right, it still doesn't follow that that is how human beings, as moral agents, ought to behave. Aristotle presumes that what is given in nature has to be normative in ethics, but that is far from obvious. He is inevitably selective in what he takes to be "given" in nature and therefore morally licit: since the "order of nature" also comprises animals that sometimes kill humans (usually in self-defence), as well as slaves and women who are not always naturally, or easily, enslaveable, the argument cannot simply be derived from the observation of nature. Aristotle may have replied here that he was concerned with intellectual power rather than mere physical power, so that the slave may well be physically stronger and yet is enslaved by virtue of his intellectual "inferiority." But that only reinforces the puzzle, since it is unclear why reason should have the *moral* right to exercise power.

The problem, then, is knowing *how* the putative natural inferiority of one being over another constitutes a morally relevant difference. If "inferiority" means that the being concerned is non-sentient, that is, incapable of feeling, one could easily grasp its relevance. But since, as Primatt indicated, mental prowess does not, of itself, render one being more or less liable to suffering than another, and since suffering is a relevant factor in making a moral decision, it is difficult to see the basis for differential moral treatment.

Stripped to its essential point, Aristotle's position seems to hinge on the exercise of power or, rather, his perception of how power should be exercised. Certainly, it is "rational" power, or power exercised according to reason, but it is power nonetheless. Aristotle might have responded that the one with the intellectual mastery of thought is the one who makes decisions, but even so the connection between intellectual decision making and exclusive moral solicitude is not demonstrated.

There seems something oddly amoral about Aristotle's conception of the rule of reason. Although natural systems may indeed exhibit an indifference to moral standards, it is difficult to see how rational, moral agents can be so exempt. As C. S. Lewis commented: "It is our business to live by our own law not by hers [nature's]."[11] Should rational power—that is, power exercised by reasoning people who are also moral agents—be exercised with no moral limitations? Should not a *rational* ruler care for his or her subjects? Again, Aristotle might have claimed that the hierarchy is not so much the ruthless imposition of power, but a kind of protection: the man has to think for the woman since she cannot do so. That being so, the exclusion of animals from moral solicitude is even more anomalous.

St. Thomas's argument, however, has a theological twist. He coupled together both notions of natural order and divine providence; he both utilised Aristotle and provided an additional line of defence. Subordination is justifiable *because God has ordained it*. It is not just how things are, but how they should be. God has willed an ordered creation with one part subordinate to the rest. The principal difficulty with this argument is that the conclusion does not follow from the premise. Even if we grant that humans have been given dominion or power over animals, it doesn't follow that *every* use of power is justifiable. St. Thomas was clear that human dominion is to be exercised without "hindrance"—that is, without moral limits. The only possible exception is where cruelty practiced on animals might adversely affect the human perpetrator.[12]

But is it true that God—at least according to the scripture that St. Thomas cited—cares nothing for animals or their ill treatment? Not so. There are scriptural passages that speak of God's care for creation (Psalm 145:9), specifically of God's covenant with "all living creatures" (Genesis 9:8–17), and of how the "righteous" care for their animals whereas "the mercy of the wicked are cruel" (Proverbs 12:10). Even more, subsequent to making humans in the divine image and the bestowal of dominion in Genesis 1:27–29, humans are then given a strictly vegetarian diet (1:29–30), a position only reversed after the fall and the flood in Genesis 9:3. In other words, divinely sanctioned human power over animals that does not (in its original intention) even allow the killing of other creatures for food (and instead requires a vegetarian diet) is not an obvious basis to justify an appeal to unrestrained power over other creatures.

But even if these verses did not exist, it follows logically that any power exercised by God's permission must surely reflect God's own attributes, and since these include love, generosity, mercy, and compassion, it is problematic to suppose that human power can be absolute or unlimited.

To answer our question, then, it seems clear that power cannot constitute its own self-justification. The natural order does not constitute a moral order so that we are beholden to follow whatever we observe therein. On the contrary, behaving morally sometimes involves acting contrary to what we perceive in nature, or against our natural impulses, such as the desire for revenge. The relative weakness of animals—their vulnerability to human power—cannot be a sufficient or principal ground for excluding them from moral solicitude. Again, Primatt's argument in relation to humans applies equally to sentient animals:

> Nor will he [the person who cares for justice] take any advantage of his own superiority of strength, or of the accidents of fortune, to abuse them to the oppression of his inferior; because he knows that in the article of feeling all men are equal; and that differences of strength or station are as much the gifts and appointments of God, as the differences of understanding, colour, or stature.[13]

And yet, there may be one ground for supposing that power has moral relevance, but one contrary to that intended by Aristotle and Aquinas. It is that those who have power ought to recognise the claim of the weak, even that it is their special obligation to do so. The basis for this idea is given in the very theology to which St. Thomas is indebted, namely, that the God who is (in Thomist terms) the "highest" and most "perfect" of all expresses divine power not in lording over "inferior" creatures, but in taking human form and suffering and dying for their sakes. In other words, the doctrine of the incarnation involves the sacrifice of the "higher" for the "lower," not the reverse. And if that is the true model of divine generosity, it is difficult to see how humans can otherwise interpret their exercise of power over sentient creatures. Lordship—from a Christological perspective—is inextricably related to service, and if that perspective is correct, human power over animals needs to be seen in a wholly different light. Far from justifying each and every use of animals, power—defined Christologically—ought to be more properly defined as "the power to serve."[14] This point is developed further in relation to the *imago Dei* (see section 1.2.vi).

(ii) Non-rational beings

Animals, we have been taught, are "brutes," "dumb," non-rational creatures. Those brought up within the Christian tradition will know the terminology well. Rational subordination was, as we have seen, key to Aristotle's defence of slavery both human and animal. St. Augustine, too, took rationality as the basic dividing line between humans and animals. In his attack on the Manichaeans (to whom he attributed the view that killing plants is wrong), he stated:

> Put aside, then, these ravings [of the Manichaeans], if, when we say Thou shalt not kill, we do not understand this of the plants, since they have no sensation, nor of the irrational animals that fly, swim, walk or creep, since they are dissociated from us by their want of reason, and are therefore by the just appointment of the Creator subjected to us to kill or keep alive for our own uses; if so, then it remains that we understand that commandment simply of man.[15]

It is worthwhile asking what "reason" meant in this context. As Gillian Clark explains, "reason" was understood to be the intellectual and spiritual force in human beings. "When a Greek philosopher says that humans have *logos*," she writes, "this means both that we can make sense of the world and that we can express our understanding in words; and our understanding includes awareness of God and of the choices we should make in our own best interests."[16] Augustine stands within this tradition, except that he saw animals as also subject to us by God's design.

Likewise, according to St. Thomas, animals are devoid of the life of reason and should be subject to the control of rational—that is, human— creatures:

> For that which acts only when moved by another is like an instrument, whereas that which acts by itself is alike a principal agent. Now an instrument is required, not for its own sake, but that the principal agent may use it. Hence whatever is done for the care of instruments must be referred to the principal agent as its end; whereas any action directed to the principal agent as such, either by the agent itself or by another, is for the sake of the same principal agent. Accordingly, intellectual creatures are ruled by God as though He cared for them for their own sake, while other creatures are ruled as being directed to rational creatures.[17]

Thus, in Aquinas and in subsequent Catholic (and not only Catholic) tradition, rationality is used as a trump card to vanquish any non-human claim to moral consideration in itself. But is rationality a morally relevant difference?

The underlying assumption (at least as it is utilised in contemporary debate) is that rational incomprehension makes suffering less morally considerable because the suffering of rational beings is incomparably greater. Rational comprehension might heighten suffering if, for example, it involves anticipation of harm or death, which animals cannot experience. It is sometimes claimed, for example, that they have no anticipation of death and are therefore spared that ontological anxiety which besets human beings. If that is true, then, it must be granted that humans may be liable to more suffering in those situations.

Another example is when, for example, a prisoner of war is told that his country has been destroyed, or that his family has been killed or will be killed. Verbal threats or abusive comments may cause considerable suffering, while such threats (as long as they remain purely verbal) would not increase the suffering of an animal. Again, in these cases, it should be accepted that humans suffer more or, rather, that they suffer in ways in which animals cannot.

But is it true that rational comprehension *always* or *generally* heightens suffering? The general claim is less well founded. Consider the case of wild animals, for example, non-human primates who are captured, taken from the wild, and then subjected to captivity in zoos or laboratories. The animals concerned do not know why they have been captured, why they are being transported, and what will happen to them. They experience the raw terror of not knowing. And since the implication of the argument is that animals live closer to their bodily senses than we do, the frustration of their natural freedoms may well induce more suffering than we allow. Human suffering, on the other hand, can be softened by an intellectual comprehension of the circumstances. When, for example, I visit the dentist and he performs procedures on me ranging from the uncomfortable to the traumatic, I can at least console myself that they are for my own putative good. No such consolations are available to animals who are denied their liberty and who have procedures performed upon them that are equally, if not more, uncomfortable or traumatic and likely not for their own good.[18]

It seems reasonable that the imposition of captivity upon free-ranging animals constitutes a considerable harm—what has been termed "the harm of deprivation."[19] Captive animals are frequently denied the opportunity to express even elementary patterns of behaviour. Is that harm lessened by intellectual incomprehension? Not obviously. If it is true that animals are non-rational, then it follows that they have no means of rationalising their deprivation, boredom, and frustration. They have no intellectual means of escaping their circumstances, for example (as far as we can tell), by use of the imagination. They cannot, like Terry Waite in captivity, intellectually appreciate the forces that led to their capture and resign themselves, as he did, to a heroic policy of "no self-pity." Waite at least had the benefit of communication, however limited, with his captors—an amelioration always unavailable to captive animals. Neither can they, like Waite, write novels in their heads.[20] Such considerations also extend to a range of other situations in which we manage or use animals.

The claim, then, that rational incomprehension is a morally relevant difference only stands if it can be shown that comprehension increases liability to suffering, or that its absence makes the experience of suffering less acute. In some instances, it surely does so, but equally there are grounds for supposing that the contrary is true in others. The bottom line is that animals and humans suffer in varying ways. Humans will suffer more in some situations, animals more in others. Rationality is only one of many factors (notably, bodily sensibility) that may intensify suffering. It cannot be singled out as the only, or even the main, factor capable of justifying the privileged position that human suffering now occupies.

(iii) Linguistically deficient

It is useful to recall Clark's point that animals were judged by Greek philosophers to be devoid of *logos* and that one demonstration of this was that animals do not use words. "They were often referred to as *aloga zôa*," meaning "living creatures without *logos*," which has been commonly translated as "irrational animals."[21] Not possessing language or, to be more precise, not possessing a human language or a language that humans can understand has been traditionally regarded as a morally relevant difference. But is it?

Thomas Hobbes famously argued that the possession of language allows for many "advantages." These principally include the ability to use numbers and to count; the ability to teach others; and, most especially, he said, "that we can command and understand commands is a benefit of speech, and truly the greatest."[22] The latter means that there can be "society" among humans who can mutually agree and understand "covenants" or "contracts" between them. But Hobbes also pointed out that there are certain "disadvantages" to the possession of language:

> Because man, alone among the animals, on account of the universal
> signification of names, can create general rules for himself in the art of living
> just as in the other arts; and so he alone can devise errors and pass them on for
> the uses of others. Therefore man errs more widely and dangerously than
> can other animals.[23]

It follows that "man" can also "teach what he knows to be false from what he hath inherited; that is he can lie and render the minds of men hostile to the conditions of society and peace; something that cannot happen in the societies of other animals."[24] Judged in itself, then, the possession of language is not an unambiguous good; it has potentialities for both good and evil. Hobbes concluded: "Therefore by speech man is not made better, but only given greater possibilities."[25]

These potentialities, fairly stated by Hobbes, do not obviously lend themselves to be classified as morally relevant differences. But so much has been built upon them that one modern philosopher, Michael Leahy, can maintain that the absence of language variously indicates the absence of self-awareness to the extent that creatures without language cannot have any independent interests. For example, he asserts, "Lacking language, animal behaviour does not have *meaning* for them as it can for us."[26] Again: "Language is the key which unlocks horizons light-years beyond those of animals. With it we make the thoughts of others our own, can share their hopes and contemplate our personal past and future."[27] People who speak of animals' interests are charged with "cognitive excess baggage": "The needs of brutes . . . cannot be guided by their own view of themselves, for they cannot have any."[28] In short: animals are linguistically deficient "primitive beings."[29]

Let us assume that even this highly minimalistic picture is correct. Does it follow that animal suffering is therefore less morally significant?

The first thing to note is that Leahy is not, as was Hobbes, seeking to present differences for impartial consideration. Rather, he has an axe to grind. He doesn't just state differences, but couples them with an undisguised denigration of what is different. In response to the objection that on issues such as hunting and the fur trade, he "misses completely the objection based on the relative triviality of the human interest served," Leahy replies:

> Many pinkish academics find sport and champagne trivial. I think them important. Many business people find academics, of any hue, trivial. Many cultured Spaniards revere bull-fighting, which has for them the status of high art. For numerous jockeys and trainers, to win the Grand National (remember horses are killed routinely) is preferable to eternal salvation. In like manner, field-sports are serious business for sensible and civilised citizens who respect and appreciate the natural habitats of animals.[30]

The logic of Leahy's position seems clear: *any* human interest if it is regarded as serious by human beings, even if it involves gratuitous cruelty—as in the case of bull-fighting—is justified.

But what of Leahy's general claim that possessing human language unlocks a "richness" of life that animals cannot experience? Consider that mammalian life *without* human language, but with its own symbolic communication (which we cannot understand) may be (to them) as rich as ours. The "my experience is richer than your experience" argument is an argument from ignorance since we know so little of the interior lives of non-human animals, other than what may be reasonably supposed by sentience. Rather than privileging one set of human experiences, it seems more reasonable to take stock of the sheer range of actually or potentially rich experiences open to other creatures. We do not know what it is like precisely to howl, or meow, or to create birdsong. We do not know what it is like to fly through the air, or possess extraordinary capacities for sight and sound, as well as a range of other senses vastly superior to our own. It seems a fair assumption that there are multiple riches—even spiritual ones—inherent in these experiences that are inaccessible to us.

Consider also: as Hobbes rightly discerned, language possession is not an unambiguous good. While it opens up the possibilities of communication, it also enables the spread of falsity and deceit. In Hobbes's telling line: "on account of the ease of speech, the man who doth not think, speaks; and what he says, he believes to be true, and he can deceive himself; a beast cannot deceive himself."[31] Language may well unlock a richness of experience, but one cannot impartially declare it to be, even in its own terms, an unmixed moral good. The apparent inability of animals to deceive themselves might, on a less prejudiced understanding of the world, place them in a higher moral category.

The bottom line, however, is that, even if Leahy is right in his description of animals as linguistically deficient, primitive beings, it doesn't follow that their suffering isn't as significant for them *in their own terms* as ours is for us. As Peter Singer indicates: "Even if Leahy were right about the limits of animal consciousness . . . it is not clear that the pain they can feel is any less painful, nor why it should matter less than the pain we feel."[32]

But there is another aspect to this argument that is rarely given its due weight. It follows that those who have a common language can also communicate their wants and feelings. Specifically, they are able to give or withhold their consent. But animals, obviously being unable to speak to us in a way that we understand, cannot consent to certain forms of human behaviour in relation to them. One example may suffice: scientists sometimes speak of animals "sacrificing" themselves for research. But that use of language masks the reality, which is not that animals have sacrificed themselves, but that we have sacrificed them. So often, the powerful *presume* consent where there is none. The same presumption operates with regard to less powerful humans. Noam Chomsky reports how he came across a gravestone inscription, placed by the national parks "as a testimonial." It read: "Here lies an Indian woman, a Wampanoag, whose family and tribe gave of themselves and their land that this great nation might be born and grow." As Chomsky rightly comments: "she and her family didn't 'give of themselves and their land.' Rather they were murdered by our forefathers and driven out of their land."[33] However we may rewrite the history of human losers, the point is that animals never even have the chance of consenting. That is widely recognised, but its moral implications are not.

Consider the importance placed on consent in human experimentation. During the twentieth century—and, indeed, up until the present—there have been experiments on both human and animal subjects. These have included experiments on children, the mentally unwell, people of colour, and prisoners of war.[34] The latter were of course so notorious that they became the subject of actual charges against the Nazis during the Nuremberg trials. Article I.5 of the Declaration of Helsinki adopted by the World Medical Assembly in 1964 (and revised by the same body in 1975) reads: "concern for the interests of the subject [in human experimentation] must always prevail over the interest of science and society." Article III.4 (the final provision of the declaration) reads: "in research on man, the interest of science and society should never take precedence over considerations related to the well-being of the subject." This declaration is in turn a development of the Nuremberg Code of 1947, "which was a by-product of a trial of physicians for having performed cruel experiments on prisoners and detainees during the Second World War."[35] The code states as its first principle: "The voluntary consent of the human subject is absolutely essential." It continues: "The person involved should have the legal capacity to give consent; should be situated as to be able to exercise free power of choice, without the intervention of any element of force . . . or other ulterior form of constraint or coercion."[36]

That principle of voluntary consent has become central to discussions of medical ethics and of ethics more generally. Indeed, it has been strengthened by the use of the preceding word "informed," which implies that experimenters must not only ensure consent, but also inform the subject of all the possible consequences—a far from easy task. In law, the concept of consent is also central. Consent can make the difference between consensual sex and rape or between acts of sadomasochism and torture. Both ethically and legally, the notion of informed consent has become indispensable in assessing the acceptability of a given act.

Consider further: if that principle is morally sound, the absence of the capacity to give consent, informed or otherwise, must logically tell *against* the abuse of animals. It makes the infliction of injury not easier, but equally difficult, if not harder, to justify. As Tom Regan extols when weighing the relative risks and harms involved in experimentation: "Risks are not morally transferable to those who do not voluntarily choose to take them."[37] The Nuremberg Code explicitly states that the subject should be able "to exercise free power of choice, without the intervention of any element of force"[38] but, since animals are incapable of doing so, it must follow that every act which makes them suffer is an act of coercion.

While the non-possession of a language is not in itself a morally relevant difference, the absence of an ability to give or withhold consent (itself contingent upon the presence or absence of a communicable language) certainly is. It means, inter alia, that animals cannot vocalise their own interests, and, without our benign representation, their interests can easily go unrecognised and unappreciated—as indeed is often the case. The inability of animals to consent cannot imply a diminished moral obligation on our part. On the contrary, our responsibility increases as we recognise that the relevant factor is absent.

(iv) Not moral agents

One of the best exponents of this view is Samuel Pufendorf in his *Law of Nature and Nations*, published in 1688. Pufendorf began by noting that Roman jurisconsults defined the law of nature as "what nature taught all animals," not just human beings. Thus: "on this hypothesis, whatever brutes and man are understood to be attracted to in common, or in common to avoid, belongs to the law of nature, and consequently a law is postulated which is common both to men and brutes."[39] This, Pufendorf rejected as depending upon a disputed theory of a common soul, metempsychosis.

However, there is a "great difference" between humans and animals since actions "among beasts . . . come from the simple inclination of their nature, while man performs them from a sense, as it were, of obligation, a sense which brutes do not have."[40] When we speak of justice, pity, or bravery in relation to animals, we only use "figures of speech" which have no objective grounding. From this, it follows:

> [W]e do not understand that the law of nature by its absolute authority
> enjoins us to cultivate friendship and society with brutes, nor are they capable
> of sustaining an obligation arising from a pact with men. From this defect of a
> common right there follows a practical state of war between those who can
> mutually injure each other, and are understood on probable reasons to be able
> so to desire. . . . And yet this state of war with brutes is very different from the
> war in which men meet at times, the latter being neither universal nor
> perpetual, and not extending promiscuously to every kind of licence.[41]

Pufendorf continued that it is "vain" for some to deny that it follows from this lack of a common right that we may not "injure" animals for our purposes. Neither can such activity be opposed as illicit because of God their Creator:

> [I]t is a safe conclusion from the fact that the Creator established no common right between man and brutes, that no injury is done brutes if they are hurt by man, since God himself made such a state to exist between man and brutes.[42]

Is possessing a sense of obligation a morally relevant difference? Well, clearly it is relevant to human beings who are moral agents, but it is difficult to see how it can pass muster as an argument against the extension of moral considerability. It would be easier to argue the converse: humans have no duties to animals because humans are *not* moral agents. If humans are morally superior (in the sense that we are moral agents), it more reasonably follows that our superiority should, in part at least, consist in acknowledging duties to animals that they cannot acknowledge towards us. While animals are not moral agents, they are, nevertheless, "moral patients," in that while they cannot choose morally, they can be harmed by the deliberate choices of moral agents.[43] The same is true of some human subjects.

If animals are not moral agents, then they must be morally innocent or blameless. This must follow if they have no consciousness of right and wrong, no free will, and no moral accountability. That animals are innocent in this sense is commonly recognised (as the argument itself demonstrates), but not its implications.

Consider: some people hold that the infliction of pain can sometimes be justified as a means of moral reformation. For example, some parents believe that smacking children can be justified if it checks morally regressive behaviour. And some judge that it is right to punish those people who have committed serious offences—simply on the basis that punishment is what they deserve. But a moment's reflection will tell us that these justifications cannot apply to animals: they cannot merit pain as part of a plan to reform behaviour (because they are not morally responsible) and cannot deserve pain as part of a policy of retributive justice (because they do not consciously commit immoral acts).

The inability, then, of the infliction of suffering to morally benefit animals must tell *against* all such activity. In the words of C. S. Lewis: "so far as we know beasts are incapable of sin or virtue; therefore they can neither deserve pain nor be improved by it."[44] That means that most of the explanations and justifications extended to human subjects cannot apply to animals. It is conceivable, for example, that a human being incarcerated in a prison as a result of being found guilty of a crime could endure the pain of captivity as a means of teaching the wrongness of his or her actions and the need to change behaviour. However unlikely (given what we know about most prisons), it is at least a possible scenario. Again, a parent may try to justify violence (however mild) meted out to a child as an attempt to improve character or (perhaps paradoxically) to stamp out anti-social behaviour, such as bullying. But, whatever we may make of these justifications, we cannot properly use these, or similar ones, to justify the infliction of suffering on animals.

The absence of moral agency, then, renders the infliction of suffering upon animals problematic. It is the unmerited and undeserved nature of their suffering, and our inability to justify it by most traditional reasoning, that strengthens the case for animals.

I anticipate one objection. A utilitarian might agree that animals can never *deserve* suffering, but say that this must be distinguished from the fact that there may be times when causing animal suffering may be *justified* by reference to the greater good that might result. A utilitarian might argue, for instance, that causing pain to a vicious dog may be justified by appealing to the fact that others will not be bitten—and so harmed—by the dog in the future. True, the dog does not deserve pain, but pain may be justified in order to prevent harm to the victim or future victims. Well, I accept that there may be a strong *utilitarian* justification for the infliction of harms, even on moral patients (animal or human) in the interests of *direct* self-defence. But that acceptance does not render the previous considerations invalid. If, to take the case of an aggressive dog, one resists being bitten by means of a strategy of self-defence (which may involve the infliction of harm), it does not follow that one has any right to extend that qualification further—by, for example, vivisecting *all* dogs on the ground that some might be aggressive, or engaging in revenge attacks on the supposition that some dogs may dislike humans. In other words, even if a utilitarian justification is allowed for some very limited situations of direct self-defence that does not render the previous considerations unimportant nor allow for general, as distinct from very specific, dispensations. I use the word "direct" here in relation to self-defence because the attempt to generalise the concept (such as researchers are prone to do in relation to, say, "waging war" on cancer) runs the risk of justifying continuing direct harm on moral subjects for the sake of some hypothetical good, which is one of the reasons that experimentation on animals is so morally problematic.

In short, then, even allowing for exceptions in the case of direct self-defence does not invalidate the considerations that ought to apply to moral subjects. Even at the moment when one is attacked by an aggressive dog or an insane human, one's right to self-defence must be limited (that is, to the disabling of the aggressor); the attack cannot justify any wider application, nor can there be any legitimate resort to "punishment." Moreover, the aim of self-defence, as I understand it, is not to do harm but to render the aggressor harmless; any harm committed is accidental or incidental, where-as I am concerned here to oppose the *deliberate* infliction of suffering.

I now consider two specifically theological arguments that have been used to limit the solicitous treatment of non-humans.

(v) Soulless beings

The notion that animals are devoid of immortal souls has, historically, played a major part in Christian attitudes. It is worth noting that, following Aquinas,[45] Catholic tradition has never denied that animals have souls as such. As E. L. Mascall explains, Thomist theology (that is, theology derived from St. Thomas Aquinas), in turn influenced by Aristotle has distinguished between three kinds of soul: "vegetative" for vegetables, "sensitive" (meaning "animate") souls for animals, and "incorporeal"—that is, rational—souls for humans:

> Turnips and wart-hogs, as well as men, possess souls, for they, too, in their humble and different ways, are alive; when more precision is needed, the soul of the turnip is described as "vegetative," that of the wart-hog as "sensitive" and that of a man as "rational"; there is no implication that a soul necessarily survives the death of the body or that it is, in the modern sense of the word "religious."[46]

The apparent lack of rationality in animals, then, disqualifies them for immortal soul possession. Only rational beings have worth in themselves, according to St. Thomas, because they are valued by God for their own sakes. But there are other theologians, such as Paul Badham, who accept that animals are "thinking" beings, but also deny that they have immortal souls:

> One might well agree that animals are not machines but are feeling, thinking agents with purpose, wills, and rights which should be respected, without wanting to commit oneself to the view that they possess an eternal destiny beyond bodily death. . . . Much of the desire to claim souls for animals or foetuses ignores the question of whether it is actually intelligible to suppose that they could live apart from their bodies.[47]

Then he goes on to reinstate rationality (with an emphasis upon language) as a criterion:

> As far as we can judge, animals appear to live very much in the present and their thoughts and purposes concern their immediate needs. Indeed, without

a complex language it is hard to see how it would be possible to have a developed, reflective individual life and a fully developed power of reasoning such that one could identify one's selfhood with that capacity. Yet unless the subject's selfhood can validly be identified with its capacity for reflective reasoning it would not be possible to say that that "self" could exist in a disembodied state.... Though one cannot any longer accept the clear-cut distinctions of the Aristotelian-Thomist tradition, there does seem to be a point in its judgment that a soul which was only sentient would be mortal whereas a rational intellectual soul could enjoy immortality.[48]

Badham reinforces his view with reference to the "religious dimension." He writes that, "as far as we can see (with the possible exception of dolphins!), animals do not worship" and hence, "a mode of existence which was given intelligibility by the thought that in it God would become the most real feature of our experiencing would not be a mode of existence which would ensure continuity of identity for animals."[49]

Leaving aside for a moment Badham's connection between worshipping God and a continuing identity capable of surviving death, the issue of identity is worth some attention. One increasingly common rejection of the moral claims of animals is based on the idea that they are not persons. To be a person requires not only being a subject of mental states, but also persisting through time (i.e., a person is a persisting subject of mental states). Many might argue that this is precisely what animals are not; they may be subjects of mental states, but they do not persist through time. Therefore, they are not persons. Evaluating a claim of this kind is far from straightforward. Despite the considerable emphasis laid upon "persons," especially by Trinitarian theologians (derived from the classical definition of God as three persons in one substance), it is remarkably difficult to find a coherent account of the notion, particularly of how it might specifically privilege *human* persons and their moral claims against those of animals.[50]

But let us suppose that the claim is true and that—in the current philosophical jargon—an animal's body "contains" not a person, but a succession of "person stages." In such an animal, suffering can in no way be mitigated by considerations of narrative significance (as when, for example, I come to understand that my life is a story where the rough follows the smooth, that things will soon get better, and so on). One might also think of the trauma of teething, when young infants experience excruciating pain from the emergence of their first milk teeth. No parent (and I speak here as a father of four children) can be anything other than disturbed at the onset of this pain, which occurs when infants are wholly incapable of comprehending what is happening to them. Infants may be potential persons, but they are surely not capable of a "self-narrative" at this early stage of their life. So the question is: is their suffering or the similar sufferings of animals (who are likewise unblessed by a personal narrative) thereby less morally significant? On the contrary, if true, it seems that we have a stronger, not a weaker, obligation to minimize the suffering of both.[51] What a poor parent it would be who withheld an analgesic to a teething child crying in pain because it is not yet a full person with a philosophically defensible self-narrative.

Again, because animals cannot worship God and do not, apparently, experience the divine, they cannot, according to Badham, have a "continuing identity" capable of surviving physical death. But if true, does it follow that they deserve—for that reason alone—less moral solicitude? Surely, the reverse is the case. If animals are not going to be recompensed in some future life for the suffering that they have had to undergo in the present, it follows that their current suffering acquires even greater significance. Lewis addressed this issue in the context of vivisection, and his logic cannot be faulted:

> The Christian defender [of vivisection], especially in Latin countries, is very apt to say that we are entitled to do anything we please to animals because they "have no souls." But what does this mean? If it means that animals have no consciousness, then how is this known? They certainly behave as if they had, or at least the higher animals do. I myself am inclined to think that far fewer animals than is supposed have what we should recognize as consciousness. But that is only an opinion. Unless we know on other grounds that vivisection is right we must not take the moral risk of tormenting them on a mere opinion. On the other hand, the statement that they "have no souls" may mean that they have no moral responsibilities and are not immortal. But the absence of "soul" in that sense makes the infliction of pain upon them not easier but harder to justify. For it means that animals cannot deserve pain, nor profit morally by the discipline of pain, nor be recompensed by happiness in another life for suffering in this. Thus all the factors that render pain more tolerable or make it less than totally evil in the case of human beings will be lacking in the beasts. "Soullessness" in so far as it is relevant to the question at all, is an argument against vivisection.[52]

As a matter of justice, then, the present condition of animals subject to suffering without any understanding of why it happens, any personal narrative that would explain their suffering, any communication with the divine, and any hope of heavenly recompense (if that is really the case) is surely the most pitiable of all, and calls out for more, not less, moral solicitude.

(vi) Devoid of the divine image

This putative difference has its principal basis in the biblical declaration in Genesis 1:26–28, in which God makes human beings in the divine image. The difficulty, of course, is understanding what the *imago Dei* really means.

Perhaps the most important work on the meaning of the image is Guunlaugur A. Jónsson's little-known but masterful survey titled *The Image of God: Genesis 1:26–28 in a Century of Old Testament Research*, in which he painstakingly reconstructs the range of interpretations offered by scholars and theologians during the period 1882–1982.[53] The century begins with work by August Dillmann (1823–1894) and Samuel Rolles Driver (1846–1914), who argue (following many of the scholastics) that the *imago* refers primarily to the "mental endowment" of human beings over and against animals, what Driver calls the "possession by man of self-conscious reason."[54] Humans have the ability "to know in a sense in which animals do not know, and involving the capacity of apprehending moral and religious truth."[55] From that altogether traditional definition, the image is variously defined as consisting in "man's external appearance" (Theodor Nöldeke and Hermann Gunkel), as deputising for God (Gerhard von Rad), as proof of the "higher category" of humankind (Emil Brunner), as expressive of divine trinity reflected in sexual differentiation (Karl Barth), as indicated by the upright posture of humans (Ludwig Köhler), and as the "holistic" view of Theodorus C. Vriezen that the image refers to the "totality of the human being embracing not only its corporeal but also its spiritual capacities."[56] The twists and turns of exegesis are too numerous to follow here in detail, but I would like to bring the survey up to date with the latest view which now commands wide agreement among Old Testament scholars.

This interpretation (variously advanced by scholars including Robert Davidson, Heinrich Gross, Helmer Ringgren, and Waldemar Janzen) locates the meaning of the image in the context of the priestly narrative in the first creation saga in Genesis (1:1–2:3) and sees it as inextricably related to the granting of dominion over animals in Genesis 1:28. Without necessarily limiting the concept to the notion of dominion (as some scholars have done), David A. Clines summarises the view that sees, at the very least, an inextricable relation between the two:

> That man is God's image means that he is the visible representative of the invisible, bodiless God; he is the representative rather than the representation. The image is to be understood not so much ontologically as existentially: it comes to expression not in the nature of man so much as in his activity and function. This function is to represent God's lordship to the lower orders of

creation. The dominion of man over creation can hardly be excluded from the content of the image itself.[57]

The importance of this "functionalist" interpretation is that it provides the grounding for an ecological- and animal-friendly interpretation of the human presence in creation. Far from being a simple reinforcement of human supremacy, this view requires us to view human specialness as consisting (at least in part) in exercising God-like power over animals—a power that also requires God-like responsibility. "Dominion" in this context is far from the despotism it suggests to human ears; rather, it is a limited and accountable authority: limited because humans are to represent *God's own* benevolent care for other creatures, and accountable because humans are uniquely responsible *to God* for how they exercise that authority. The picture that emerges is of a God who creates humans with God-given capacities to care for creation as God's own representative on earth. In short, humans have to be that kind of unique creature (in terms of possessing a spiritual and moral sense that animals do not possess) *in order to care for* creation as God intended.

In case this is thought to be just one opinion among others that will change (as invariably all ideas do over time), it is worth noting how established the consensus among scholars has become. As Jónsson indicates, this creation-friendly interpretation has gained "an ever increasing acceptance" among scholars. "There is no doubt," he writes, "that during the period 1962–1982 an obvious general shift in scholarly opinion has taken place," so that "the functionalist interpretation . . . is now the predominant view." Indeed, Jónsson goes so far as to say that were it not for one or two dissenting voices, there would be a *"complete* consensus among OT scholars" on this issue.[58]

Understood theologically (with the help of modern scholarship), we can report that the divine image only warrants a more careful, diffident, and conscientious stewardship of creation, and animals in particular. The moral relevance of this difference works entirely in favour of animals, rather than against them. This must, logically, be true if the image in whose God we are made is a holy, loving, and just God who cares for all creation.

This brings us back to our opening discussion about the nature of human power over animals (see section 1.2.i). The issue is sharpened still more if the further step is made to understand this God-given power over animals from a Christological perspective. In that sense, St. Thomas was not entirely wrong in seeing a kind of implicit moral hierarchy in the world—except that he misunderstood it at its most important and relevant point, namely, that the "higher" should serve the "lower," rather than the reverse. The notion of human "mastery" is replaced by the notion of "service," and humans become not the "master" species but the "servant" species.[59]

1.3. A TEST CASE: HUMAN INFANTS

So far, we have been concerned with examining the differences and considering whether they are morally relevant. In order to test their relevance, let
us examine an analogous case—that of suffering inflicted on infants.

Suppose that you happen to be staying in the house of an old friend of
yours (we shall call him John), and you wake to the sound of screaming. You
go upstairs and there you find John beating his son, an infant of no more
than one year old (we shall call him Stephen). Astonished by John's behaviour, you decide to remonstrate with him. But, as your friend is a philosopher older and wiser than yourself, you decide that the best way forward is
to engage in philosophic discussion.

The child is put back to bed, and you go downstairs and ask why John has
been beating his child. Distinguished philosopher that he is, he is not bereft
of serious arguments.

"I know you think I am heartless," he says, "but you have to understand
I am the child's father. Stephen always cries for no apparent reason, and my
sleep is needlessly disturbed, which prevents me from undertaking my
important teaching duties the following day. My interests are superior to
his, and I have the natural right to make him subject to me and my
interests."

"But," you object, "power cannot be its own justification. Stephen may
well be subject to you, as indeed all children are subject (in a sense) to their
parents, but that cannot be sufficient justification for beating an infant."

"Ah, well, you have to understand," he replies. "I've never gone in for this
political correctness that says we are all equal. There is no equality in the
natural world; one being is naturally subject to another. One being serves
another. God designed the world like that: the big fish does not greet the
little fish, but eats it." And he adds: "Power has rights."

"But is it a *moral* right?" you question. "Yes, there are inequalities in
power, but don't the weak have a claim on the strong—not least of all your
own child?"

"Well, you need to look at the basis on which I exercise this power. It isn't
arbitrary; there are real differences between Stephen and me. Though I care
for him dearly, he really hasn't the same interests as I do. Mine are obviously
superior. For example, I am much more intelligent than he is. It isn't just
that I have three university degrees and a distinguished record of research
and publication. Unlike Stephen, I can think and reason. I am a rational
being, whereas Stephen isn't much more than a brute animal who cannot
reason at all."

"Yes," you protest, "all that may well be true, but Stephen still feels, he can
experience pain just as we do. It is surely heartless to beat him."

"Do you really think so?" John replies. "I wouldn't deny that he feels *some* sort of pain, but without a mind, what kind of pain could it really be? I have thought about this, you know. I mean, he cannot suffer ontological anxiety—I mean, real *angst* about whether life is worth living or whether he is going to die. Dear chap, I don't think he even knows what death is. What can suffering mean if you can't even think about tomorrow or remember much of yesterday? Yes, he feels something, but suffering such as you or I experience it would be far too grand a claim."

"But," you protest, "I grant it may be very different pain, even (in your terms) less important than your own, but it is still suffering of sorts. If you cut him, he bleeds; if you beat him, he suffers. How do you know that his feelings matter less to him than yours do to you?"

"Well, there's another point," John answers. "Stephen has no language, and without language, there can be no conceptualisation, no understanding, no depth of experience. You know, I don't even think he has a conception of himself, and without self-awareness how can anything have meaning for him—as life has for us?"

"But when Stephen cries, is that not a form of communication, a kind of language? Does that not tell you that he is in distress, that he needs attention?"

"That's sheer sentimentality, I think. Yes, of course, he groans and cries, and I hear him—though who knows really what he is feeling? After all, he cannot tell us anything about it. It might as well be the gurgling of his stomach or the letting out of wind. He cannot actually speak or make me understand."

"But shouldn't you give him the benefit of the doubt?" you ask.

"You mean, by imagining that he might actually be experiencing the heights of intellectual vexation or cognitive dissonance? Come, come! He is just an infant. He has no mind, no language, and precious little feeling—at least as we would understand it."

"I still can't help feeling that poor Stephen is suffering when you beat him."

"My dear, you really are taken with terrible, untutored thoughts about the world. You see suffering everywhere. I mean, Stephen isn't a moral agent; he has no duties or responsibilities. There can be no rights without duties; otherwise, even beasts would have them. What you really don't seem to grasp is that Stephen isn't *like us*—he's not intelligent, he's not articulate, he's not a responsible being."

"I still think I heard cries of suffering," you declare. "It would be inhuman not to respond to them, not to take them seriously, even if all the things you say are true."

"Inhuman!" John shouts, now getting angry. "This is getting ridiculous. Stephen *isn't* human like us—that's the whole point. You can engage all these fantasies as much as you like, but you haven't presented me with one solid reason why my behaviour is wrong, whereas I have given you plenty in response. We can't have a philosophical discussion if you are just going to be dogmatic. There's much more to philosophy, you know, than mere feeling. If you give way to feelings, you can become submerged in all kinds of irrationalities."

The scenario is imaginary, but not entirely fanciful. For most of Western history, children have been regarded as little more than appendages, even as the property of their parents. The Christian tradition has underwritten not the rights of children, but the rights of parents, including the right of physical chastisement. The UN Convention on the Rights of the Child was not even promulgated until 1979, and still awaits full ratification in many countries, including the United Kingdom.

The test question is: if we regard John's arguments as morally irrelevant in the case of his child, Stephen, what grounds could there be for regarding them as relevant in the case of animals?

One obvious reply is that, while there is no intrinsic difference, there is a huge *relational* one: John is related to his son in a way that he is not related to any non-human animal, namely, in being a human. Moreover, it may be stressed that this unique commonality imposes duties and responsibilities among its members that do not exist when this relationship (that is, humanity) does not exist. In effect, there is a solidarity that exists among humans that doesn't exist between human and non-human animals.

The problem with this relational argument is that, if it is sound, it ought to cut both ways. If the justifiability of inflicting suffering depends not upon an impartial weighing of interests, but wholly on one's *relation to* the subject in question, then we cannot consistently protest about those who prefer their animal "companions" over human ones. Consider, for example, the case of an elderly woman (we shall call her Griselda) who was deserted by her children but who spends her life with her companion cat (we shall call him Harry). Harry, although feline (or perhaps because he is feline), offers Griselda unconditional love and daily companionship. Her life is immeasurably enriched by this experience. Unsurprisingly, Griselda dotes on him. So far, so good, one might think. But suppose one day the parents of one of the neighbouring children complain that Harry is spiteful to their child (we shall call him Jimmy) and scratches his face, and Griselda replies, not with appropriate solicitude for the welfare of children, but rather with "Well, Harry is my companion; I care for him more than your children. Your children are not my companions or my relatives; they can go to blazes." Now, of course, some aspects of this story are far-fetched. Cat lovers are also, in my experience, child lovers. Moreover, no cat gratuitously scratches without having been provoked. But leaving these details to one side, we

would surely judge that Griselda was acting inconsistently in caring everything for Harry and nothing for Jimmy. We couldn't morally commend her
response nor credit her evaluation. Do not both Harry and Jimmy suffer
pain? It is inconsistent to care for Harry's well-being and not also for
Jimmy's.

If we had to counsel Griselda, we would surely want to say that, however
understandable her preference for her animal companion, it should not
override the general concern she should have for Jimmy and, indeed, for all
other children. Particular preferences and loves, especially intense loves, are
liable to make for partial perspectives. That doesn't mean that we shouldn't
have them, nor that they are not entirely natural and understandable, nor
that they can't constitute specific obligations in particular contexts. But they
cannot morally be sufficient; that's the point. From an impartial perspective—whether it is someone we love or hate—both are capable of suffering
and both are worthy of our solicitude.

The counter-argument may come that "Jimmy is a *human*, and therefore
he deserves more solicitude." But that is precisely the point. Unless we are to
adopt the position of blind species loyalty (that is, no matter the situation,
human suffering alone matters or always matters more), we need an impartial perspective in order to judge competing claims. Saying that we should
put humans first because we are human is clearly not an impartial standpoint. I am reminded of the argument of C. S. Lewis as regards vivisection.
Noting that vivisection is defended by those who see no fundamental
distinction between man and animals since "man" is simply regarded as
"the cleverest of the anthropoids," he comments that it must follow that we
"sacrifice other species to our own not because our own has any metaphysical privilege over others, but simply because it is ours":

> It may be very natural to have this loyalty to our own species, but let us
> hear no more from the naturalists about the "sentimentality" of anti-
> vivisectionists. If loyalty to our own species, preference for man simply
> because we are men, is not sentiment, then what is? It may be a good
> sentiment or a bad one. But sentiment it certainly is. Try to base it on logic
> and see what happens![60]

Of course, there will be some who claim that humans have some "metaphysical privilege" over animals, as I do myself. But if my reading of
"dominion" and the *imago Dei* is correct, Christians of all people cannot
claim that they are *unrelated* to fellow creatures. We are all creatures of the
same Creator; our life (*nephesh*) is God-given and, in both cases, the work of
the Spirit. Our metaphysical privilege consists in being set in such a relationship to the earth and its creatures that we are required (as part of our

very humanity) to exercise God-like care, even of a costly and sacrificial kind. There is no *Christian* privilege that doesn't involve service.

1.4.   RECONFIGURING THE DIFFERENCES AND THEIR RELEVANCE

The difficulty with almost all of these arguments is not that they isolate differences as such (even, sometimes, important ones). What is problematic is that they most usually couple these differences with implicit or (more usually) explicit denigration of what is different. And they do so as a means of denying or lessening moral solicitude.

Nevertheless, these arguments contain intimations of moral relevance that cut across the original intention of their defenders. Reconfigured, these differences do, paradoxically, point to particular considerations that should apply to weaker and more vulnerable beings. Briefly summarised, they are as follows:

(a) *Animals cannot give or withhold their consent.* As already noted, it is commonly accepted that "informed consent" is required in advance from anyone who wishes to override the legitimate interests of another. The absence of this factor requires, at the very least, that we should exercise extraordinary care and thoughtfulness. The very (obvious) fact that animals cannot agree to the purposes to which they are put increases our responsibility.

It might be claimed that, although animals cannot talk consensually and non-consensually, their actions may manifest consent and the lack thereof. So, for example, an animal that fights (and howls perhaps) to stay out of a kennel may be presumed to register her will against being placed in a kennel. So maybe animals can behaviourally, and even vocally, manifest their lack of consent.

While not denying the importance of these behavioural indications, they obviously fall short of what humans mean when they speak of voluntary, informed consent. Consent only makes sense, logically, if an individual is presented with alternative possibilities and has both the knowledge of what these possibilities represent and the freedom to choose one of them, and that without coercion. When an animal cries, or howls, or reels in pain, she registers displeasure at her predicament, but registering displeasure (or pleasure) is not voluntary consent. In any case, it is to be doubted whether any domestic animal, routinely subjected to human control, can exist without coercion. In short, we can sometimes know how animals feel (mostly negatively) about their state (and we do well to be sensitive to such indications). In that sense, we do often (rightly or wrongly) presume consent, but *presuming* consent is still a long way from *voluntary*, verbal consent as we know it between human beings.

(b) *Animals cannot represent or vocalise their own interests*. Individuals who cannot adequately represent themselves have to depend upon others to do so. The plight of animals, like that of children or of the elderly who suffer from dementia—precisely because they cannot articulate their needs or represent their interests—should invoke a heightened sense of obligation.

Again, it may be claimed that animals can and do represent their interests—as, for example, an animal found scouring rubbish bins may be said to "represent his interest" in getting food. In such ways, animals may be said to "speak to us" so we have some sense of their interests. But one cannot logically insist upon the "linguistic deficiency" of animals (as so many philosophers have done) and then refuse its conclusion that animals cannot properly represent themselves—at least in terms that we can verbally understand. Of course, those who wish to exploit animals pretend to know only too well what "their" animals "want." But, in fact, while we can and should take behavioural indications seriously, our general (and sometimes specific) unknowing should be counted in their favour.

(c) *Animals are morally innocent*. Because animals are not moral agents with free will, they cannot—strictly speaking—be regarded as morally responsible. That granted, it follows that they can never (unlike, arguably, adult humans) deserve suffering nor be improved morally by it. Animals can never merit suffering; proper recognition of this consideration makes any infliction of suffering upon them problematic.

The point remains valid, even if some moral theorists, notably utilitarians, conclude that some infliction of pain—in self-defence, for example—may be justifiable. Inflicting pain on those who can never deserve nor merit it increases our responsibility; it raises the bar of moral acceptability even higher, and that is true even if some decide that it may still be justified by reference to the greater good. Whether we are utilitarians, virtue theorists, or deontologists (or a combination of all three), the special claim of animals remains that their suffering cannot be justified by the means that might conceivably apply in the case of human subjects.

(d) *Animals are vulnerable and defenceless*. They are wholly, or almost wholly, within our power and entirely subject to our will. Except in rare circumstances, animals pose us no threat, constitute no risk to our life, and possess no means of offence or defence. Moral solicitude should properly relate to, and be commensurate with, the relative vulnerability of the subjects concerned, or with what might be termed "ontologies of vulnerability."[61]

The massive vulnerability of animals to humans is like and unlike other vulnerabilities. It is like the vulnerability of children (particularly infants), comatose patients, and the mentally unwell. These beings are most readily subject to us; in fact, almost everything we do to them is done without consent, even though they are blameless. Such actions incur heavy responsibilities when they involve calculations of the subjects' own interests, and especially when the activity involves harm. Few would dissent from this line of reasoning in relation to these subjects.

But, in relation to animals, the case is equally strong, if not stronger. Animal vulnerabilities are *unlike* others in that they, especially managed animals, are almost completely vulnerable and subject to massive exploitation. We do not breed, choose to create, artificially inseminate, nor genetically engineer infants or the mentally unwell. Our institutional control of animal lives is without parallel, except perhaps in the case of non-sentient plants. In the case of many domestic and farm animals, we choose not only that they should exist, but also determine the pattern and shape of their lives. We change the "nature," that is the physical appearance, of animals through, inter alia, de-barking, de-clawing, ear cropping, tail docking, and so on, and those are the "lucky" ones that we supposedly care about. And in the case of farm animals, we now genetically modify their lives. Our almost total control over animals, properly understood, involves us in near-total moral responsibility.

Moreover, vulnerable human subjects are usually (though not always) accompanied by advocates who at least feel and understand what it might be like to be so physically constrained, or subject to others, and who are able to articulate with some precision their needs and interests. But in the case of animals, many humans, it seems, do not even grasp the full sensitivity of the animal subjects with which they regularly interact. Our dominant philosophy, religion, and science all keep us from grasping the immensity of their suffering and appreciating its moral significance. People sometimes remark disparagingly on the number and range of animal protection organisations worldwide, but in truth such welfare work (which is what in most cases it still is) falls far short of what protecting animals from abuse actually entails. The ontologies— that is, the various "beings," kinds, and natures of animals—are subject to the domination of human kind in every country and culture.

The presence of just one of these factors should be enough to merit moral consideration; together, they form the rational basis for a compelling case. It bears repeating that the key point is that all these considerations make the infliction of suffering on animals not *easier* but *harder* to justify.

1.5. CHILDREN AND ANIMALS AS SPECIAL CASES

By "special" is meant something "exceptional." Exceptional because animals do not fit into most established ethical theories, such as correlated rights and responsibilities, mutual contracts, or (most forms of) virtue ethics, and they ruin well-crafted theories of justice, merit, and deserts. Albert Schweitzer likened the history of Western philosophy to that of a person who cleans the kitchen floor—only to find that the dog comes in and muddies it with paw prints.[62] Animals do make a mess of anthropocentric philosophy and theology. As a consequence, they have been relegated to the periphery of moral thinking, since their inclusion poses too great a threat to established ethical systems to be worth the effort. But if my thesis is correct, the very differences which have been appealed to in order to buttress this exclusion also contain the seeds of a radical reconfiguration.

The practical upshot is that we cannot continue to privilege human suffering as if it stands alone as a unique source of moral concern. Some animal-friendly philosophers advance solicitude for animals on the basis that they are, inter alia, *like us*. But my thesis is that their very alterity in many respects should underpin their moral claim. The usefulness of animals, paradoxically, is that they help us to grapple with the moral relevance (as well as irrelevance) of difference. Neither is it sufficient to argue on the basis of "equality" or "equal consideration."[63] The rational grounding for animals cannot be done justice by concepts that flatten out obligations.

One concluding linkage is inescapable. Our present society is characterised by an increasing ethical sensitivity to children and a particular abhorrence at their violent or abusive treatment. Is this newfound sensitivity well founded rationally? In order to provide such an account, it would be necessary to bring these considerations into play: children (young children and infants especially) are vulnerable, they cannot articulate or represent themselves nor fully comprehend, they cannot give or withhold consent, they are morally innocent and totally dependent upon us. It will not have escaped the reader's attention that these are also the very rational considerations that should ground solicitude to animals. If the considerations are morally sound in one case, they are morally sound in both. It is precisely these considerations that should mark both infants and animals as justifying special solicitude.

1.6. A THEOLOGICAL JUSTIFICATION

Some might ask how this thesis could be justified from a specifically theological perspective. So far, the impact of theological ideas has been seen to be largely negative in relation to animals. Indeed, the Christian tradition has been the ideological mainstay (or at least one of them) of those who want to exploit animals. But Christian theology comprises more than the Aristotelian-Thomist tradition, however practically indebted it may be to it. To look at the matter from a fresh perspective, we need to ask why the sufferings of vulnerable, innocent, uncomprehending, unprotected, defenceless beings might be theologically significant.

One answer is given in a little-known sermon by John Henry Newman preached when he was the vicar of St. Mary's University Church, Oxford, on Good Friday in 1842. Like most of Newman's sermons, this one merits careful attention. Newman began in a devotional way by saying that we cannot love Christ unless we feel heartfelt gratitude, and we cannot feel that gratitude "unless we feel keenly what he suffered for us."[64] While feeling is not enough, it is an essential component of our response to Christ. He then posed the question: "*how* are we to feel pain and anguish at the thought of Christ's suffering?"[65]

He offered three ways in which this can be done. The first is by reference to the suffering of animals. His text was from Isaiah 53:7, which compares the coming Messiah to "a lamb that is led to the slaughter, and like a sheep that before its shearers is dumb, so he opened not his mouth." Newman noted that Christ was "as defenceless and innocent, as a lamb is," and stated that since scripture compares Christ to this "inoffensive and unprotected animal," so "we may without presumption or irreverence take the image as a means of conveying to minds those feelings which our Lord's sufferings should excite within us."[66]

But Newman did not stop there. He specifically addressed the issue of cruelty and, in the process, made a remarkable claim:

> I mean, consider how very horrible it is to read the accounts which sometimes meet us of cruelties exercised on brute animals. Does it not sometimes make us shudder to hear tell of them, or to read them in some chance publication which we take up? At one time it is the wanton deed of barbarous owners who ill-treat their cattle, or beasts of burden; and at another, it is the cold-blooded and calculating act of men of science, who make experiments on brute animals, perhaps merely from a sort of curiosity. I do not like to go into particulars, for many reasons; but one of those instances which we read of as happening in this day, and which seems more shocking than the rest, is, when the poor dumb victim is fastened against a wall, pierced, gashed, and so left to linger out its life. Now do you not see that I have a reason for saying this, and am not using these distressing words for nothing? *For what was this but the very cruelty inflicted upon our Lord?* He was gashed with the scourge, pierced through hands and feet, and so fastened to the Cross, and there left, and that as a spectacle.[67]

What is significant about this passage is not the particular sympathy shown to animals as such, but the placing of such suffering within a Christological context. With the question: "For what was this but the very cruelty inflicted upon our Lord?" he posited nothing less than a moral equivalence between the suffering of animals and the suffering of Christ himself. He underlined this by illustrating how the suffering of a hapless animal in a particular experiment mirrored the physical suffering of Christ on the cross. But the issue is not just about the physical similarity of the torture inflicted; Newman went on to explain the rationale for our abhorrence of cruelty in both cases:

> Now what is it that moves our very hearts, and sickens us so much at cruelty shown to poor brutes? I suppose this first, that they have done no harm; next, that they have no power whatever of resistance; it is the cowardice and tyranny of which they are the victims which makes their sufferings so especially touching. For instance, if they were dangerous animals, take the case of wild beasts at large, able not only to defend themselves, but even to attack us; much as we might dislike to hear of their wounds and agony, yet our feelings would be of a different kind; but there is something so very dreadful, so satanic in tormenting those who have never harmed us, and who cannot defend themselves, who are utterly in our power, who have weapons neither of offence nor defence, that none but very hardened persons can endure the thought of it.

And to make the parallel exact, he continued:

> Now this was just our Saviour's case: He had laid aside his glory, he had (as it were) disbanded his legions of angels, he came on earth without arms, except the arms of truth, meekness and righteousness, and committed himself to the world in perfect innocence and sinlessness, and in utter helplessness, as the Lamb of God.[68]

And Newman concluded: "Think then, my brethren, of your feelings at cruelty practiced upon brute animals, and you will gain one sort of feeling which the history of Christ's Cross and Passion ought to excite within you."[69]

Newman was doing much more here than using our feelings about cruelty as an aid to religious reflection. He was explicitly recognising a moral equivalence between two kinds of suffering. Moreover, and this is the crucial point, in so doing, Newman uncovered the all-important rational ground for positing that such cruelty is nothing less than (in his word) "satanic."

1.7. CHRIST-LIKE SUFFERING

So, if we ask again our question with which we began—namely, why should the sufferings of vulnerable, innocent, unprotected, defenceless beings be judged to be theologically significant?—the answer must be that there is something Christ-like about such suffering. It ought to compel a moral response, as ought the sufferings of Christ himself. We are right to be, in Newman's words, "moved" and "sickened" because that kind of suffering—whether of humans or of animals—of the innocent, unprotected, and vulnerable is morally unconscionable.

One further connection should be made, and it goes to the heart of the issue about Christian believing and suffering generally. Given the close correspondence between these two kinds of suffering, and their identical moral underpinning, it should follow that those who are properly sensitised to the sufferings of the crucified ought—for the same reasons—to be sensitive to the suffering of all vulnerable and innocent beings. That is further illustrated by Newman's second example, concerning the suffering of children. Newman asked: "How overpowered should we be, nay not at the sight only, but at the very hearing of cruelties shown to a little child, and why so?" He replied: "for the same two reasons, because it was so innocent, and because it was unable to defend itself."[70] The same pattern of argument repeats itself: there should be a common revulsion at the infliction of suffering on all innocent and vulnerable beings. Newman was sagacious, even prophetic, in grasping the underlying philosophical justification for opposition to both animal and child cruelty.

1.8. SUMMARY OF MAIN POINTS

1. The assumption is frequently made that human suffering matters more than any other kind of suffering. This position may not be wholly rational nor supported by rational considerations. At the very least, my argument is that we owe animals more than is commonly supposed.

2. Those who wish to justify or minimise animal suffering frequently argue that animals are different from humans. But the question is whether any of these are *morally relevant* differences that could justify differential treatment (1.1).

3. My concern is not to dispute the accuracy of these differences, but rather to show that the moral conclusions drawn from these differences are almost entirely mistaken, and that another completely opposed conclusion follows (1.2).

4. Six putative differences are considered for their moral relevancy:

(i) *Animals are naturally slaves* either by the design of nature or by divine providence. This argument, stripped of inessentials, is about power and whether power can be its own self-justification. It cannot stand, by itself, as a ground for refusing moral solicitude to animals, but should rather, at least on one mainstream theological account, be reckoned as morally relevant—in favour of increased sensitivity to the weak and the vulnerable (1.2.i).

(ii) *Animals are non-rational beings.* The argument only works if it can be shown that rational comprehension increases liability to suffering and is therefore morally relevant. In some cases, rational comprehension may increase suffering, but there are grounds for supposing that incomprehension may also increase liability to suffering in others. Animals and humans suffer in varying ways. Humans will suffer more in some situations, animals more in others (1.2.ii).

(iii) *Animals are linguistically deficient.* Possession of a language that humans can understand may unlock a richness of experience but so, too, may the possession of a complex range of non-human characteristics, as well as a symbolic language that *we* cannot understand. Even if the minimalist picture of animals as linguistically deficient, "primitive" beings is true, it doesn't follow that their suffering isn't as significant for them *in their own terms* as ours is for us (1.2.iii).

(iv) *Animals are not moral agents.* Our moral superiority (in the sense of possessing moral agency) should more reasonably be displayed by acknowledging duties to animals that they cannot acknowledge towards us. The absence of moral agency renders the case of animals problematic, since animal suffering is necessarily unmerited and undeserved, and we are unable to justify it by most traditional reasoning (1.2.iv).

(v) *Animals are soulless.* According to traditional theology, animals do not have rational and, therefore, immortal souls. But beings that will not be recompensed in another world for their suffering in this one logically deserve more, not less, moral solicitude (1.2.v).

(vi) *Animals are devoid of the divine image.* The consensus of Old Testament scholars now locates the meaning of the image within the biblical narrative that sees humans as divinely commissioned to look after the world and other animals. Moreover, if a Christological understanding of power is engaged, human power over animals means responsibility, even service (1.2.vi).

5. A test case concerned the beating of a human infant. The question is: if we regard John's arguments as morally irrelevant in the case of his child, Stephen, what grounds could there be for regarding them as relevant in the case of animals? (1.3).

6. It may be objected that, while there is no intrinsic difference, there is a huge relational one since Stephen is a human being. But this relational argument, if sound, cuts both ways—both for and against animals. But either way, however understandable, they are morally insufficient. Impartiality requires us to go beyond species loyalty (1.3).

7. The arguments from differences contain intimations of moral relevance that cut across the original intention of their proponents. Reconfigured, these differences point to considerations that *are* relevant:

animals cannot give or withhold their consent;
animals cannot represent or vocalise their own interests;
animals are morally innocent; and
animals are vulnerable and defenceless.

The presence of just one of these factors should be enough to merit moral consideration; together, they form the rational basis for a compelling case. When judged impartially, these make the infliction of suffering not easier, but harder, to justify (1.4).

8. Both animals and children, specifically infants, constitute special cases. Similar considerations apply to both. We cannot continue to privilege (adult) human suffering, as if it stands alone as a unique source of moral concern. The "felt" emotional case for animals and children has strong rational foundations (1.5).

9. This case can be supported by a mainstream theological argument that the suffering of the vulnerable and the innocent have a Christ-like quality. Such suffering ought to compel a moral response, as should the sufferings of Christ himself (1.6–7).

10. It follows that those who are sensitive to the sufferings of the crucified ought—for the same reasons—to be sensitive to the sufferings of all vulnerable and innocent beings (1.7).

2

How We Minimise Animal Suffering and How We Can Change

The last chapter outlined the considerations that oblige us to regard animal suffering as a special case. But since almost everywhere animal suffering is regarded as minimally important, and sometimes not important at all, the question might naturally be asked: if, as I have suggested, the case for animals is so strong and rationally well grounded, why has it so often been overlooked?

2.1. CONFRONTING THE POWERS

My aims in this chapter are twofold: first, to identify and illustrate what might be described as "the powers that be"—intellectual mechanisms that prevent us from recognising sentience in animals or that help to limit its significance. I then draw out the challenges involved in attempting to speak impartially, or at least less prejudicially, about animals. Second, I aim to consider ways in which animal abuse is socially perpetuated through the phenomenon called "institutionalisation." Then, with the help of some

Chomskian analysis, I suggest ways in which moral perceptions about animals need to become embodied in new institutions.

(i) The power of misdescription

The first is what Denys Turner has called "that most powerful of human tools, the power of misdescription." In a paper provocatively titled "How to Kill People," he argues:

> Let me tell you how to kill people efficiently; or rather, here's how to get yourself, and, if you are in the business of doing so, here's how to get others to kill people. First you have got to call your proposed victims names. . . . if we propose to kill a fellow human being and justify it, we have to redescribe him in such a way that he no longer belongs to us, becomes an alien being . . . and in that way the inhibition against killing is effectively weakened.

He provides the examples of how some newspapers, in the time of the Falklands/Malvinas War, described the Argentineans as "Argies" or "wops," and how, in the Vietnam War, U.S. soldiers called the North Vietnamese "gooks." Apparently, General William Westmoreland once commented that the Viet Cong could be killed with less scruples because they had an "Eastern" attitude to death and the value of human life.[1] These examples are not intended to pass moral judgments on either war, but to illustrate that we cannot easily kill human beings without first degrading them verbally. In order to kill or abuse, we need to create an *artificial* distance from the one who is to be killed or abused.

Similarly, we have created an artificial distance between ourselves and other animals. We have seen that there are differences, sometimes important ones, both between and among species. It is not the citing of difference per se, but rather the *denigration* of difference that is questionable. It is how we *use* differences to justify unjust treatment and, specifically, how these are embodied in our language. Consider the historic language we use about animals: "brutes," "dumb brutes," "unfeeling brutes," "critters," "sub-humans," "beasts," "wild beasts," and the adjectives "brutal," "beastly," and "bestial."[2] The Anglican *Book of Common Prayer*, which is still in use, recommends that marriage should not be undertaken "to satisfy men's carnal lusts and appetites, like brute beasts that have no understanding." By definition, it is difficult to champion the rights of "beastly," "brutal," or "bestial" life.

So pervasive is this language that it is difficult even for "animal advocates" (itself not an unambiguous term) to find an alternative nomenclature. Our

Dumb Friends' League was the actual title of an animal-friendly organization (now called the Blue Cross) founded in 1898. The term "non-human animals" (used by pioneering animal advocates in the 1970s) is hardly unprejudicial either. As one Buddhist friend of mine recently remarked: "I am getting fed up with being called a *non*-Christian—who wants to be defined by what one is not?" In a class on sexual ethics at Oxford, one student said how much he opposed adultery because it was "ratting on one's partner." I had to point out that some rats are more monogamous than some human beings. In doing so, I had, as it were, to "take the bull by the horns," not "let sleeping dogs lie," "be as sly as a fox," even act as "a snake in the grass"—the point to be grasped is that these are not just libels on human beings.

Unless we address the power of misdescription, we shall never be able to think straight, let alone see straight (that is, impartially or, at least, with some measure of objectivity). Even "animals" is itself a term of abuse (which hides the reality of what it purports to describe, namely, a range of differentiated beings of startling variety and complexity). The language we use is the language of *past* thought. We shall not possess a new understanding of animals unless we actively challenge the language we use, which is the language of historic denigration. The challenge is how to create a nomenclature—born of moral imagination and a sense of fellow-feeling—that does justice to animals.

(ii) The power of misrepresentation

It is important to grasp that the artificial distance between ourselves and other animals does not arise from nowhere. It has been fuelled by both religious and scientific ideologies.

In Christianity, that ideology is Cartesianism: the doctrine, largely originating with Descartes, that animals are unthinking automata. The reasoning goes like this: because animals possess no rational (and therefore immortal) souls, they cannot think, they cannot possess self-consciousness and language, and, therefore, they cannot experience pain. In short, they cannot feel pain because they do not have the mental wherewithal to do so. Supporters of Descartes often want to absolve him of callousness to animals, and perhaps they are right because it is difficult to discover one line that absolutely denies that animals feel any kind of pain. But it is the clear logic of what he writes that creates the conclusion that animals are little more than machines. Consider, for example, this tortuous argument:

> I know that animals do many things better than we do, but this does not
> surprise me. It can even be used to prove they act naturally and mechanically,

like a clock, which tells the time better than our own judgment does. Doubtless when the swallows come in spring, they operate like clocks. The actions of honeybees are of the same nature, and the discipline of cranes in flight, and of apes in fighting, if it is true they keep discipline. Their instinct to bury their dead is no stranger than that of dogs and cats who scratch the earth for the purpose of burying their excrement; they hardly ever actually bury it, which shows that they act only by instinct and without thinking. The most that one can say is that though the animals do not perform any action which shows us that they think, still, since the organs of their body are not very different from ours, it may be conjectured that there is attached to those organs some thoughts as we experience in ourselves, but of a very much less perfect kind. To which I have nothing to reply except that if they thought as we do, they would have an immortal soul like us.[3]

In other words (and at the very least), animals are unthinking organisms that operate by instinct. We cannot assume that their organs, though similar to our own, carry the same, or even similar, sensations since this is the function of the rational soul, which is unique to human beings. The argument is entirely a priori. It is difficult to see how any empirical evidence could count against it.

The effect of Cartesianism was to give those who wanted it a theoretical basis for disregarding the pains of animals. The Cartesian model was taken up by specific discourses—the sciences in particular—that are helped by the idea of the animal-machine. But it also specifically hardened religious attitudes to animals. Although, prior to Descartes, the dominant voices within Christianity were largely negative about animals, there were various sub-traditions that commended fellow-feeling and even kindness, as exhibited in the lives of many canonised saints of East and West.[4] Descartes' followers, the Port Royalists, reportedly "kicked about their dogs and dissected their cats without mercy, laughing at any compassion for them, and calling their screams the noise of breaking machinery."[5]

It is doubtful whether the Jesuit Joseph Rickaby could have written in 1889, "we have no duties of charity, nor duties of any kind to the lower animals, as neither to stocks or stones,"[6] without the influence of Cartesianism. And even Charles Raven, professor of divinity at Cambridge (and a biologist), writing as late as 1927, maintained, "it may be doubted whether there is any real pain without a frontal cortex, a fore-plan in mind, and a love which can put itself in the place of another, and these are the attributes of humanity."[7] No matter the differences between their positions, Descartes would have heartily approved of Raven's tying of sentience to altruistic love.

Cartesianism was paralleled by a scientific doctrine called "behaviourism." Behaviourist ideology—which has so influenced American and British psychology—only allows for descriptions of *learned* behaviour. Subjectivity in animals is jettisoned. As Bernard Rollin explains: "A major victim of this ideology was the notion of felt pain in animals."[8] In order to preserve scientific objectivity, scientists "totally ignored any subjective dimension of feeling, and dealt only with the neurological and chemical substratum, the 'plumbing' of pain."[9] The result, as Rollin indicates, was an extreme scepticism about the existence of animal pain:

> Animal anaesthesia was known only as "chemical restraint" throughout most
> of the twentieth-century, and the first textbook of veterinary anaesthesia,
> published in the United States in the middle of the 1970s, does not list
> control of felt pain as a reason for anaesthetic use.

Again: "Anyone doing a literature search on animal analgesia in the late 1970s would have found literally no journal articles on the topic, and such theoretical lack of concern was replicated in laboratories, and in veterinary practice."[10] Amazingly, according to Rollins, the International Association for the Study of Pain still maintains a definition of pain that makes the possession of language a necessary pre-condition.

It is useful to digress at this point and remind ourselves of how strong the evidence for sentience in mammals has become. "Sentience" is defined in some dictionaries as "sense perception," but I shall use it to denote the capacity for suffering; it is most regularly used nowadays by philosophers to denote the capacity for pain and pleasure. There is ample evidence in peer-reviewed scientific journals that mammals experience not just pain, but also suffering, to a greater or lesser degree than we do ourselves. The scientific reason for that is straightforward. Animals and humans show a common ancestor, display similar behaviour, and have physiological similarities. Because of these triple conditions, these shared characteristics, it is perfectly logical to believe that animals experience many of the same emotions as humans. Logic tells us this and we do not need special data to believe in the suffering of animals.

In fact, the onus should properly be on those people who try to deny that animals have such emotions. They must explain how, in one species, nerves act in one way and how they act completely differently in another. They must explain why we believe that a child who cries and runs away from us after we have stamped on his foot is unhappy while a dog who behaves in precisely the same manner is said to present us with insufficient information for us to believe that the dog is unhappy. In the words of Konrad Lorenz: "The similarity [between humans and animals] is not only functional but historical, and it would be an actual fallacy not to humanise."[11]

Indeed, as early as 1872, Charles Darwin devoted a whole book to *The Expression of Emotions in Man and Animals* in which he detailed, inter alia, the emotional responses of wild and domestic animals.[12] Since then, there has been a wide range of scientific, especially ethological and epistemological findings on animal learning, tool making, and self-consciousness. One of the founders of the field of animal cognition, Donald R. Griffin, argued in 1992, "What scientific understanding can provide is evidence against the notion that all animals are incapable of suffering and therefore totally undeserving of sympathy."[13] And David DeGrazia in his authoritative study published in 1996, concluded:

> The available evidence, taken together, suggests that many species of animal—indeed, there is some reason to think, most or all vertebrates—can experience anxious states of mind. . . . Additionally, given the close—probably overlapping—relationship between fear and anxiety, it is reasonable to conclude that these animals can also experience fear. Supporting this proposition is the fact that all vertebrates have automatic-nervous systems and limbic systems, which contain the basic substrates of anxiety and fear. In conclusion, the available evidence suggests that most or all vertebrates, and perhaps some invertebrates, can suffer.[14]

The misrepresentation of animals is paralleled by the misrepresentation of their advocates. Jeremy Paxman introduced an item on BBC2's *Newsnight* concerning the Great Ape Project by asking: "should we give human rights to apes?" In fact, no animal advocate (to my knowledge) wants to give apes human rights.[15] The notion conjures up—as one suspects it was designed to do—visions of apes in polling booths, ape MPs, apes demonstrating for better pay, ape trade unions, and so on. By the misuse of one word, the case for not harming apes was subjected to public ridicule. One Canadian newspaper, in the course of attacking the International Fund for Animal Welfare's anti–seal hunt campaign, described it as "the International Fund for putting Animals on Welfare." In an increasingly welfare-unfriendly world, that charge betokens fraudulent activity. It conjures up pictures of animals as rival welfare claimants, drawing benefits, claiming the dole, and squandering tax-payers' money. Another welfare fraud. The power of the media to misrepresent can frighten us out of most moral sensibilities. Who wants to be known as a "bunny hugger," a "Bambi lover," a "friend of the dumb brutes," or a "sentimentalist"? And, now, fuelled by the lamentable violent tactics of a tiny minority, animal advocates are likely to be classed as "extremists," "fanatics," "animal fascists," and even (most horribly of all) "animal terrorists."

The second challenge, then, is to seek non-pejorative, even convivial, representations of animals and less-partial labels for those who try to protect them.

(iii)   The power of misdirection

By the power of misdirection, I mean the way in which suffering in animals, even when acknowledged, is minimised, obfuscated, or its moral significance belittled. There are five arguments worth briefly examining:

(a) *The "we can't really know" argument.* Academics frequently exhibit the "scepticism of the wise" tendency.[16] When presented with what to most ordinary mortals appears to be a case of abuse, if not downright cruelty, they invariably inflate uncertainty, and in so doing misdirect our attention away from the harm inflicted. Here is an example:

TV INTERVIEWER: Don't pigs suffer when immobilised in these crates?

RESPECTED SCIENTIST: You are assuming, of course, that pigs suffer just like we do. We do not really know that. It's a very complex question.

TV INTERVIEWER: But don't most animals have the need to turn around?

RESPECTED SCIENTIST: But, again, you're assuming that the needs of pigs are identical to our own. We have to move beyond naïve anthropomorphism.

TV INTERVIEWER: So you're saying that they aren't suffering then?

RESPECTED SCIENTIST: I think we would need a great deal more research in order to reach a definite conclusion about such a complex question. We can't simply assume that pigs suffer in circumstances that would make us suffer.

TV INTERVIEWER: So what do you think should be done?

RESPECTED SCIENTIST: I think we need much more research. We don't know how animals feel because they can't tell us about it. We should set up a scientific committee to explore this question, obtain research grants, make experiments, and find really objective ways of measuring what may be at issue here.

TV INTERVIEWER: Thank you, Professor, for your eloquent insights.

The interview is imaginary, but not wholly fictional. Such are the legacies of Cartesianism and behaviourism that academics find it as difficult to talk about emotion in animals as (it is claimed) nineteenth-century clergymen found it difficult to talk about sex, something that they could not easily do without blushing. Researchers open themselves up to the most dreaded accusation that can be levelled at any academic, namely, being a "sentimentalist." For most academics, agnosticism is a lifelong "faith"—and I use that word deliberately. Scepticism has its good side (we surely need people committed to rigorous enquiry), but it misleads us when it becomes an end in itself. In the not wholly unfair definition provided by George McLeod: an academic is "someone who can hold a vital issue at arm's length for a lifetime."[17] What is worrying is that this professional scepticism (which, in other contexts, we should welcome) is increasingly taken over by government ministers and officials, and especially represented by government committees (which usually comprise appropriately sympathetic academics) so that government policy becomes itself unreasonably sceptical about animal sentience. Peter Roberts provides a classic example. In a symposium contribution titled "The Experts Say This Is Not Cruel . . . ," he refers to how the State Veterinary Service Report to Parliament maintained that there was "no suffering detected in the keeping of a calf in a 22-inch wide veal crate night and day for all its life, and unable to turn round." The report maintained, "[I]t is not in the calf's interest to be able to turn round."[18]

Philosophers have sometimes compounded the scepticism of scientists by reason of their own agnosticism. Modern discussion has been influenced by Thomas Nagel's well-known essay "What Is It Like to Be a Bat?"[19] His answer (not surprisingly) is that we cannot know much—actually nothing—about what it is like to be a bat. But we do not need to know precisely how a bat thinks, or feels, or mentally encounters the world in order to know basic things about how it can be harmed, for example, by mutilation, by deprivation of its instincts, by isolation from its peers, by subjecting it to invasive procedures, and by the infliction of adverse physical stimuli. We can, and do, know these things, without scientific evidence and without knowing everything possible, philosophically or scientifically, about the mental consciousness of a bat. We can know these things at least *as reasonably* as we know them in the case of most humans. The same is also true of the many millions of mammals that we regularly harm in research, recreation, and farming. We should not allow not knowing everything to prevent us from acting ethically on what we can reasonably know.

In short, academics exhibit two principal tendencies. The first is professional scepticism of an epistemological kind (about what can be known and by what means). This is a useful and necessary tool, but is most readily directed *against* animals by inflating uncertainty. It is seldom used consistently by also, for example, interrogating the claims of those who abuse animals. Without evidence of consistency, it is fair to say that academics, often unwittingly, bolster existing prejudices about animals and, in so doing, become the willing intellectual tools of the established world view. The second tendency is political quietism: the still-entrenched view that academics should not get involved in political activity, even on the basis of intellectual conviction. The latter view still predominates in many universities, but its consequence is to render mute those who sometimes have the most interesting things to contribute to public discussion. Both tendencies cramp the style of academics in relation to moral issues, and especially (with some honourable exceptions) in relation to the cause of animals.

(b) *The "we must have scientific proof" argument.* The desire for data, for evidence of all kinds, rather than simply assertion, is to be welcomed in moral debate, but when it comes to animals, that desire is frequently hardened into a pre-condition of judgment. We shall examine the Burns Report on hunting when we consider the morality of hunting with dogs in chapter 3, but I simply want to mention here one example from Burns of how the argument is utilised. Commissioned postmortem evidence, detailed in the Burns Report, showed that hunted foxes died from "massive injuries to the chest and vital organs." Yet, the report concluded that there is "a lack of firm scientific evidence about the effect on the welfare of a fox of being closely pursued, caught, and killed above ground." Hunting is judged to "seriously compromise the welfare of the fox,"[20] but it is not "cruel." Lord Burns, in a subsequent speech in the House of Lords, explained why:

> Naturally, people ask whether we were implying that it was cruel but in true Sir Humphrey style were not prepared to say so. The short answer to that question is no. There was no sufficient verifiable evidence or data safely to reach views about cruelty. It is a complex area. . . . One cannot ask an animal about its welfare or know what is going on inside its head.[21]

Cruelty is sometimes defined as the act of *deliberately* harming, but it is not cruelty in that sense to which Burns appears to be referring. By "cruelty," he seems to mean "real suffering," and to reach that judgment one apparently needs "sufficient verifiable evidence" *in addition to* physical postmortem evidence. Thus, even prima facie evidence of injury is not taken as sufficient to reach a definite judgment about suffering. But the idea that there must be "sufficient verifiable evidence" before we can know that a fox suffers when it is being disembowelled by dogs is as unreasonable as supposing that we cannot know that lashing a whip across a child's back is "cruel." If Burns's attitude of extreme scepticism were maintained in the face of similar evidence of cruelty to children, the noble lord would justifiably be the subject of public ridicule, even though infants cannot tell us "what is going on inside their heads" either.

(c) *The "we mustn't be anthropomorphic" argument.* We need to distinguish between good and bad anthropomorphism. The bad principally focuses on the attempt to project specifically human needs and emotions onto animals. Although Beatrix Potter fans will hate me for saying this, I have always been less than enamoured of her imaginative world in which, inter alia, animals dress up in human clothes and enjoy gardening. Some might say that this is a harsh judgment on Potter since her kind of anthropomorphism is generic, a literary technique especially widespread among writers of children's fiction, and it is conceivable (though I have no evidence for supposing it) that her work has a positive impact on the way children conceptualise animals. Even so, the danger of the technique is in viewing animals as mini-humans, rather than as beings in their own right. Animals have to become humans, or acquire human-like characteristics, in order to merit attention, whereas, in my view, it is the very *unlikeness* of animals that should, inter alia, arouse our moral and imaginative concern. At its worst, the technique invites us to a child-like fantasy land which, whatever its immediate merits, is rightly discarded as children become adults. Feeling for animals is thus seen as a subject for children—and therefore, by definition, something that adults grow out of.

Good anthropomorphism, on the other hand, accepts as a reasonable assumption that all non-human mammals suffer to a greater or lesser extent than we do. Grasping this essential similarity between human and animal suffering should not, however, extend to supposing that all aspects of animal life should be viewed through the human model. Much damage has been done to animal protection by people who cannot conceive, it seems, of sensitive creatures without imagining scenes of animals in human garments. The good anthropomorphic view was well expressed by the "ethical approach" of the former Farm Animal Welfare Advisory Committee in 1970: "the fact that an animal has limbs should give it the right to use them; the fact that a bird has wings should give it the right to spread them; the fact that both animals and birds are mobile should give them the right to turn around, and the fact that they have eyes should give them the right to see."[22]

Yet, making that fairly minimal assumption appears to some a step too far. Colin Tudge, for example, argues, "many of the things done to animals in the name of farming *seem* cruel. It seems cruel to stand a sow in a stall, too small for her to turn round.... It seems cruel to make a cow lie on concrete." But, he continues: "We cannot assume that animals are unhappy simply because they are in situations that would make us unhappy; we cannot assume they are unhappy because they look unhappy to the casual observer."[23]

In fact, it is a very reasonable assumption that animals denied the use of most, or all, of their natural instincts—without any compensating factors— are "unhappy." That is exactly what we *can* and *should* assume. We do not need science to know that intensive farming harms animals, deprives them of their natural lives, and makes them liable to suffering. In 1974, Professor John Napier, then chair of the Farm Livestock Advisory Committee of the Royal Society for the Prevention of Cruelty to Animals (RSPCA) stated, "No good ethologist would regard even a modicum of anthropomorphism as the proper way to present a case [for animal welfare] in the long run."[24] Thus began a thirty-year industry in which academics have occasionally been paid large sums to investigate whether animals in intensively farmed conditions are "suffering." But if anthropomorphism is so "unscientific" and so flawed, why is it that subsequent research has vindicated almost all of the objections to factory farming, based on "naïve anthropomorphism," that were advanced as early as 1964? The very systems that attracted criticism—battery cages, sow stalls, veal crates—have all been shown to make animals liable to harm or to engender suffering.

(d) *The "everything has feelings" argument.* Those who want to reject the idea that animal suffering matters apparently see pain and suffering everywhere. The case of fish is instructive. Although the case for sentience in mammals is stronger than in the case of fish, some apparently regard fish as wholly insensible. Three scientists applied bee venom and acetic acid to the lips of trout and learned that they had "adverse behavioural and physiological effects."[25] The conclusions were hardly surprising and, despite the claims, had already been anticipated by earlier research.[26] Nevertheless, even this evidence was not enough for some. In the words of a columnist of *The Times*: "We should ignore this codswollop [*sic*] hook, line, and sinker." The argument is that, if we allow ourselves to be persuaded by evidence of pain in fish, "it is illogical to deny the possibility that your lawn cannot feel a thing when you attack it with your flymo."[27]

There is no evidence or reason, however, to suppose that plants are sentient, but that does not prevent our columnist from making the argument that PETA (People for the Ethical Treatment of Animals) will, we are assured, shortly become the "People for the Ethical Treatment of Vegetables."[28] Those who place their hopes in science might like to reflect that, for some, evidence of whatever kind will never count against their opinions. The issue, as always, is not about science, nor even about the sensibility of fish or plants, but about *our* moral sensibility. Konrad Lorenz may have overstated the point, but it is nevertheless worth recalling that he recommended suicide for "any man who finds it *equally* easy to chop up a live dog and a live lettuce."[29]

(e) *The "they may feel pain, but not as we do" argument.* This one is reminiscent of Mr. Spock's famous line in *Star Trek*, "yes, it's life, but not as we know it." The origin of this view is the idea, so central to Cartesianism, that animals are incapable of rational thought, and therefore cannot really suffer like us. But, as we have seen, the moral issue is not whether their suffering is identical in all respects to our own, but rather whether their suffering is *as important to them as ours is to us.*

Mention should perhaps be made here of the view of philosopher Peter Carruthers that animals experience pain "non-consciously." He writes:

It may be that the experiences of animals are wholly of the non-conscious variety. It is an open question whether there is anything that it [sic] feels like to be a bat, or a dog, or a monkey. If consciousness is like the turning on of a light, then it may be that their lives are nothing but darkness.[30]

And the ground for this extraordinary view is that since mental states are either conscious or non-conscious, "there is no reason to believe that animals are capable of thinking about their own thinkings in this way, [so] none of their mental states will be conscious ones."[31] The claim that there is "no reason" to believe that animals can exercise reflective consciousness is breathtakingly dismissive of accumulated scientific evidence. It has the nature of an a priori metaphysical speculation. That *some* mental states (in both humans and animals) may be non-conscious, as for example when one is injured in a car crash and yet not immediately aware of it (the example that Carruthers gives), cannot be taken, in itself, to imply that *all* the mental experiences of animals are non-conscious.

Carruthers derives his conclusion from the so-called higher-order thought (HOT) model of consciousness, according to which for a mental state to constitute consciousness, the subject of that state must have a thought about it—a thought to the effect that she is in that state. Since animals can't have thoughts of this sort, all their mental states are unconscious. Of course, if this is true, the same applies to young children also. Any sane defender of the HOT model will regard this implication—with respect to both children and animals—as hugely embarrassing, indeed a *reductio* of the entire theory, should it prove to be a genuine implication. Thus, in practice, the strategy of almost all defenders of the HOT account is to try and show that this isn't really an implication of that account. Only Carruthers embraces this implication, and it is difficult to know what to say about someone so out of touch with the reality of both children and animals that he doesn't think they have any conscious states.[32]

In any case, Carruthers makes clear that his is no impartial enquiry into truth. He rather gives the game away when he claims in his preface to The Animals Issue that "popular concern with animal rights in our culture [is] a reflection of moral decadence," thus people concerned with animals are morally like "Nero [who] fiddled while Rome burned."[33] An attempt to discredit a cause by name calling in advance of examining the evidence betokens extreme partiality. It is a pity that he didn't take up the moral significance of his initial statement that "animal sufferers are always blameless," which could have led him to a different form of enquiry.[34] Carruthers has since modified his stance, arguing that even though these states may lack "phenomenological properties," this need not prevent those states from being "appropriate objects of sympathy and moral concern."[35] But it is doubtful whether this later adjustment has undone the damage of his previous work, which has buttressed Cartesian-like indifference to suffering.

There is a kind of snootiness (I can't think of a nicer word) about the way in which humans regard their own interests or pleasures as self-evidently more important than those of other species. It was epitomised some years ago when a researcher on television defended animal experiments on the ground that animals are incapable of writing poetry. Well, every individual—both within and between species—has different interests and pleasures. Mine happen to include reading political biographies, smoking Three Nuns pipe tobacco, arguing about theology, watching romantic films, and consuming cheap red wine. My half-Persian cat, on the other hand, enjoys being tickled on the chin, chasing table tennis balls, stalking in the long grass, and reclining on my wife's pillow. What gives pleasure to other animals—and other humans—is often different, sometimes very different, from what gives *me* pleasure, but I can see no *rational* ground for supposing that our ability to enjoy pipe tobacco—rather than, say, an ability to chase table tennis balls—justifies any of us in supposing that our suffering or pleasure matters more to us than theirs does to them.

Doubtless, for those whose worlds are divided into only "rational" and "non-rational" beings, the presumed non-rationality of the lives of animals counts for little or nothing. Commenting on this dualism, which has so distorted Christian thought, Alec Whitehouse writes, "Those who believe that man's chief end and highest good is to glorify God and fully to enjoy him for ever are frequently disposed to treat as fully actual, and envisage as finally actual, only what is incorporated into the activity of [presumed] rational agents."[36] These people, not unfairly described as "aristocrats of the mind," "are unwilling to be comfortably or uncomfortably at home along with the world's minerals, vegetables, and animals."[37] It is wrong, of course, to despise specifically human rationality, but that is a separate matter from supposing that such rationality is the highest good, or the only thing of value in the world.

The third challenge, then, is to find the moral and intellectual resources to face the full reality of animal sentience without trivialisation or obfuscation.

(iv) The power of misperception

I turn, lastly, to the power of misperception (or, rather, the power of perception). I begin with an example that I have used before.[38] The university where I used to work as chaplain was situated in acres of eighteenth-century parkland. From my office, I was able to look out over the undulating hillside, which was populated with rabbits. At first, I used to just notice things moving here and there as I occasionally looked up from my computer. But as the weeks and months progressed, I slowly began to marvel at the complexity, intricacy, and beauty of their lives. I used to say—only half-jokingly—that "it was worth coming to the university to see the rabbits." Whenever visitors came, I used to point out the rabbits, and some would indeed say, "How wonderful," but for many others, it was as if I had pointed out the dust on the carpet, or the faded colour of the paint. Whatever they saw, they did not *see* rabbits.

I may be labouring the obvious here. But many people still do not *see* animals. They may have seen things moving, objects out there, even "pests" that invade "their" territory. But they have not yet seen other living, sentient beings. Our language, our philosophy, our science, our history, our theology, our culture, by and large, prevent us from seeing. We should not be surprised that, since major voices in our history have regarded animals as machines, in the end we treat them as machines. It was Ruth Harrison's prophetic work in 1964 on farm animals, titled *Animal Machines*,[39] that helped us to appreciate how we had reduced other creatures to just that. I recall after lecturing one day in Oxford, a student came up to me and said: "Well, Dr. Linzey, I found all your arguments very interesting, but there's something I don't understand. What are animals for, if they are not to be eaten?" The person concerned was being perfectly serious and sincere. She just had not seen animals as anything more than lumps of meat. We need to move from an anthropocentric—indeed, gastrocentric—view of animals.

The change of perception—or insight—can be stated quite simply: it is the move away from ideas that animals are machines, tools, things, commodities, resources here for us, to the idea that animals have their own value—what we may call an "intrinsic value." Animals are not just "objects" out there; they are—in the words of Tom Regan—"subjects of a life," and they bring *subjectivity* into our world.[40] As I have put it elsewhere, "this is a moral and spiritual discovery that is as objective and important as any other fundamental discovery, whether it be the discovery of the stars or the discovery of the human psyche."[41] It is the "Eureka!" experience, the "Aha!" experience, the moment when the penny drops experience. It is when we make the *moral* discovery that animals matter in themselves, that they have value in themselves, and that their suffering is as important to them as ours is to us. We need to recognise that there are still human beings out there who just have not had this insight. They do not think that animals matter, or that there are other creatures of value in the world. They think that human beings matter, but that the rest is just "the environment," a theatrical backdrop to what really matters, namely, themselves.

There is, however, the alternative possibility that some, perhaps many, are all too able to see the reality, but refuse to do so. It certainly sounds naïve to think that the majority of people are so blind about the nature of animals that they can only understand them as meat. The issue here is not that we live with ignorance, but with *willed* ignorance: we refuse to see what is right before our eyes. So, on this account, we have a more active relation to animals (as those who *choose* not to see) rather than that of simple passive ignorance. This possibility cannot be discounted, not least of all because of the investment that most humans have in the current arrangements that obviously serve their interests. But it also seems a rather low argument involving the imputation of less than honourable motives to one's opponents, so that, while tempting as it may be and plausible though it may seem at least in some situations, it should be generally avoided.

Whatever the truest explanation, one fact more than all others needs to be factored into our thinking, namely, our investment in *not changing*. Humans profit from animal suffering. The reason that it is often so difficult to get a serious hearing for animals is because, unlike many other ethical issues, humans not unnaturally suspect that granting animals moral solicitude will involve major changes to their lifestyles. It is understandable that some people will view this indebtedness and conclude that humans are simply incapable of making the necessary changes if animals are to be treated properly. There is a silent despair about the possibility of moral change that informs a resignation to much abuse and suffering—and not only that of animals.

2.2. MORAL CHANGE AND RESISTANCE TO CHANGE

In order to counter this despair, we need to indicate the means by which moral change can happen, and may yet happen in relation to animals. The following points are obviously made with the animal issue in mind, but they are also relevant to some other social issues.

We need to begin by reminding ourselves of the dimensions of the problem. Some animal abuse may result from the actions of people who deliberately intend to be cruel. Such people need corrective therapy so that they learn to understand the harmful effects of their actions and are helped to mend their ways. But it is a mistake to understand animal abuse simply in terms of *individual* pathology. Doubtless, there are people with dispositions towards cruelty or, more generally, individuals who are unthinking in their attitudes towards animals, and the same is true of other forms of abuse as well.

But where animal abuse differs from most others is that it is socially legitimised and institutionalised. Cruelty to children, for example, is thankfully already illegal in most of its manifestations. The anti-cruelty cause in relation to children enjoys wide social approval and is making strong progress. That does not mean, of course, that all is well. The UN Convention on the Rights of the Child (1979) has still to be fully ratified by many countries, and even in countries where anti-cruelty legislation exists, there is still a continuing need for education, prevention, and inspection.[42] Some forms of child abuse are certainly institutionalised—for example, child labour—but what most characterises animal abuse is its widespread social acceptability and consequent institutionalisation.[43] It is the highly developed and entrenched nature of that institutionalisation that makes change so highly problematic.

It is important to grasp how institutions—for good or ill—shape our lives and give meaning to them. They are multivalent in their power and influence. An institution is defined as an "established law, custom, or practice."[44] And in that definition, the word "established" is probably the most important, since all institutions embody power through their influence. We live our lives through our participation in institutions, which provide us with our identity, or (at the very least) we are influenced by the effects they have on us. Families, schools, colleges, universities, businesses, trade unions, local councils, newspapers, television, government, and so on—no person lives without being defined in some way by these corporate identities of which he forms a part. From the time we are born, institutional influence shapes us. Parents begin the process by socialising children and guiding us (often in subtle ways) about what to think or how not to think, if, indeed, we are encouraged to think at all. Thus, early on, our attitudes towards animals—and how we should react to their suffering—are shaped by parental guidance and control, and they are later reinforced by schooling, university education, and subsequent careers. And, most especially, such attitudes are bolstered by daily contact with the media.

We do not, therefore, come to the animal issue with clean hands nor, indeed, with a clean mind. The range of our use of animals is enormous: we hunt, ride, shoot, fish, wear, eat, exhibit, factory farm, and experiment on millions, if not billions, every year. None of us are untouched by our use of animals, and all of us, directly or indirectly, benefit from it. This means that we are never able to decide our actions from a position of impartiality based on first principles, as if we were encountering an entirely new moral problem for the first time. Rather, we find that the issue has already been determined for us, and by the time we begin thinking (if we do), we find that we are already compromised by our existing involvement. That recognition should give us pause. Whatever the strengths of rational argument, it is always difficult, sometimes even impossible, for people to change deeply ingrained habits of life, especially ones that bring specific benefits. Much more work needs to be done—by psychologists, educators, and ethicists—on the nature of moral change and development in individuals. Far too many campaigners assume that all individuals are prepared, able, or willing to change when faced with rival moral perceptions or rational arguments. We know that the situation is not so simple, and it remains an open question whether humans are ever really able to withstand the immense power of their own conditioning and upbringing. But the moral response is not simply to despair (however understandable that may be at times) but to think creatively about how these institutions that so govern our lives can be adapted and transformed, even how we can create new ones.

It is also important to grasp that almost all these institutions are not morally neutral as regards animals. Sometimes, they can be positive, but most usually they are negative for this simple reason: they reflect and reinforce *past* attitudes and *past* thought in relation to animals. They act, therefore, as agents of what George Orwell called "thought control."[45] Reflecting on Orwell's 1984, Noam Chomsky comments:

> I also think he [Orwell] missed the main techniques of thought control and indoctrination in the democracies. For example, in England and the United States we do not use the devices for control he described: crude vicious use of highly visible power. That's not the way thought control works here. It works by more subtle and much more effective devices . . . Orwell completely missed this.[46]

Chomsky isolates institutional influence, especially the media, or "the propaganda system," as he calls it, as the principal, at least most effective, form of social control. When asked how we can "get at what is real, get at the truth," Chomsky replies:

> [W]hat one has to do is adopt towards one's own institutions, including the media and the journals and the schools and the colleges, the same rational, critical stance that we take towards the institutions of any other [countries'] power. For example, when we read the productions of the propaganda system in the Soviet Union or Nazi Germany, we have no problem at all in dissociating lies from truth and recognising the distortions and perversions that are used to protect the institutions from the truth. There's no reason why we shouldn't be able to take the same stance towards ourselves [U.S.–style propaganda], despite the fact that we have to recognise that we're inundated with this constantly. A willingness to use one's own native intelligence and common sense to analyse and dissect and compare the facts with the way in which they're presented is really sufficient.[47]

Chomsky is specifically referring to U.S. foreign policy and the justifications given for going to war, but his view has a much wider application. Whether one agrees or not with Chomsky's general position, the plea for the utilisation of "critical intelligence" seems unassailable. Its relevance will be obvious, since the language and concepts that we use about animals have overwhelmingly been forged by those who want to justify their use of animals and protect their position. An attitude of critical distance—what Paul Ricoeur has called the "hermeneutics of suspicion"—is called for.

The need, then, in our context, is to cultivate a critical perspective on contemporary portrayals of animals that seek to justify abuse. "I don't think it's really hard," Chomsky assures us:

> Once one perceives what is happening, they [those who want to know the truth] have to take the first step of adopting a stance that is simply one of critical intelligence towards everything you read, in this morning's newspaper or tomorrow's newspaper or whatever, and discover the assumptions that underlie it. Then analyse those assumptions and restate the account of the facts in terms that are really true to the facts, not simply reflections of the distorting prism of the propaganda system. Once one does that I think the world becomes rather clear. Then one can become a free individual, not merely a slave of some system of indoctrination and control.[48]

2.3. CULTIVATING AND INSTITUTIONALISING CRITICAL AWARENESS

With the help of Chomsky's insights, let us examine some of the obstacles to change and the possibilities of overcoming them.

(i) Discovering the facts

Chomsky's emphasis in this regard may surprise us, given what we know of how facts, not to mention figures, can be distorted or manipulated. But discovering how facts are distorted is immensely significant. It helps us to grasp the underlying perspective that the distortions actually serve. Once we have understood that, we can begin to make the necessary intellectual corrections to what we read, hear, or see in the media. In the case studies in part II, it will be seen that I frequently investigate the factual bases of the claims made by those who wish to exploit animals. This is one of the most useful ways in which to begin ethical analysis and to discover what the issues really are.

Now, of course, facts cannot deliver values, as every ethicist will (or should) say. Facts by themselves do not constitute argument. All facts have to be interpreted and seen against a larger backdrop. All that is true, but in order to discover what partiality or perspective is at work in any given debate, there is no better way than checking the putative facts. I do not mean to imply that only animal advocates know the facts or use them accurately. On the contrary, all advocates can and do play fast and loose with factuality, and not only advocates, it should be said, since the same applies to government officials, even, and especially, government reports. No matter how understandable the reasons for manipulation on either side, rational debate on animals requires, inter alia, due reverence for the facts of the case.

(ii) Retaining the focus on the ethical

One of the reasons that we so seldom hear or read a rigorously ethical discussion of our treatment of animals in the media is because defenders of abuse have become adept at sidestepping the ethical issues. Strenuous efforts are made to divert discussion from the ethical issue at hand: the morality of hunting, for example, is viewed in terms of the need to "control vermin" or the special needs of those who live in the countryside; the morality of experimentation on animals in terms of effective "models" of research; the morality of farming in terms of trade and commerce. Whatever the legitimate place of these considerations in ethical debate, to allow them to dominate all moral discussion is to fail to give ethics its proper due. It is only when the ethical becomes the primary focus that people are enabled to *see* the issue and make connections.

Animal people are not always the best advocates of their cause in this respect. Aware of the way in which defenders of the status quo frequently focus on non-ethical issues, they sometimes focus on these aspects as well and thereby help to obfuscate the central moral issue. This is best illustrated by the way in which some anti-vivisectionists respond to the claims about utility by counter-claiming that all animal testing is useless, fraudulent, or misleading. Now, there is an important scientific critique of the utility of animal testing,[49] but to claim that the results of *all* animal tests are useless is to go way beyond the evidence. Much more important, it focuses the argument on the utility rather than on the morality of animal testing.

Likewise, some advocates make the "scientific" case for animals, sometimes speaking of "scientific animal welfare," the "science of animal suffering," or "animal science," as if science by itself is able to determine the morality of the issues. Of course, there needs to be a healthy respect for facts and scientific evidence—as I have already argued. But ethical terms, like right and wrong, good and bad, are not reducible to non-moral terms. Moral issues cannot be turned into scientific ones, nor subsumed under scientific categories.

But even when the media addresses the moral issue, there seems to be only one kind of moral philosophy that media commentators understand or can cope with, and that is popular utilitarianism. Classical utilitarianism, as developed by philosophers like J. S. Mill and Jeremy Bentham and as advanced (with some qualifications) by contemporary philosophers like Peter Singer, is indeed capable of taking animal suffering into account, but popular utilitarianism, as espoused almost daily by the media, is invariably antipathetic to animals. That is because it invariably takes as its measure of right and wrong the simplest rule of thumb, namely, "does it benefit us?" When that is combined with the unexamined assumption that human suffering is self-evidently more important than animal suffering, the result is that, even when the media does address moral issues, it does so crassly by posing questions such as: "How can you place the suffering of a few rats over the needs of medical research that is essential to saving lives?" or "Aren't suffering children more important than laboratory animals?" By this technique (used even by experienced or reputable broadcast journalists), the moral issue is addressed and disposed of at the same time. What is at the heart of the issue of course is *what kind* of utilitarian calculus is being employed, *and by whom*, that is, what is real benefit and who is calculating it?—but television discussion hardly ever reaches that level of analysis. Slogans win out over argument.

Indeed, it is astonishing to see how frequently even trained ethicists lapse into popular or simplistic utilitarian considerations when it comes to debating our duties to animals—considerations that in other contexts they would hardly dare to employ. Just imagine the reaction to a person who proposed that child pornography could be justifiable because it provides jobs. Ethicists of course, like the rest, have their blind spots and their prejudices. One sure way of detecting such partiality is to ask oneself whether such consequentialist considerations would also be given such weight in comparable situations concerning human subjects.

(iii) Recognising the limitations of the media

Most people who are subject to the media every day soon begin to absorb not just the dominant perceptions presented but also the forms of argument. We learn, in other words, by sound-bites (an unlovely term that, in my view, describes an equally unlovely thing). Complex arguments are deliberately reduced to their barest simplicity. This technique is understandable given the attempt to reach a mass audience and to present the "news" in an accessible form. But anyone who actually knows anything about the news being reported is only too aware of how partial, simplified, or dichotomised the reporting often is. Since none of us can know everything about everything, we inevitably rely on media reporting, even if we discount it in areas where we have personal knowledge or experience.

The result of this technique, however understandable in other areas, is devastating when it comes to any in-depth analysis, especially of an ethical kind. That is because, in order to engage in ethical thinking, one invariably needs to be reflective, to think further and deeper than sound-bites, and ethical arguments are often complex depending upon different world views or philosophies. The problem is expressed by Chomsky in this way:

In two minutes, between two commercials, or in a few hundred words, you can say some conventional things. For example, if I'm given two minutes on the radio and I want to condemn the Russians for invading Afghanistan, that's easy. I don't need any evidence, I don't need any facts, I can make any claim that I want, anything goes because that's conventional thought, that's what everybody believes anyway, so if I say it it's not surprising, and I don't have to back it up.

But for those who want to question conventional thought or socially accepted practices, the position is different:

On the other hand, suppose I were to try in two minutes to condemn the U.S. invasion of South Vietnam, or the U.S. attack against Nicaragua. That sounds crazy. The U.S. isn't attacking people! So within two minutes between two commercials it sounds absurd, in fact any unconventional opinion sounds absurd. The reason is that if you say anything in the least way unconventional, you naturally, and rightly, are expected to give a reason, to give evidence, to build up an argument, to say why you believe that unconventional thing. The very structure of the media in the United States prevents that, makes it impossible. The result is that what's expressible are conventional thoughts and conventional doctrine. That's a very effective technique for blocking thought and criticism.[50]

In other words, all unconventional thinkers face the difficulty of "concision," which is required by almost all the media. To make a case, and to make it rationally, requires more argument than the short interview, head-to-head confrontation, or media slot generally allows. If I may speak personally here: I know from twenty-five years' experience of being interviewed just what a desultory experience it can be. Except in rare situations, conventional thinking always sounds best, and attempts to invoke wider considerations often appear to miss the point. For this reason, I now seldom agree to speak to the media unless there is at least a chance of a fair hearing. How exactly can one indicate the rational grounds for extending moral solicitude to animals—innocence, vulnerability, inability to articulate and consent—in a twenty-second sound-bite? Others may well be more skilled in this direction than myself, but even so it is a challenge for the best of communicators to create those twenty seconds that provoke people to a deeper sense of the issue.

The other problem that Chomsky highlights is the nature of the print media especially. Many people assume that newspapers are financed by the people who buy them, whereas it is advertising revenue that overwhelmingly funds newspapers. It follows that newspapers are not going to promote positively any philosophy that is detrimental to the majority of their advertisers. Once grasped, the point is obvious. But it helps to explain why the "editorial" line of many newspapers (quite apart from the views of individual proprietors) is often hostile to the development of a strong pro-animal position. Some newspapers, it is true, are more generous than others in allowing space for dissident opinions. I am not saying that the pro-animal position is never allowed space nor reported fairly. But the most usual editorial positions, the ones reflected in space given to columnists as well as in "factual" reporting, are overwhelmingly reflective of current thinking and vested interests.

One example may illustrate this. In 1996, there was extensive media coverage of the first cloned animal, a sheep called Dolly. Journalists were invited to see Dolly in her pen, and she was photographed profusely for the world's press. A healthy, attractive animal obviously makes good copy. But almost no journalist asked the question that should have been asked: what was the cost (to the animals) of this development? Most published accounts of the first experiments failed to report significant abnormalities: "In addition to death through malformed internal organs, one lamb had to be delivered by caesarean section because it had grown to twice its normal size in the womb, and all but one of the five cloned lambs were at least 20 per cent larger than they should have been."[51] Almost everyone has heard of Dolly by now, but how many people know of the 200 or so experimental Dollys that went so badly wrong and the harm that they suffered?

The above, while gloomy, needs to be counter-balanced by an awareness that—despite the inherent difficulties—it is sometimes possible through careful preparation and sheer opportunism to utilise the media to make pro-animal arguments. The opportunities are limited, but that doesn't make the task impossible. What is needed is a far more professional approach among animal advocates and a determination to learn and use the necessary skills.

(iv)   Establishing alternative sources of information

When asked how he is able to sustain his unconventional critique of state power, Chomsky indicates that he is the recipient of many communications from individuals who provide alternative accounts, including press cuttings, of major events.[52] By this means, he is able to use the media against itself, by locating the facts they choose to minimise, or misrepresent, or represent poorly. By this kind of careful news analysis, new perspectives can emerge, and one can be freed from the stereotypical news coverage that predominates in most of the media.

In addition, there is now the possibility of establishing frequent contact with alternative news sources at the press of a button. Despite the many criticisms that one can legitimately make of the Internet, it has undoubtedly enabled individuals to search for information beyond the usual boundaries. We know, for example, that the chief reason that China enforces tyrannical control of the Internet is because it wants to impose ideological control and to limit access to alternative viewpoints. It may not be long before other countries pursue the same course. But, for the present time at least, we are free as never before to think differently from the prevailing nostrums of orthodoxy in relation to many moral issues, including animals. Animal advocates have yet to use this opportunity to its fullest extent, although some animal organisations are beginning to do so. Through e-mail lists, chat rooms, and blogs, individuals and groups are freer than ever before to create a new critical awareness of the powers supporting animal abuse.

Despite these useful sources, there can be no substitute for painstaking reading and the careful weighing of arguments that comes principally through the medium of books. Since the 1970s, there has been a considerable growth of high-quality works on animal abuse, which chronicle the harm done to animals and offer thoughtful and challenging perspectives from a range of disciplines within the sciences and the humanities. There are now so many of them that it is almost impossible for one individual to have read all the texts and to keep up with the arguments in every field. But, however demanding, there is (in my view) no alternative to patient study. Unless one is constantly reading the evidence and sifting the arguments in some depth, it is impossible to counter conventional views and utilise one's critical faculties to the fullest.

(v) Institutionalising critical awareness

I lay stress here on the word "institutionalising." Since, as I have said, so much of our lives is influenced by institutions, it follows that there can be no possibility of effecting lasting change unless moral insights about animals are embodied in institutional change. The agenda is vast, so I will select just three areas:

(a) *Through law making.* To understand the importance of this, one need only look at the history of animal protection in the United Kingdom. Pioneering animal advocates in the nineteenth century insisted upon the need for both changes in moral sensibility and changes in laws to protect animals. The two were seen to go hand in hand, and this was the key to their success. It was not enough that people should think and feel differently about animal suffering, it was also necessary that this sensibility should be reflected in laws. Looking back now, it is hardly possible to credit the enormous resistance to even the most basic reforms that sought to prevent gratuitous cruelty through "sports," such as bear- and bull-baiting, cock-fighting, and cock-throwing (throwing sticks at a cock tied to a post). But advocates learned early the lesson that has to be re-learned in every generation: only changes in laws secure lasting protection. Not only are laws the principal instrument of protecting animals, they are also the dominant means through which people change social behaviour. I make the moral case for the inclusion of animals within the sphere of legal protection at some length in part II, and I will not pre-empt that discussion now except to say that legislative change is, and has to remain, the cornerstone of building a society that respects animals.[53] Such legislative advances may well have to be piecemeal, pragmatic, even opportunistic, but without that overall goal, lasting institutional change is impossible.

(b) *Through consumer choice.* At first, this might seem a rather slight mechanism through which to establish change. Consumer choice does not, of course, constitute an institution as such, but it can lead to the institutionalisation of such choices. In capitalist societies, those who buy, or refuse to buy, have great power. To those who say that the great multi-nationals that govern the lives of so many people on this earth cannot change, my answer is that, however improbable it may seem, they are, due to their very capitalist nature, vulnerable to change. That is simply because they depend, in the last analysis, upon people being prepared to buy or consume their products. This is where the ethical consumer (in sufficient numbers) can make change happen. Two examples may suffice. The sale of organic foods in the United Kingdom has grown since the 1970s from a wholly negligible part of agriculture, almost everywhere derided, to sales worth £1.12 billion to retailers, and organic foods are growing at twice the rate of the general grocery market.[54]

The important point is that this has been a consumer-led, grassroots revolution: concerns about animal welfare, concerns about the use of pesticides, and opposition to genetically modified products have made possible a new kind of choice in the supermarket. Another example is the emergence of meat-substitute products, which have grown exponentially since the 1980s. To take one example: Quorn—one of the largest producers of meat-substitute products—helped to boost its parent company, Premier, to a pre-tax profit of £27.9 million in a mere six months in 2006.[55] Such developments are paralleled in Europe and the United States. Of course, all such figures need to be qualified in various ways: for example, an increase in meat substitutes is not always accompanied by a decrease in meat eating per se (meat eaters also use substitutes), and not all consumption of organic produce is driven by animal welfare concerns. Nevertheless, even when all the various qualifiers have been allowed, both developments indicate the radical possibilities inherent even in amoral capitalism. I return to this point at the end of this chapter.

The major point to be grasped is that ethical choice has resulted in institutional change. There is no part of capitalism that is more susceptible to change than the food industry—and none more influenced by consumer choice. Food producers or retailers do not risk investment in new products without extensive market research and without early evidence of consumer acceptance. That products are now being developed without harming animals and without involving intensive farming is the most tangible evidence we have of how ethical sensitivity can change the face of capitalism. Of course, much more needs to be done, and should be done. It is often said that consumers will not pay for more humanely reared animal products. Well, if mandatory labelling were introduced (explaining precisely how the animal lived and how it died), then we would all have the possibility of making an *informed* choice. And we know, when put to the test (as in the case of battery eggs), there are many people prepared to pay more.

(c) *Through education.* It is astonishing that humane education finds no place in the national curriculum of British schools, nor of most schools in the United States and Europe. Whether pupils gain any sense of the need to respect other life forms or are encouraged in compassionate behaviour towards them is wholly dependent on enlightened teachers or animal-friendly parents. In the light of this lamentable lack, it is surprising that people are not crueller than they actually are. Finding formal space within the curriculum for some expression of the need for humaneness is an urgent task if institutionalising animal protection is to become a reality.

Of course, positive insights about animals cannot be programmed or, even worse, indoctrinated. But animal advocates have been too hesitant about insisting that animal-friendly insights should, at least, be on the programme. While others have been shameless in promoting their concerns for the educational agenda, animal advocates have hardly begun to articulate the case for theirs. There are few examples of where the possibility of seeing animals differently forms part of the curriculum at any level of education: primary, secondary, tertiary, or higher. In many courses, whether in animal husbandry, animal conservation, animal science, or even sometimes in animal welfare, students are not required to challenge, or even address, the dominant perceptions of animals as commodities, resources, tools, machines, or things.

Indeed, courses in animal conservation seem to miss the point entirely, for they often presuppose that animals are not individuals, but just collectivities or species. Hence, so-called conservationists are in the forefront of killing ruddy ducks, hedgehogs, and grey squirrels, in order to "preserve" other species.[56] Conservationists see species, but they fail to see *individual* animals that deserve our protection. Similarly, courses in animal science are often so "scientific" that they fail to see animals as anything more than objects of dissection or complex machines. It seldom seems to occur to zoologists, any more than to conservationists, that animals are not just animals but *individual* animals—each with her own unique individuality.

That said, there are some signs of significant change in higher education. If humane education for children is in short supply, animal ethics for university students is currently a growing area. A range of new academic posts and new courses in animal welfare, animal studies, philosophy and animals, religion and animals, animal law, and even animal theology have slowly but surely emerged since the 1970s. Moreover, in many classes devoted to ethics, religious studies, or philosophy, normative questions about the status of animals are now being raised and critically examined—buttressed by an increasing number of high-quality anthologies and texts that serve as bases of informed discussion.[57] This is by far the most exciting and important development in animal advocacy for many years. Education needs to give people the chance to think and imagine differently, to conceive of other, better worlds for humans and animals. There should be courses, centres, institutes, degrees, even universities dedicated to new perspectives on animals. The challenge, then, is to find ways of institutionalising, embodying, and incarnating new perceptions of animals so that, as a matter of course, all students—at all levels—are encouraged to rethink the dominant intellectual paradigm.

2.4. VISION AND PRACTICALITIES

What needs to be grasped and pondered is that the institutions that govern our lives are themselves the result of our vision, or lack of it. "History," according to Walter Benjamin, "is written by the winners."[58] What we see all around is the embodiment of what was once thought. All our existing practices are ineluctably the result of past thought, whether they are zoos, animal circuses, bull-fights, animal laboratories, or factory farms. They are the living embodiments of the old view that animals are simply commodities, tools, machines, or resources. In order to break free, we need to think creatively about, invest in, and plan practical means of institutionalising new patterns of relationships.

In case all this appears too visionary, it is worth considering how science, which like religion and philosophy has historically supported the old paradigm, could be brought into service of the new. In an article written with Dr. Jacky Turner (then a lecturer in crystallography at Birbeck College, London) for *Biologist* (the journal of the Institute of Biology), we envisaged alternative futures in three areas. First, in animal farming:

[S]cientific ingenuity has been placed almost entirely at the disposal of agribusiness, which seeks to maximise yields, even and especially at the expense of the animals concerned. In their enthusiasm to strengthen links with industry, government funding agencies also support intensive animal farming. Geneticists are now promising us a future where herds of farm animals will be composed of identical, optimised animal-protein machines. But biology doesn't have to follow this route. Scientific ingenuity could be harnessed to a wider vision, which insists that if animals are to be killed for food, humane (or, rather, something closer to humane) farming is absolutely essential. What is needed here is a scientific commitment to the creation of genuinely animal-friendly forms of husbandry, in which the lives of the animals concerned are enhanced rather than diminished. Such research is thoroughly practical. Bovine Spongiform Encephalopathy (BSE), the prevalence of *Salmonella* and *Campylobacter* infection, and the threat of antibiotic resistance, are making it increasingly clear that the move away from intensive animal farming is long overdue.

Second, in medical research:

At the moment, the use of animal models for human problems is still central to biomedical science. Here again, scientific expertise has undoubtedly been used to intensify the exploitation of animals, but this trend can and should be reversed. There is after all something perverse, if not downright inconsistent, in attempting to improve the quality of life for humans *at the expense of* the quality of life of animals. The same scientific ingenuity which has facilitated the massive use of laboratory animals worldwide could be directed to the discovery of non-sentient alternatives and the exploitation of bioinformatics. This is already happening in the drug discovery industry, partly to save time and money, and the UK Home Office has said [in 1998] that it sees "an irresistible momentum for change." The ban on cosmetic product testing in the UK provides an opportunity for a fundamental rethink. For more than 20 years, cosmetic manufacturers have been saying "There's no alternative to animal tests." Now, at least in one part of the globe, there will have to be.

And, third, in food production:

Already the market for plant-based protein has significantly increased in recent years, even to the extent that high-street supermarkets are now supplying their own brands. Business follows the market, and the market now includes a considerable and increasing number of vegetarians, demi-vegetarians and vegans, especially among the young. Science and technology, which once led the way in the intensification of animal farming, could now lead the way in the opposite direction, towards the development of alternatives to animal protein which would allow animal farming to be de-intensified.

We further argued that scientists should choose to become pioneers because many of them, particularly biologists, know better—especially about the degree of sentience in mammals. And we concluded: "such knowledge is far from complete, but it is already sufficient for a radical ethical assessment. Biologists and animal rights advocates have never been easy friends, but they do not have to be enemies: they could even be collaborators."[59]

2.5. SUMMARY OF MAIN POINTS

1. This chapter attempts to answer the question: why, if the rational case for animals is so strong, has it so often been overlooked? Intellectual mechanisms that prevent us from recognising animal suffering or that help to limit its significance are examined (2.1).

2. The first mechanism is the power of *misdescription*, whereby animals are denigrated as "dumb brutes," "beasts," "sub-humans," and so on. The same technique is also used in characterising animal advocates. A new understanding of animals requires that we actively challenge the language we use, which is the language of historic denigration. The challenge is how to create a nomenclature that does justice to animals (2.1.i).

3. The second is *misrepresentation*. The artificial difference between animals and humans is fuelled by Cartesianism and behaviourism, which variously deny felt pain in animals, whereas there is ample evidence of suffering in mammals. The challenge is to seek non-pejorative representations of animals, and less-partial labels for those who try to protect them (2.1.ii).

4. The third is *misdirection*. Various arguments are deployed:

(a) The *"we can't really know"* argument. Excessive scepticism about animal suffering is still exhibited by academics, especially scientists and philosophers, which in turn has fuelled government scepticism. But we should not allow not knowing everything about mammals to prevent us from acting ethically on what we can reasonably know (2.1.iii.a).

(b) The *"we must have scientific proof"* argument, which means in practice that such data become a pre-condition of judgment. But that argument flies in the face of what we can reasonably know, and would never be employed in analogous cases of human suffering (2.1.iii.b).

(c) The *"we mustn't be anthropomorphic"* argument. There is a good and a bad anthropomorphism. Good accepts as a reasonable assumption that mammals suffer to a greater or lesser extent than we do (2.1.iii.c).

(d) The *"everything has feelings"* argument. Those who want to reject the idea that animal suffering matters morally apparently see pain and suffering everywhere, even in plants, so leading to the view that no dividing line can be drawn. But there is no evidence that plants are sentient, and drawing the line at mammalian suffering (at least) is evidentially based (2.1.iii.d).

(e) The *"they may feel pain, but not as we do"* argument. The origin of this view is the idea that animals are incapable of rational thought, and therefore cannot really suffer like us. But the moral issue is not whether their suffering is identical in all respects to our own, but rather whether their suffering is *as important to them as ours is to us*. The challenge is to find the moral and intellectual resources to face the full reality of animal sentience without trivialisation or obfuscation (2.1.iii.e).

5. The fourth is *misperception* or, rather, the power of perception. The view that animals are little more than lumps of meat has historically dominated ethical discourse. But there is an emerging change of perception away from ideas that animals are machines, tools, commodities, or resources here for us, towards the idea that animals have their own intrinsic value. Many have yet to experience this change, and there is a colossal investment in *not* changing because of the benefits that result from exploitation (2.1.iv).

6. What characterises animal abuse, unlike some other types of abuse, is that it is institutionalised. Institutions, for good or ill, shape our lives. None of us are untouched by our use of animals and all of us, directly or indirectly, benefit from it. That means that we are never able to decide our actions from a position of impartiality based on first principles, as if we were encountering an entirely new moral problem for the first time. Rather, we find that the issue has already been determined for us, and by the time we begin thinking (if we do), we find that we are already compromised by our existing involvement (2.2).

7. Few institutions are morally neutral as regards animals because they reflect and reinforce past attitudes. They act as agents of thought control. What is required is the cultivation of a critical perspective to help counteract the dominant ideology about animals perpetuated by the media in particular (2.2).

8. Chomskian insights can help us to illuminate some of the obstacles and the means of overcoming them:

(i) *Discovering the facts.* By learning how facts are distorted or misrepresented, we are enabled to see the underlying perspective that the distortions serve. Facts cannot deliver values, but are important in order to begin ethical analysis (2.3.i).

(ii) *Retaining the focus on the ethical.* Defenders of exploitation are adept at sidestepping the ethical issue (a technique even imitated by advocates themselves), which means that the ethical issue is obfuscated. This is also helped by a popular utilitarianism among media spokespeople, based on the assumption that only human suffering really matters (2.3.ii).

(iii) *Recognising the limitations of the media.* The media invariably privilege the status quo because arguing for unconventional positions requires more time than is normally allowed. Advocates need to be aware of the problematic nature of imposed concision, while striving to present the rational case (2.3.iii).

(iv) *Establishing alternative sources of information.* Being free of most of the stereotypical news coverage requires access to alternative viewpoints through the Internet and patient book reading. Alternative information sources can help to cultivate critical intelligence (2.3.iv).

(v) *Institutionalising critical awareness.* Individual awareness is not enough; lasting change requires new perceptions to become embodied in institutions, inter alia:

(a) *Through law making.* Changes in legislation provide lasting protection for animals and help to change social behaviour (2.3.v.a).

(b) *Through consumer choice.* Capitalism is inherently vulnerable to consumer choice. Ethical choices can lead to institutional change, as we are witnessing in the areas of organic farming and meat substitutes (2.3.v.b).

(c) *Through education.* Humane education is still under-represented in the formal curriculum. But there are signs that normative questions about how we should treat animals are being asked in higher education, as witnessed by the growth of new academic posts and courses. The challenge is to find ways of ensuring that all students are encouraged to rethink the dominant intellectual paradigm (2.3.v.c).

9. The institutions that govern our lives are the result of past vision, or lack of it. But they can and should change. For example, science has become the principal means of implementing past ideology, but scientific ingenuity could be harnessed to realising new ethical possibilities in the fields of farming, research, and food production (2.4).

Part II

THREE PRACTICAL CRITIQUES

3

First Case

Hunting with Dogs

Some might think that organised hunting with dogs, specifically fox-hunting, is a uniquely English pastime. In fact, hunting packs exist throughout the world, especially in European countries, and—excepting Britain—the largest number (including drag hounds) exists in the United States. Figures for hunting packs are Belgium 4, France 5, Germany 28, Holland 6, Italy 3, Portugal 1, United States 191, Canada 13, Australia 23, New Zealand 29, India 1, Kenya 1, and South Africa 2.[1] Although there is no moral objection to drag-hunting (following a pre-set course with an artificial scent), many of the packs pursue a live quarry, usually a fox or a deer.

While fox-hunting in North America is less widespread than in Britain, it appears to be growing. According to the Masters of Foxhounds Association of America (MFHA), there are 11 fox packs in Canada and 154 in the United States.[2] Although the MFHA was not founded until 1907, fox-hunting in the United States has a long history. The first pack was instituted by Thomas, the Sixth Lord Fairfax, in 1747 in northern Virginia. The MFHA claims that American hunting has "evolved its own distinct flavour which is noticeably different from the British," with an emphasis upon "the chase rather than the kill" (with coyotes also being hunted). But there is no doubt that American foxes are also killed by dogs, and otherwise the hunt follows the usual English pattern, though "stopping-up" (blocking the earth so the foxes cannot go to ground) is officially against the MFHA code of practice.[3]

Fox-hunting is likewise an established tradition in Ireland. The Irish Masters of Foxhounds Association was founded in 1859 but traces its history back some 600 years. The Muskerry Hunt, the oldest pack in the country, was established in 1743, and in 2008, there were 39 active fox-hunts.[4] Although shooting (what is usually termed "hunting" in the United States) is more popular in the United States and Europe, France also has a developed tradition of hunting with dogs, which targets deer, rabbits, boar, and foxes. The French Association of Hunting Packs claims that *la venerie à cheval* (hunting on horseback) comprises 38 packs for red deer, 85 packs for roe deer, and 30 packs for boar. And there are, in addition, 240 packs of foot hunts, comprising 80 fox packs, 115 hare packs, and 45 rabbit packs.[5] French hunting with dogs, mounted or on foot, is as old, if not older, than its European or North American counterparts. There are more than 1.5 million licensed hunters (mostly shooters), an estimated 700,000 hunting dogs in the country, and hunting seems to be an increasing tourist attraction.[6] What characterises hunting with dogs is not just the usual kill, but the chase, in which the prey is pursued over distances, sometimes for many hours.

Although this chapter concentrates on hunting with hounds in the United Kingdom, the ethical critique applies to hunting in Europe, North America, and elsewhere. Some might think that hunting is dead and gone as an issue in Britain, given the passing of the UK Hunting Act of 2004, which made the hunting with dogs of foxes, deer, hares, and mink (and organised hare coursing) illegal. In fact, hunters have continued to hunt—exploiting whatever ambiguities they can find in the act—buttressed by the remarkably quiescent attitude of law enforcement agencies. Thus, despite some successful (mainly private) prosecutions, hunting with dogs still continues, and a change of government in Britain (from Labour to Conservative) would almost certainly result in the repeal of the act.

The history of attempts at prohibition in the United Kingdom, and the ethical debate that has been engendered, has more than passing significance; it is central to understanding what hunting involves, why it continues, and why it is ethically objectionable.

3.1. THE DRAWN-OUT DEBATE

The 2004 act was prefaced by lengthy and frequently acrimonious parliamentary debates. Indeed, the whole business was an astonishingly drawn-out process. Two private members' bills to ban or restrict hunting were introduced as early as 1948, but both failed to make progress. During the course of its first parliament, the 1945 Labour government responded to these attempts at abolition by setting up the Scott Henderson Inquiry, and it reported in 1951. Opponents of hunting claimed (not without justification) that the committee was chosen to produce a pro-hunting report, since it comprised members sympathetic to hunting. The inquiry concluded, "Fox hunting makes a very important contribution to the control of foxes, and involves less cruelty than most other methods of controlling them" and so should be "allowed to continue."[7]

With the election of Labour governments in 1964, 1966, and 1974, further attempts were made at legislation. In 1969 and 1975, the House of Commons passed legislation to ban hare coursing, but neither bill became law. Three further private members' bills were introduced in the 1990s—the first by Kevin McNamara (Wild Mammals [Protection] Bill) in 1992, the second by Tony Banks in 1993 (Fox Hunting [Abolition] Bill), and the third by John McFall in 1995 (Wild Mammals [Protection] Bill)—all of which similarly failed to become law, although the latter won (for the first time) majority support in the House of Commons.

The election of a new Labour government in 1997, with a manifesto commitment to protect wildlife and specifically to allow a "free vote" on hunting, raised new hopes of abolition. A private member's bill was soon introduced, this time by Michael Foster, and received massive support (411–151 at the second reading in the House of Commons) but ran out of time without government support. Indeed, it soon became apparent that many senior members of the government, including Jack Straw (the secretary of state for the Home Office) and the Prime Minister Tony Blair, were reluctant to see the end of hunting. In a climate of political uncertainty, the government in 2000 commissioned its own report on hunting, known as the "Burns Report."[8] Unsurprisingly, it was feared that Burns would do what Scott Henderson had done, and find ways of keeping hunting in existence.

And so it has proved, since Burns recommended a system of licensed hunting, and the government subsequently introduced an "options bill" in which Members of Parliament were allowed to choose among a ban, licensed hunting, and self-regulation. In what follows, I provide a close analysis and critique of the Burns Report, and I do this for four reasons.

The first is that Burns represents the most substantial body of writing to attempt some kind of impartial analysis of hunting. Since it is the most detailed account of hunting ever published, it deserves serious scrutiny. Engagement with Burns involves addressing all the arguments for hunting. Second, and not surprisingly, the report became the foremost point of reference for all sides of the debate. One only has to look at *Hansard* (the verbatim report of parliamentary debates) to see how often, and variously, Burns was cited and taken as an objective source. Third, for all its manifest inadequacies (as I see it), it is likely to remain a continuing focus point and reference for continuing debates on the subject. The last and most important reason is that Burns provides an example of how *not* to deal with a moral issue, nothing less than a text-book case of how a moral issue can be obfuscated by a government report.

3.2.   THE ODDNESS OF THE BURNS REPORT

At the outset, it is the sheer oddness of the Burns Report that needs to be appreciated. That can be immediately grasped by looking at its terms of reference, which were to

> inquire into the practical aspects of different types of hunting with dogs and its impact on the rural economy, agriculture and pest control, the social and cultural life of the countryside, the management and conservation of wildlife, and animal welfare in particular areas of England and Wales; the consequences for these issues of any ban on hunting with dogs, and how any ban might be implemented.[9]

The first oddity, then, is that the ethical issue was specifically *excluded* from the remit of the inquiry. Animal welfare comes a poor seventh (actually last) in the list of items to be addressed by the inquiry, preceded by matters as wide as "the social and cultural life of the countryside" and as question-begging as "pest control." The moral argument receives no attention at all. Clearly, if the remit were to be followed (as it largely was), then issues relating to welfare would be given short shrift and the ethical issue largely ignored. Both were the case, as we shall see. The second oddity is that none of the Burns Committee had qualifications in moral philosophy, ethics, or theology. In matters relating to moral issues, we have become accustomed for there to be at least *one* token ethicist on government committees, but in this case even tokenism was abandoned. These two facts are remarkable given the fact that hunting is widely regarded as a moral issue and opposed largely on moral grounds.

It is important to pause at this point because, if my argument from the previous chapter is correct, it is the sidestepping of the ethical that most confounds discussions of animal issues. Once that focus is lost, all else becomes a matter of trying to weigh largely unquantifiable factors, such as the "social and cultural life of the countryside," and what may or may not constitute adverse consequences. Framing the question is the issue—in fact, is always the issue—in official reports, enquiries, and commissions. Bias is almost always detected most easily at this point. Without in any way questioning the integrity of the committee, it has to be said that, if one wanted to produce a report that avoided the moral issue, down-played animal welfare, and concentrated on the largely unquantifiable issues—the remit given to Burns would surely be the means of doing it.

Few reports on contentious issues can be free of value judgments, and the Burns Report is no exception. It makes a range of judgments concerning the economic, social, and welfare aspects of hunting, all of which have implications for future legislation. It does so, however, without an explicit, or considered, ethical framework. It offers, at numerous points, opinions and prescriptions with a greater or lesser degree of argumentation but, of necessity, fails to confront the central moral issue. The result is that the report, for all its admirable qualities, encourages ethical avoidance, which in turn leads to ethical obfuscation.

3.3. FLAWED METHODOLOGY

In the first place, Burns makes no attempt to situate concern for animals historically. We are not provided even with a brief sketch of the movement for animal protection in Britain, how it evolved, what it has tried to achieve, and the influences, both social and political, which have propelled the issue of animals to political centre stage. While we are provided with detailed explanations of hunting and lengthy expositions of its putative social, economic, and cultural importance, not one insight is offered into the social and political history of animal protection and its contemporary significance.[10]

Second, there is no attempt to explain or understand the philosophy or goals of the humanitarian movement which emerged in the nineteenth century, and its effective continuance to the present day in contemporary debates about the rights and wrongs of how we treat animals. Someone reading the report and new to the issue could be forgiven for failing to see what the fuss is all about, since nowhere does the report even note the philosophy of animal protection, which has become such a significant feature of contemporary ethical debate. There is an increasing, even voluminous, amount of literature on this topic, which is now widely regarded in both developed and developing countries as a moral problem. Arguably, no other moral issue has received such sustained and detailed philosophical consideration, especially since the 1970s.[11] The Burns Report nowhere helps us to understand the contemporary moral debate and precisely what the issues of justice, welfare, and rights are all about.

Third, while Burns rightly defines animal welfare as "concerned with the welfare of the *individual* animal,"[12] it then offers a reductionist conception of animal welfare as "a scientific discipline, which has developed rapidly in recent years."[13] This is reductionist because while it is true that there is a scientific aspect, concern for animal well-being is as old as the pre-Socratic philosophers (who in some instances anticipated contemporary philosophical discussion).[14] In many periods throughout the history of philosophy, one finds an undercurrent of concern for animal well-being. Most of the celebrated names in philosophy and theology—including Plato, Aristotle, Aquinas, Descartes, Hobbes, Locke, Hume, Berkeley, Kant, Leibniz, Rousseau, Herder, Schopenhauer, Bentham, Mill, and Nietzsche—have at various times, and sometimes at length, explored fundamental questions about the nature of animals, including their capacities for reason, language, self-consciousness, and soul possession, and the nature of our rightful use of power over them.[15] However adequate their thought may be, it is wrong to give the impression that animal welfare concerns began with the first empirical studies in the early seventies; the RSPCA was founded in 1824 and even before then there was a sizeable body of thought—philosophical, ethical, historical, social, political, and theological—on this topic. By limiting animal welfare to its (comparatively recent) scientific aspect, Burns is able to subsequently posit uncertainty and unclarity in a range of matters where no precise scientific evidence obtains. The report accepts, for example, that there is "a large measure of agreement among the scientists that, at least during the last 20 minutes or so of the hunt, the deer is likely to suffer,"[16] but then maintains that the "available evidence does not enable us to resolve the disagreement about the point at which, during the hunt, the welfare of the deer becomes seriously compromised."[17] In other words, even scientific *agreement* is not sufficient; there must be *demonstrable* evidence of suffering at each significant stage of hunting. This is such a high standard of evidence that one wonders whether comparable cases of cruelty to domestic animals or children could possibly meet it. It opens the door to a kind of agnosticism in the face of evident physical suffering, which is socially and morally regressive.

Fourth, no less unsatisfactory is Burns's method in dealing with animal welfare issues. Consider this paragraph, for instance:

> We also consider that it is important, in examining the arguments about the welfare of animals subjected to hunting, not to judge them in isolation. In our view, this means not only considering the relative welfare advantages and disadvantages of different forms of culling—assuming that there is a need to kill the animal concerned—but also taking into account of [sic] what we know, and can reasonably assume, about the extent to which they would be likely to be used in practice in the event of a ban on hunting.[18]

No arguments are adduced in favour of the first statement or the second. The Burns Report is welcome to its opinion, but without argument or evidence, it remains just that. In fact, the report's approach to the question is far from neutral. It will not go unnoticed that it has been a favourite argument of hunters (echoed by the Scott Henderson Report) that, taken as a whole, hunting inflicts less suffering than other methods, or less than the suffering that wild animals might occasionally endure in their natural state, and Burns simply takes over their perspective without qualification or even an attempt at argument. But it is questionable whether this is a satisfactory method of proceeding, and for two reasons. The first is that it assumes that all such killing is in principle justifiable (precisely what needs to be determined), and second, it assumes that all such (legal) practices are on a level footing morally (which is precisely the point that needs to be determined). It is, to say the least, a question-begging procedure. Consider, for example, how satisfactory it would be for a dog owner to justify his cruel treatment of a domestic dog by reference to the possible or actual lives of abandoned, neglected, or abused dogs that live on the streets. Proper moral analysis, on the other hand, requires attention to, inter alia, the object, intention, motivation, and consequences of a specific act regardless of what may or may not be done by others.

3.4. SUFFERING? WHAT SUFFERING?

Fifth, Burns minimises the reality of suffering. As we have seen, there is ample evidence that mammals experience not just pain, but also suffering, that is, stress, terror, shock, anxiety, fear, anticipation, trauma, and foreboding, and that to a greater or lesser degree than we do ourselves. And yet, evidence of sentience and comparable emotional response is never given the weight that it deserves. Indeed, Burns seems to give it no more weight than another "opinion," for example:

It has been argued that, in view of what is known about the fox's ecology and social systems, the hunted fox, whether being pursued by hounds or being dug out, is bound to experience fear and distress, but others dispute this, arguing that this simply amounts to anthropomorphism and that there is *no evidence to support this assertion.*[19]

Burns does note that two postmortems of foxes from the University of Bristol reveal that death "was caused by massive injuries"[20] other than to the head and neck, and accepts that the killing of the fox "is *not always* effected by a single bite to the neck or shoulders by the leading hound."[21] But the report concludes: "There is a lack of firm scientific evidence about the effect on the welfare of a fox of being closely pursued, caught and killed above ground by the hounds."[22] Comparable treatment of a domestic dog would not need "firm scientific evidence," since it is widely understood that a number of dogs biting and killing a cornered dog would be considered cruel in the extreme. Anyone who asked for scientific evidence in this case would, legitimately, be an object of mirth. Dog-fighting is, of course, illegal in the United Kingdom.

The report concludes, "We are satisfied, nevertheless, that this experience seriously compromises the welfare of the fox."[23] But this is an ambiguous and unsatisfactory phrase, as indicated by the dictionary definition of the word "compromise," namely, a "settlement of a dispute by mutual concession."[24] This is a highly reductionist way of describing a cruel death by disembowelment, unless it was intended, perhaps in an unforeseen way, to have political connotations. It certainly does not mean "cruel," as Lord Burns himself made clear in a subsequent debate in the House of Lords, and as we have already noted.[25] One wonders whether there will ever be the kind of evidence which would finally satisfy Lord Burns on this matter, or whether any such evidence could ever be provided in the case of either humans or animals. Since, however, prosecutions against cruelty to domestic animals are successful, one can only posit that the standard of evidence that Burns requires is simply not met in most criminal or civil cases. In fact, as we noted, there is ample evidence that all mammals experience suffering, and to suppose that being chased for prolonged periods, disembowelled while alive, or baited by dogs is other than cruel is to be pusillanimous before the facts.

In this section, one other point needs to be made. Burns repeatedly asserts that foxes, hares, and mink die "in seconds." For example: "In a proportion of cases it [the death of the fox] results from massive injuries to the chest and vital organs, although insensibility and death will normally follow within a matter of seconds once the fox is caught."[26] Again, in relation to hares: "death and insensibility will normally follow within a matter of seconds."[27] But these assertions mask the point that *just one second* of excruciating pain while being torn apart by dogs is morally objectionable, let alone many seconds. But how do we know that it is only a "few" seconds and not five, ten, fifteen, or many more? It should be noted in this context that the government's own advisory committee, the Farm Animal Welfare Council, supported a ban on religious slaughter on the grounds that such slaughter rendered the animals liable to suffering for an average of seventeen to twenty more seconds than traditional slaughter.[28]

Again, we have an example of how the Burns Report, in the absence of the scientific evidence it says is essential to make firm judgments, conjectures only to minimise the gravity of animal suffering. In fact, however, Burns accepts that, in the case of hares, there can "sometimes be a significant delay [unaccountably unquantified] ... before the 'picker-up' reaches the hare and dispatches it (if it is not already dead)."[29] And, moreover, in the case of deer, there is scientific agreement that the animal may be liable to suffering for at least *the last twenty minutes of hunting.* Even given these minimal figures, distinct from the suffering caused through the chase itself in the case of foxes, mink, and hares, or through the activity of digging out, we have good reason to posit a cruel and certainly less than instantaneous death.

Sixth, although the rationale for hunting is frequently stated, we are provided with no such account in relation to animal welfare. The chapter on animal welfare is one of the shortest in the report and consists, inter alia, of a number of repetitious statements and little argument. By focusing solely on the "scientific" aspect of animal welfare, the report provides an incoherent account of why animals may be thought to matter morally. It is not enough to say that animals should not suffer or that suffering is wrong, what is needed is an account of *why* that is so. Only when this case has been made, as we have done in chapters 1 and 2, can we fully appreciate the strength of the moral obligation to avoid harm. But there is no indication that the report's authors attempted to understand the rational and moral case against animal abuse.

3.5. ADDRESSING THE MORAL ISSUE

Seventh, we now need to articulate the moral dimension that the Burns Report fails to address. Hunting offends two basic moral principles. The first is that *it is intrinsically wrong to deliberately inflict suffering on a sentient mammal for purposes other than its own individual benefit* (for example, in a veterinary operation). This, I submit, is the most satisfactory definition of "cruelty." Historically and legally, the term "unnecessary suffering" has been used and in its time may have had its pragmatic uses. But with hindsight, we can see that this term involved the problematic implication that there are "necessary" cruelties, or that cruel acts *could* be morally licit. From the considerations we have discussed in chapters 1 and 2, it follows that there are certain acts against the vulnerable, the innocent, and the defenceless (both human and animal) which are prima facie unacceptable, and the deliberate infliction of suffering is surely one of them. We do not speak, for example, of "necessary rape" or "necessary torture" or "necessary child abuse," and neither should we do so in the case of the deliberate infliction of suffering on animals.

It is sometimes argued that hunters simply imitate the "cruelties of nature." But this view is based on a misunderstanding of the nature of moral actions. Animals are not moral agents and are not therefore responsible for their actions, whereas human beings are both. Free will is absolutely basic to the notion of morality. Without choice, there is no morality: we do not blame someone for doing something that she could not help doing. We may not like the action, but we do not morally condemn. The so-called cruelty of nature, however, is not based on choice. If the lion does not kill the antelope, the lion starves and dies: the lion has no real choice. On the other hand, foxes, deer, hares, and mink are not threatening our survival, and neither is it essential to eat them in order to live. Our choices clearly fall within the realm of morality. There is thus a fundamental distinction between the accidental or non-intentional harming of animals or humans (for example, by an earthquake) and the deliberate, intentional infliction of harm by moral agents. It is the deliberate infliction of suffering by moral agents who can and should know better that is central to the moral objection to hunting.

Nowhere does Burns consider the possibility that the deliberate infliction of suffering is intrinsically objectionable. By failing to do so, he fails to understand the basic moral case against hunting. But there is also a second, even more fundamental principle, namely, *it is intrinsically wrong to deliberately cause suffering for the purposes of amusement, recreation, or in the name of sport.* It is sometimes argued that not all hunters enjoy the pursuit of their quarry or its death and that may be true. But that hunters are involved in a collective activity that has the definite and deliberate aim of harrying a living creature to its death (which in the process causes suffering) is indisputable.

3.6. PLEASURE IN SUFFERING

Here we reach, perhaps, the most unsatisfactory part of the report. Burns accepts that "pleasure" is a motivation for hunting,[30] that "hunting is itself partly a *social* event,"[31] and the report refers to surveys which indicate that "farmers in the Midlands often cite *sport* as a reason for killing foxes."[32] It further recognises that, in the event of a ban on all forms of hunting, "farmers would lose the benefit of a *recreation* they value,"[33] and it accepts that hare hunting and coursing "are essentially carried out for *recreational* purposes,"[34] but it does not consider the moral implications of any of these admissions.

Burns also accepts that hares are "maintained at high levels for shooting and hunting/coursing purposes"[35] and also that hundreds, perhaps thousands of such animals are actually transported for this purpose,[36] but lamely notes:

> In the case of hare hunting and coursing it is difficult to disentangle the conservation efforts made in the interests of hunting and coursing from the game management (such as predator control) undertaken in the interests of shooting hare and other game such as partridges and pheasants.[37]

However difficult it may be for Burns to "disentangle," the unmistakable implication is that hares are preserved only so that they may be killed by hunting and coursing. The same is also true in the case of foxes where artificial earths are provided. Burns, to its credit, censures such activity and argues, "The active use of artificial earths, with a view to hunting, is inconsistent with the stated objective of controlling fox numbers through hunting."[38] Burns notes that the Countryside Alliance (a coalition of predominantly pro-hunting organisations) saw nothing morally objectionable about this practice and sought to justify it.

We cannot avoid the evidence, then, that animals, such as foxes and hares, are preserved for hunting. No other reading is possible of these admissions. What does not seem to be appreciated here is that preservation—far from being simply an "inconsistent" activity—vitiates the entire case for "control." And without such a case, hunting is revealed for what it is: the pursuit of a live creature purely for the purposes of sport. For if, as is often alleged, the "kill" is a practically irrelevant issue for those who enjoy hunting—indeed, they even dislike the very thought (we are assured)—why cannot such enjoyment be found in drag- or bloodhound hunting (where the kill is not the object)? The only conceivable answer is that those who go hunting do so because they enjoy and take pleasure in the pursuit of a *live* animal to its death. Burns notes that, inter alia, the appeal of drag hunts is less because they "do not have the same 'rhythm' as a typical foxhunt,"[39] but the question must be asked: what "rhythmic" difference is there, save that of specifically enjoying the prolonged and cruel chase of a sentient creature? The case against hunting is nowhere better summarised than by the frank admission of Baroness Mallalieu: "Hunting is our music, it is our poetry, it is our art, *it is our pleasure. . . .*"[40]

As an aside, Burns castigates those involved in illegal coursing, suspecting that they "do so for base motives and have little regard for animal welfare."[41] It is striking that Burns claims to know, from the inside, what the motivation of illegal hare coursers must be, but since what is done by illegal coursers differs little in practice from legal coursing, and since from the animals' standpoint the end result is identical, we might ask why such perspicacity and moral indignation are not displayed equally in the direction of *legal* coursers as well.

It is important to understand why taking pleasure from the cruel death of an animal is nothing less than morally evil. In order to do so, we need briefly to give some account of some of the major theories of normative ethics. Roughly, they can be divided into three: (1) deontological theories, which hold that there is an objective standard of right and wrong and that there are duties incumbent on each individual, some of which are absolutely binding; (2) virtue theories, which hold that the standard of right or wrong consists in acts or behaviour likely to promote individual virtue or the "virtuous life"— specifically the classical virtues, such as prudence, justice, courage, and temperance; and (3) utilitarian theories, which broadly hold that the best consequences will be those that include the greatest possible balance of pleasure over pain. These theories differ in the accounts given of our obligations to animals (and most, as we have noted, are hardly animal-friendly), but the important thing to note is that all these theories, and their classical and modern exponents, would draw an absolute line at taking pleasure from cruelty.

Representatives of each theory are adamant. Immanuel Kant, who explicitly opposed "cruelty for sport," held that "[h]e who is cruel to animals becomes hard also in his dealings with men" whereas "tender feelings towards dumb animals develop humane feelings towards mankind."[42] St. Thomas Aquinas (not known for his enlightened views on animals) similarly posited that the purpose of scriptural prohibitions is "to remove man's thoughts from being cruel to other men, and lest through being cruel to animals one becomes cruel to human beings."[43] And even within utilitarianism, it is worth noting that, among its main historical exponents, John Stuart Mill was an early supporter of the (then) SPCA, and Jeremy Bentham was expressly opposed to hunting. Indeed, Bentham famously wrote of animals, "The question is not, Can they *reason?* Nor, Can they *talk?* but Can they *suffer?*"[44]

It is therefore odd to see a vague, non-principled utilitarianism utilised (perhaps unconsciously) throughout the Burns Report as if the rightness or wrongness of hunting could be determined by general appeals to usefulness alone, and as if a utilitarian calculus would unambiguously approve of hunting. This kind of loose utilitarian talk, so much in vogue today, which supposes that any demonstration of useful ends justifies any means, would be abhorrent to classical theorists. A utilitarian uses the principle of utility to judge which actions are right, which actions produce the greatest happiness for the greatest number. This calculation of pleasures and pains "applies to the whole sentient creation," according to Mill. He also said:

> According to the Greatest Happiness Principle ... the ultimate end, with reference to and for the sake of which all things are desirable (whether we are considering our own good or that of other people) is an existence *exempt as far as possible from pain*, and as rich as possible in enjoyments.[45]

James Rachels, in a commentary, explains that, for a utilitarian, "what matters is *not* whether an individual has a soul, is rational or any of the rest. All that matters is whether he is capable of experiencing happiness or unhappiness—pleasure and pain."[46] Thus, for a classical utilitarian, the pain of animals must always be taken into consideration when coming to a moral decision. Certainly, the death of any animal and its pain would outweigh the pleasure achieved in hunting, and one would thus have to conclude that hunting cannot be morally justified. And, moreover, the taking of pleasure in pain or making a sport of it would deserve the highest kind of moral censure.

Unsurprisingly, Peter Singer, perhaps the leading contemporary utilitarian ethicist, is resolutely opposed to hunting and asserts, "The trouble is that the authorities responsible for wildlife have a 'harvest' mentality, and are not interested in finding techniques of population control that would reduce the number of animals to be 'harvested' by hunters."[47] Suffice to say, it would take a tortuous calculation to justify recreational hunting by reference to orthodox utilitarian theory.

3.7. HUNTING AS ANTI-SOCIAL BEHAVIOUR

Of particular importance is the united view expressed by classical theorists that cruelty has anti-social implications. Nowhere does Burns even ask whether hunting might have adverse consequences for the wider society. The unexamined and unargued assumption throughout is that the various utilities—social, cultural, and economic—all point to the justifiability of hunting. But there are other, admittedly less immediately tangible, factors on the other side that should, in the course of any proper evaluation, be considered, for example, the loss of moral respect for animals manifested by the various activities of hunting, the instrumentalist attitudes to nature encouraged by treating animals merely as objects of sport, the acceptance that cruelty is a "normal" or "natural" way of life in the countryside, and the spiritual poverty in regarding animals as merely means to human ends. Not least of all, we should not overlook the capacity of human beings to become desensitised through habitual exposure to practices that involve suffering and violence to animals. This has been, as we have seen, a frequent concern of philosophers and moralists. The question has to be faced: what example of respect or, rather, disrespect for animals is learned through hunting? John Locke, writing as early as 1693, maintained that the education of children must abhor any tolerance of cruelty since "the custom of tormenting and killing beasts will, by degrees, harden their minds even toward men; and they who delight in the suffering and destruction of inferior creatures, will not be apt to be very compassionate or benign to those of their own kind." Specifically, when unchecked, "unnatural cruelty is planted in us; and what humanity abhors, custom reconciles and recommends to us, by laying it in the way of honour. Thus by fashion and opinion, that comes to be a pleasure, which in itself neither is, nor can be any."[48]

That there is a public moral interest in preventing cruelty has already been established over many decades by legislation, and not only by the pioneering bills against cruel sports. Yet Burns writes of the potential incompatibility of a ban on hunting with the European Convention on Human Rights, maintaining:

> If it were the case that private life is interfered with, the issue of a legitimate objective (i.e., the protection of morals) seemed to the committee to be crucial. That question seemed to the committee to turn on two key factors: first, whether hunting with dogs is viewed as inherently or necessarily causing suffering; second, whether, if it was so seen by members of the public or Parliament, this could constitute sufficient "moral" grounds in the absence of objective, scientific evidence.[49]

The idea that "objective, scientific evidence" is required before the UK government could act in a matter deemed to be in the interests of public morality is extraordinary, especially if it presupposes Burns's own method of calculating suffering. But the point is in one sense irrelevant, since the government already legislates against practices on the basis of "public morality," as we shall see in the next chapter.

3.8.   THE "NO CONTROL" CONTROL

We now turn to the issue of control. Some utilitarians might be amenable to the argument for control if there were good evidence in favour of it, namely, if there were overwhelming advantages and few or no disadvantages, and if there were no preferable alternatives. But what is clear from the report is that, even if there is a case for control, Burns does not make it. It is astonishing how, when it comes to issues of establishing suffering, Burns requires the highest "scientific" standard possible, whereas the "need for control" is almost entirely unargued and rests largely on the repeated *perceived* need for such control:

[Upland areas]... where there is greater *perceived* need for control.[50]

Many farmers too would no doubt *feel* they had suffered a financial loss if hunting was banned.[51]

[Farmers]... would *feel* that they had suffered an economic loss since a free "pest control" service would have been removed: they would *expect* more predation of lambs, poultry, piglets and game birds.[52]

Although foxes are widely *perceived* as a pest.[53]

It is clear, however, that the great majority of land managers do *consider* it [fox-hunting] necessary.[54]

Not everyone accepts that it is necessary to manage the fox population: some argue that it would be satisfactory to rely on self-regulation. In most areas of England and Wales farmers, landowners and gamekeepers *consider that it is necessary* to manage fox populations.[55]

Again:

[Upland areas]... where there is a greater *perceived* need for control.[56]

There is a world of difference between *perceived* and *actual* needs; similarly, needs, feelings, and expectations do not establish *facts*. That the Burns Report, to its credit, so prefaces its remarks on so many occasions indicates the dearth of actual, let alone "scientific," evidence.

When analysed in terms of the contribution of hunting to the control of each relevant species, the results are startling. The "overall contribution of foxhunting" is "*almost certainly insignificant in terms of the management of the fox population as a whole.*"[57] On deer, Burns maintains that there is "virtually unanimous agreement" that red deer populations need to be culled (though, again, no evidence is supplied), but hunting with dogs "*accounts for only about 15% of the annual cull apparently required in the relevant region.*"[58] On hares, Burns is frank: "No-one argues that legal *hunting or coursing has an appreciable effect on hare numbers.*"[59] On mink, Burns again accepts that "*the contribution made by mink hunts to the control of mink populations nationally is insignificant.*"[60] All in all, then, the contribution of hunting and coursing to the *perceived* need for control of foxes, hares, and mink is non-existent or negligible, and even in the case of deer, the contribution remains small in terms of overall numbers. Given the widely canvassed view that hunting can be justified solely by reference to control, we are compelled to conclude that such a claim lacks foundation.

Much has been made of Burns's view, in the event of a ban on fox-hunting: "In upland areas, where the fox population causes more damage to sheep-rearing and game management interest, and where there is a greater perceived need for control, fewer alternatives are available to the use of dogs, either to flush out or for digging out."[61] Defenders of hunting have seized upon these words as a potential lifeline to justify the continuance of fox-hunting and even, less logically, other forms of hunting and coursing as well. Opponents of hunting, at least of a utilitarian kind, might be presented with a poser if it could be shown that the need for fox control in a particular region was established beyond doubt *and* that it had some overwhelming advantage *and* that hunting was the only available means of doing so. But, in reality, not even one of these conditions applies—as closer reading of the report reveals.

To begin with, Burns is disarmingly frank about the weakness of the case for lamb predation by foxes (a commonly held reason for controlling them):

> It is not easy, however, to establish with any certainty how serious a problem fox predation represents. Predation is not usually witnessed; it is not always possible to distinguish between the killing of healthy lambs and scavenging dead or dying ones; and other predators, including domestic dogs, also kill lambs.[62]

At most, predation of uncertain origin amounts to about 2%, and predation on piglets, just about as uncertain, amounts also to the same small percentage though even here, there has been, we are told, "no systematic study of this problem."[63] When it comes to game birds, we are assured, "In the absence of [presumably, any] fox control a substantial number of birds would be lost before the start of the shooting season,"[64] but no figures are actually specified nor is there any evidence of independent research. Unsurprisingly, Burns speaks, entirely rightly, of a *perceived* need for control, for whatever this "evidence" amounts to, it falls short of anything approximating a case of necessity. This is reinforced by what is subsequently noted about the highly problematic nature of control,[65] and the recognition that overall the contribution of fox-hunting to control is in any case insignificant. Although Burns argues that there are "fewer" alternatives to fox-hunting in upland areas, that is not the same as saying there are none, nor that fox-hunting is the only one.

One obvious point concerning the proposed justifiability of killing foxes for "game management" purposes should be made. To kill birds for sport will strike many as objectionable, but to add to this the killing of foxes simply because one wants to kill the birds oneself appears doubly objectionable. If I have understood the argument correctly, it goes like this: one kills one kind of creature only because it is perhaps decreasing one's pleasure in killing another. The reasoning that attempts to justify this kind of hunting would have to be grotesque.

Those who wish to turn Burns's tentative statement into a justification for the continuation of fox-hunting really have not understood the requirements of a proper assessment of a moral issue. Even in utilitarian terms, to subject animals to a prolonged chase and a cruel death requires much, much more in terms of moral justification. It is insufficient to point to perceived need; in utilitarian terms, any control would need to pass a series of moral tests, including genuine necessity, evidence of a direct threat, proven use, unavailability of non-lethal methods, and humaneness.

What also needs to be borne in mind is that the general case for control of any of the relevant species (with the possible exception of deer) is still remarkably weak. This is because, as Burns notes, there are a number of highly complicating factors that beguile the whole issue. The first and most obvious is that nature is an essentially self-regulating system; animals breed in relation to the food and environment available. Second, there is no obvious "equilibrium level"[66] for each species; it is now held by many scholars that populations rise and fall as a matter of course. It is believed that animal populations cycle just as do trees, grasses, and, in general, plants. Third, killing ("culling") does not necessarily "control" any species since the species itself compensates for any dent in its population. Scientists talk of compensatory reproduction. This is a well-known phenomenon; many animals compensate for losses by breeding at an earlier age, having bigger litters, and so forth. As Rory Putman explains in relation to deer:

> If population levels are lowered artificially, the density-dependent brake on population growth is released: reproduction increases, mortality declines. Lack of selectivity in the cull . . . may also exacerbate the pest problem by disrupting the social structure and organisation of the pest. This may have two consequences: a further increase in population density, and an increase in damage caused because the animals display abnormal behaviour in response to a distorted social structure.

Again: "we have repeatedly stressed that most natural populations respond to reduction in numbers by increased productivity."[67]

Fourth, as Burns again acknowledges:

[C]ulling does not necessarily produce a proportional decrease in abundance or damage.... It is therefore important to distinguish between attempted and achieved population control, and to bear in mind that a reduction in the population does not necessarily translate into a *pro rata* reduction in the perceived problem.[68]

With so many fundamental qualifications, the case for control needs a great deal more "expert," "scientific" (and moral) scrutiny.

3.9. LICENSING VERSUS ABOLITION

The Burns Report showed its real colours when it concluded by recommending licensing: "We consider that it might be productive, in the absence of a ban, to explore the possibility of introducing some form of licensing system."[69] This of course gave defenders of hunting a potential lifeline, and it was duly taken up by the government wishing for some kind of middle way. Alun Michael, then rural affairs minister, was charged with the responsibility of piloting the "options bill" through Parliament. According to Michael, the "golden thread" of the legislation consisted of two "tests," namely, "utility" and "least suffering," which should be applied "sequentially."[70] Under the bill, registration tribunals would have been set up in different parts of the country to adjudicate on these two issues and register those forms of hunting they judged to be acceptable.

But the obvious problem with this procedure is that it would have devolved responsibility for deciding the basic moral issue from Parliament to unelected regional appointees. This is as logically odd as seeking to resolve the issue about the morality of capital punishment by devolving authority to a three-person committee who would decide on a case-by-case basis. In other words, instead of addressing the moral issue in itself, the bill would have provided a mechanism by which another body (or bodies) would judge the issue.

Moreover, registration and licensing would have given hunting a legal authority, which it has never had before. Licensing, by definition, empowers or authorises what was not previously authorised. It would have legitimised, institutionalised, and, therefore, helped to perpetuate hunting. Registered hunting is worse than a fudge; the bill would have provided hunting with full legal protection and helped to make it immune from fundamental criticism. Far from seeing hunting dwindle (as some have supposed), licensed hunting would provide a spurious justification for its continuance for many decades to come, if not indefinitely. Registered and licensed hunting is not a step forwards, but a step backwards. It was said that if these "tests" were fairly administered, hunting would, and should, be banned. But even those who support licensing admit that it is very unlikely that *absolutely all* hunting would be banned in practice. Indeed, the licensing system would be predicated on the possibility that at least *some* hunting can meet the so-called tests. Otherwise, what is the point of the process?

Equally worrying was the way in which the government conceived the utility test. The language of utilitarianism, by definition, excludes the idea that there are certain acts that are always wrong in themselves. Rather, the rightness or wrongness of an action is to be judged by a consideration of utilities. According to the classical theory, as we have seen, a utilitarian uses the principle of utility to judge which actions are right—that is, which actions produce the greatest happiness for the greatest number—which in practice means assessing the likely costs against the likely benefits. Now, whatever may be the usefulness of this theory, when it comes to considering some aspects of the moral treatment of humans or animals, it obviously fails to recognise that certain actions are intrinsically wrong in themselves whatever the circumstances. By placing hunting in a wholly utilitarian context, the government implicitly accepted that there will be occasions when hunting is justifiable.

Even more, the way in which the Hunting Bill was formulated allowed for a very one-sided analysis of what constitutes these utilities. The provisions of the bill allowed for hunting by reference to a wide range of "utilities"— from damage to livestock, on one hand, to the preservation of biological diversity, on the other. But classical utilitarianism requires a calculus of "benefits." True utilitarians have to ask not only what are the advantages, but also what are the disadvantages of a course of action: they have to calculate benefits *equally*. In the case of foxes, for example, what should be taken into account is the beneficial side of a fox population, including their intrinsic value, their contribution to the ecosystem itself, and the benefits (to farmers and landowners) of their predation on rabbits and rats. No one has even asked the basic moral question—namely, whether humans can ever truly "benefit" from the deliberate infliction of suffering on animals. On any proper utilitarian view, the list of utilities proposed is simply one-sided and partial. The test simply does not provide for a proper, impartial, and full utilitarian calculation of the benefits on both sides. The government's bill, therefore, stacked the evidence against the hunted species by selective use of what it conceived the utilities to be. As one eminent philosopher said, "the problem with utilitarianism is always: who is going to decide the utilities?"

In short, by going down the route of utilitarianism and the utility test, the government sought to bypass the central moral issue by devolving authority to resolve the issue to a small (three-person) committee who would have had to decide each case according to predetermined, highly partial, utilitarian considerations. Far from resolving the issue "once and for all" (as was claimed), registration and licensing would have required voluminous paperwork, legal argument, contested adjudications, and inevitable controversy extending over an indefinite time span. If bull-baiting had been licensed rather than abolished in 1839, we would still have bull-baiting today.

In the end, Parliament had the good sense to reject the licensing option and go for full abolition. It was a major victory for animal advocates who, after enduring decades of political filibustering, wrangling, and obfuscation, finally saw the end of one particular kind of cruelty. But, of course, that was not the end of the matter. The legislation has yet to be adequately enforced, and future governments may yet re-introduce hunting, using the licensing option as a means of doing so.

3.10. CONCLUSION

Given the weakness of the case for control by hunting, it is astonishing that society should have tolerated it as long as it has, especially since comparable acts against domestic animals are illegal. That society *has* tolerated it, and that people who hunt so vehemently support it, says something about the mechanism of moral rationalisation that bedevils all attempts to think clearly and impartially about the morality of our treatment of animals. Since we now know that the case for control by hunting is negligible, we can only logically suppose that other motives are in play, be they social, cultural, or sheer pleasure seeking. It is the recognition of this latter factor, namely, pleasure seeking, that above all makes hunting so especially morally abhorrent. We may recall Macaulay's famous rebuke that the Puritans objected to bull-baiting, not because it hurt the bull, but because it gave pleasure to the spectators. But the Puritans were only half-wrong. Both the pain of the hunted and the pleasure of the hunter should equally concern us morally.

Jane Ridley, herself a hunter, in her notable social history titled *Fox Hunting*, begins her first page with the words: "Fox hunting isn't strictly necessary."[71] Given this admission, and the many others in the Burns Report about control, preservation, and recreation, it is not difficult to understand why hunting has become such a totemic issue for all concerned with the right treatment of animals. It is true that some real gains have been made for animal welfare even during the centuries in which hunting for sport has been practiced, and it is also true that the making of all legislation invariably involves some inconsistencies in the fields of both human and animal welfare. But sometimes, legislative inconsistencies are so great that they rebound upon us, and once we become aware of them, it is difficult not to be seized by the need for urgent rectifying change. For how can we logically pursue a progressive animal protection agenda, even making the case for the enlightened treatment of animals where some genuine human interest is involved, while people gratuitously hunt creatures to a cruel death for comparatively trivial reasons? Reasonable people may reasonably disagree about where we should draw the line in our treatment of animals, but hunting mammals for sport is one of the least justifiable, and the most objectionable, of all current practices.

3.11. SUMMARY OF MAIN POINTS

1. Hunting with dogs is not just an English phenomenon. Hunting packs exist throughout the world, especially in European countries, and, excepting Britain, the largest number exists in the United States. What characterises hunting with dogs is not just the usual kill, but the chase, which can extend for many hours. The debate about and attempted abolition of hunting in the United Kingdom are central to understanding what hunting involves, and why it is ethically objectionable.

2. There have been legislative attempts to curtail hunting with dogs in the United Kingdom since 1948. The 1945 Labour government set up the Scott Henderson Committee to investigate hunting, which recommended its continuance. Opponents of hunting claimed that the committee was chosen to produce a pro-hunting report, since it comprised pro-hunting members (3.1).

3. In the midst of increasing political controversy about hunting, the 1997 Labour government similarly set up another committee, this time under the chairmanship of Lord Burns. The Burns Report is the most detailed account of hunting ever produced and deserves a reasoned critique (3.1).

4. But, oddly, the ethical issue was specifically excluded from the remit of Burns, and the committee comprised no one with qualifications in ethics, philosophy, or theology. Burns could not avoid making value judgments but did so without an explicit or considered ethical framework (3.2).

5. The flawed methodology of Burns can be seen in its failure to situate concern for animals historically, by its lack of understanding of animal protection philosophy, and by its reductionist definition of animal welfare as only comprising a "scientific" aspect (3.3).

6. Burns minimises the reality of animal suffering, seeking "scientific" proof of what most reasonable people hold is prima facie evidence of injury. Hunting, incomprehensibly, "compromises the welfare of the fox,"

but is not "cruel." But, since there is ample evidence that all mammals experience suffering, to suppose that being chased for prolonged periods, disembowelled while alive, or baited by dogs is other than cruel is to be pusillanimous before the facts (3.4).

7. Most centrally, Burns fails to articulate and address the two moral objections: it is intrinsically wrong to deliberately inflict suffering on a sentient mammal for purposes other than its own individual benefit, and it is intrinsically wrong to deliberately cause suffering for the purposes of amusement, of recreation, or in the name of sport (3.5).

8. Although Burns accepts that pleasure is a motivation for hunting, the report fails to recognise the intrinsic objection to causing suffering for enjoyment. Moreover, although it recognises that foxes and hares are preserved for hunting, it fails to grasp that such activity vitiates the entire case for control (3.6).

9. In accordance with its (humanly conceived) utilitarian framework, Burns fails to admit the possibility that hunting may be an anti-social behaviour with adverse implications for society (3.7).

10. Most glaringly, Burns accepts that the contribution of hunting to control is generally negligible: "insignificant" in relation to the control of foxes; deer hunting apparently only accounts for 15% of the annual cull required; hare hunting has no "appreciable impact" on numbers; and mink hunting has an "insignificant" effect. Given these admissions, the view that hunting can be justified by reference to control lacks any foundation (3.8).

11. Burns recommended the licensing of hunting, the singular result of which was the options bill sponsored by the government. But licensing would have given hunting an authority it did not have previously and would have effectively institutionalised the practice. Licensing would have devolved the issue to appointed regional committees, with the task of adjudicating the utility of hunting compared with other methods. Clearly, licensing would have ensured hunting's continuance. It was thankfully rejected by Parliament. But licensing may yet be brought back by a future government (3.9).

12. Hunting has become a totemic issue because causing suffering for pleasure is one of the least morally justifiable activities. It is difficult to see how fundamental progress is possible while individuals are allowed to hunt creatures to a cruel death for comparatively trivial reasons (3.10).

4

Second Case

Fur Farming

While most people are aware that wild animals are trapped for their fur, many are surprised to learn that wild animals are farmed for their fur as well. The numbers involved are considerable. Around 50 million mink (*Mustela vison*) and 7 million foxes (mostly Arctic fox, *Alopex lagopus*) are bred each year to meet the world demand for their skins. According to the Fur Commission USA, based on statistics released annually by Oslo Fur Auctions, 2008 shows a world-wide "harvest" totalling 51.12 million mink pelts. Denmark leads the way with 14 million (27.2%) followed by China with 13 million (25.3%) and figures for other major producers are as follows: the Netherlands: 4.5 million, Poland: 3.2 million, the USA: 3 million, Canada: 2.3 million, Russia: 2 million, Finland: 1.9 million, the Baltic States: 2 million, Sweden: 1.45 million, Belarus: 800,000, and Norway: 660,000.[1]

According to the *Sandy Parker Reports* (the Weekly International Fur News), world production of fox (of all colours including blue frost, silver and blue shadow and white) amounted to 7 million in 2007; Scandinavia, comprising of Finland, Norway, Denmark, and Iceland led the list in production. The other countries, in order of amount of production were:

Poland, Russia, the Baltic States, Canada, the United States, and Argentina and Holland.[2] The British Fur Trade Association says that wild fur accounts for only 15–20% of the global fur trade (with Canada, Russia and USA as the main suppliers)[3] and since these are mainly for species other than mink and fox this means that the overwhelming majority of fur sold is farmed.[4]

While this chapter concentrates on the situation in Europe and the moves to legislate against fur farming, it is important to stress at the outset that fur farming is virtually a worldwide phenomenon and the associated practices vary little.[5] Animals are kept in rows of barren wire cages in open-sided sheds. A typical mink cage measures 70 centimetres long by 40 wide and 45 high, and a cage for two Arctic foxes would typically measure 110 centimetres square. Fur factory farms follow a regular calendar. Animals are mated in February and give birth in May, and the pups are weaned six to seven weeks later. Each year's offspring are killed in November at the age of just seven months. The killing of animals on fur factory farms is carried out immediately after their first winter's moult when their fur is at its best and any defects have disappeared.[6]

Since the aim of producers is not to damage the actual fur, slaughter practices have to aim for a kill by unusual means, which include electrocution (using electrodes clamped in the mouth and inserted in the rectum), gassing, cervical dislocation, and sometimes (homemade) poisoning. All these methods are controversial and largely unregulated. The United States, for example, has no federal laws that govern the humane treatment or killing of animals on fur farms. The Fur Commission USA, which mainly represents mink farmers, promulgates "voluntary" standards and recommends only CO or CO_2 gassing.[7] Only one state in the United States has specifically banned a certain type of killing method, namely, anal electrocution.[8] The issue of the inhumanity of the killing has been highlighted by evidence of grotesque killing methods in China.[9] It would be a fair summation to say that the killing practices alone (necessitated by the aim of obtaining undamaged fur) render animals liable to suffering.

This chapter defends the decision of some European governments, including the British government, to legislate against fur farming on the grounds of "public morality." It aims to show *why* there is a legitimate public interest in reducing the suffering of animals. The ban on fur farming was the first time that the British government advanced any animal protection legislation on explicitly ethical grounds.

Although the major thrust of the argument in this chapter relates to European legislation, it also has obvious relevance to non-European countries, not least of all the United States and Russia. Moreover, there is no reason to suppose that the veterinary objections to this practice, detailed

below, do not also apply to fur farming in other countries, since the practices
described are similar, if not uniform.

4.1. INCREASING LEGISLATION AGAINST FUR FARMING

An increasing number of European countries are legislating against fur
farming. Austria has banned "fur farming in six of the nine Austrian federal
states and in the remaining three, there are such strict welfare regulations,
[particularly] in relation to the availability of [water for swimming], that fur
farming is no longer economically viable."[10] In fact, "[t]here are no . . . fur
farms [left] in Austria."[11] The Netherlands decided to ban fox farming in
1995, and all fox fur production ceased on 1 April 2008.[12] In 2005, the
Swedish agricultural minister announced that stringent new welfare standards for keeping mink would be introduced into the Animal Protection
Act.[13] In Italy, new welfare standards for fur farming were adopted in March
2001 and came into force on 1 January 2008.[14] Italy's directive contains such
stringent animal welfare standards—including enriched pens, minimum
spatial requirements, access to swimming water, and provision for nest
boxes—that it is doubtful whether fur farming will survive.[15] In addition,
the Croatian government introduced a new Animal Protection Act that will
outlaw fur farming, "subject to a ten year phase out period."[16]

In 2000, the Westminster Parliament of the United Kingdom passed the
Fur Farming (Prohibition) Act, which makes it a criminal offence in England and Wales to keep animals solely or primarily for slaughter for the
value of their fur, or for breeding progeny for such slaughter.[17] A similar
measure was passed by the Scottish Parliament.[18] The principal ground
cited for this legislation within the United Kingdom was "public morality."[19]
Elliot Morley, the parliamentary secretary to the (then) Ministry of Agriculture, Fisheries, and Food, gave the following account of the government's
position:

> Morality is important when it comes to the treatment of animals. I shall
> repeat our view on the morality of fur farming. Fur farming is not consistent
> with a proper value and respect for animal life. *Animal life should not be
> destroyed in the absence of a sufficient justification in terms of public benefit.
> Nor should animals be bred for such destruction in the absence of sufficient
> justification.* That is the essence of our argument for applying morality to a
> Bill of this kind, and for justifying it under article 30 of EU regulations.[20]

One might wish that the case had been differently put, or at least more
explicitly—specifically that the issue of suffering had been more prominent

in the government's justification of its position. The issue concerns not just unjustifiable *killing* but also unjustifiable *suffering*, as we will go on to show. And what is sorely needed is some account of the rational considerations that undergird concern for the value of animal life.

But the main criticism of the government's position has concerned its appeal to the idea that our treatment of animals is a *public* moral issue. At first sight, it appears to inject a new note into the usual discussion about animal protection. Public morality suggests that there must be some public interest involved. Those who want legislative changes for animals, therefore, have an obligation to spell out precisely what that public interest is and why it can justify making fur farming a criminal activity.

The general answer is that concern for the right treatment of animals has been the subject of legislative activity in the United Kingdom since 1800, when the first animal protection bill (to abolish bull-baiting) was presented to the House of Commons.[21] Since that time, there has been a growing awareness that there must be legal constraints on the uses to which animals may be put. There is now a wide range of measures regulating or prohibiting use in almost every sphere of human activity that affects animals: these include the use of animals in commercial trade, in farming, in research, in entertainment, and even as domestic companions.[22] A consensus has emerged that these developments are conducive to a civilised society—even the complete prohibition of practices (such as cock-fighting and bull-baiting) whose abolition in Britain was attended by no little controversy.[23] These developments have been supported philosophically by a growing sense that society has a clear stake in safeguarding animals from acts of cruelty. Not only is it wrong to make animals suffer for trivial purposes, but also humans themselves benefit from living in a society where cruelty is actively discouraged and punishable by law. In the late twentieth and early twenty-first centuries, a number of factors has stimulated concern that this now commonly accepted position should be strengthened still further.

4.2. FUR FARMING, HARM, AND SUFFERING

In the first place, many previous attempts at legislation defined cruelty in specific relation to *physical* acts, such as beating, kicking, hitting, stabbing, and so on.[24] Such a definition reflects an understanding at the time that animals could be harmed solely, or principally, by the infliction of adverse physical activity. We now know, however, that animals can be harmed, sometimes severely, in a range of other ways, for example, by subjection to unsuitable environments where their basic behavioural needs are frustrated.

As early as 1980, biologists, veterinarians, and ethicists proposed "basic guidelines" for all "managed" species:

> No husbandry method should deny the environmental requirements of the basic [behavioural] needs of these animals. These needs will include the following:
>
> > freedom to perform natural physical movement
> > association with other animals, where appropriate of their own kind
> > facilities for comfort activities, e.g., rest, sleep, and body care
> > satisfaction of minimal spatial and territorial requirements including a
> >   visual field and "personal" space
>
> Deviations from these principles should be avoided as far as possible, but where such deviations are absolutely unavoidable efforts should be made to compensate the animal environmentally.[25]

Where these principles are not observed, animals suffer "harms of deprivation,"[26] which cause as much, if not more, suffering to animals than the infliction of physical pain. Our current understanding of animals—their mental states and behavioural needs—has necessitated a much wider appreciation of harm than was previously possible through simple appeals to physical cruelty. Fur farming is a case in point. Some people, unaware of the conditions on fur farms, assume that breeding animals for fur is like any other form of farming and poses no special welfare problems.[27] There are good reasons for thinking otherwise. The UK government's own advisory body, the Farm Animal Welfare Council (FAWC), made public its disapproval of mink and fox farming in 1989.[28] Its judgment makes clear the particular difficulties in subjecting essentially wild animals to intensive farming:

> Mink and fox have been bred in captivity for only about 50–60 generations and the Council is particularly concerned about the keeping of what are essentially wild animals in small barren cages. The Council believes that the systems employed in the farming of mink and fox do not satisfy some of the most basic criteria which it has identified for protecting the welfare of farm animals. The current cages used for fur farming do not appear to provide appropriate comfort or shelter, and do not allow the animals freedom to display most normal patterns of [behaviour].[29]

So severe were these strictures that the council declined to issue a welfare code for fur farming as it had done for other farming practices. The council's then chair, Professor C. R. W. Spedding, made clear in a letter to the parliamentary secretary to the Ministry of Agriculture:

One of the objects of the [press] statement is to give a clear warning that
FAWC does not see fur farming as an acceptable alternative enterprise as
currently [practiced]. We have decided against drawing up a Welfare Code for
mink and fox farming to avoid giving it the stamp of approval which a
government-backed Welfare Code would imply.[30]

This unusually strong position was subsequently confirmed by further
research. A comprehensive review of the welfare of farmed mink in 1999,
undertaken by Professor D. M. Broom, professor of animal welfare at the
University of Cambridge, and his colleague A. J. Nimon of the Department
of Clinical Veterinary Medicine, concluded:

The high level and pervasiveness of stereotypies among farmed mink, and the
incidence of fur chewing and even self-mutilation of tail tissue, suggest that
farmed mink welfare is not good. Stereotypies are associated with negative
consequences such as slower kit growth, and higher levels of feed intake
without an increase in growth.[31]

A further study, published in 2001 by the same authors in relation to the
welfare of farmed foxes, concluded:

Research on fox welfare in relation to housing shows that farmed foxes have a
considerable degree of fear, both of humans and in general, that the
barrenness of the cages is a significant problem for the foxes, and that farmed
foxes can have substantial reproduction problems. There is clear evidence that
the welfare of farmed foxes in the typical bare, wire-mesh cages is very poor.[32]

Such conclusions are further confirmed by the report *The Welfare of Animals Kept for Fur Production* published by the Scientific Committee on
Animal Health and Animal Welfare of the European Union in 2001.[33] Areas
of concern with respect to the welfare of mink include gastric ulcers, kidney
abnormalities, tooth decay, self-mutilation, and stereotypies.[34] Foxes were
found to suffer from, inter alia, "[a]bnormal [behaviours] such as exaggerated fear responses, infanticide, stereotypies and pelt-biting."[35] While ethical questions were not included within the remit of the committee, it
concluded on welfare grounds alone that "mink and foxes generally suffer
from being kept in cages because it limits their natural [behaviour] as wild
animals."[36]

In the light of these findings, it is now unreasonable to hold that fur
farming does not impose suffering on animals. The issue is not whether
direct, physical pain is inflicted upon such animals. It is rather that the
confinement of wild creatures in barren, sterile enclosures where their

behavioural needs cannot be adequately met involves the infliction of kinds of deprivation that inevitably result in suffering. Wild animals that normally travel long distances are cooped up in small cages that deny them any kind of natural life. Wire cages, typically measuring 70 centimetres long by 40 wide and 45 high, are simply insufficient to allow for the exercise of natural behaviour. In addition, mink are semi-aquatic, but they are denied access to water in which to swim.[37]

As we have seen, the problem isn't just that about 57 million animals are bred and killed for their fur. It is the conditions in which they are kept. What the figures indicate is the massive institutionalisation of the abuse of animals. Such forms of confinement cannot by their nature be made "animal-friendly"; no captive environment can adequately facilitate the full range of social and behavioural needs that are essential to the well-being of essentially wild animals. The worst aspects of fur farming may conceivably be ameliorated by some environmental improvements, but no reform can eradicate the suffering inherent in such systems.

4.3. ANIMALS AS A SPECIAL MORAL CASE

The second factor stimulating change is the growing ethical sensitivity to issues of animal protection. This sensitivity, as we have seen, has been reinforced by considerable ethical and philosophical work on the status of animals. Our use of animals in intensive farming has been the subject of particularly strong criticism. Professor David DeGrazia, for example, maintains that "the institution of factory farming, which causes massive harm for trivial purposes, is ethically indefensible."[38] While not all ethicists agree on the precise limits that should be observed in our treatment of animals, there is an emerging consensus that we have special kinds of obligations to animals and that a great deal of what we now do to them is morally unacceptable. There is, in short, a strong desire for fundamental change among ethicists who have addressed this topic.[39]

We have already spelled out in chapter 1 *why* animals should be regarded as constituting a special moral case. Without understanding that case, it is difficult to grasp why animals should be seen as having a special claim on our attention. It is not enough to simply say that the infliction of suffering is wrong; we need to provide an account of the rational considerations that make it so. These considerations are all particularly relevant to the issue of fur farming. After all, in such farming we keep essentially wild animals captive and make them subservient to our purposes; we frustrate their basic behavioural needs; and we kill them in a frequently inhumane way which makes them liable to suffering. We do all this even though they have not harmed us, and even though they do not pose any threat to our life or well-being. They cannot "assent" to their maltreatment or even vocalise their own interests. Theirs is a state of moral innocence and blamelessness; they are without means of defence and are wholly vulnerable. In short, we have *made* them entirely dependent upon us; they deserve, as a matter of justice, special moral solicitude.

It is that latter consideration that is especially relevant when it comes to fur farming. Doubtless, we have obligations to free-ranging wild animals, for example, not to harry or hunt them and to allow them to live their own lives in their own manner, except where there is some definite clash of interests with our own (and these occasions need to be weighed carefully). But these are different sorts of obligations than those owed to those beings that we specifically *choose* to breed and rear for commercial advantage. In the case of fur farming, we select wild animals and take over their conditions of life so that there is hardly an aspect that is not subject to our close control. In a secondary, but real sense, they only exist because of us. We have made them as they are and we exercise near-absolute control. That being the case, our obligations are the greater. The moral rule of thumb is: the greater the power, the greater the responsibility.

It is thus the sheer vulnerability and dependency of animals in this context that is one of the most powerful reasons for regarding them as a special moral case. Respecting their vulnerability is intrinsic to the care that must be shown in bringing them into existence in the first place.

In the past, this claim for special care has been flattened by the counter-claim that animals are our property: they can be owned like bricks and cabbages, and with as few or no moral obligations. Immanuel Kant rein-forced this thinking almost by sleight of hand: "Inasmuch as crops (for example, potatoes) and domestic animals are products of human labour, at least as far as their quantity is concerned, we can say that they may be used, consumed, or destroyed (killed)."[40] But this attitude he contrasted with what is owed humans: "This kind of argument for a right . . . is indeed valid with respect to animals, which can be owned by human beings, but it absolutely cannot be applied to a human being, and especially not a citizen." In other words, in Kant's famous phrase, a citizen is "not merely a means, but . . . an end in itself."[41] The principal reason that Kant cited for this being so is that humans (specifically, citizens) must "give their free consent."[42] But, as I have argued, the absence of free consent incurs not less, but more moral respon-sibility when dealing with subjects that can be harmed. Indeed, the history of animal protection is, in one sense, a protest against Kant and the idea that we can do what we like with what we own. Animals are not just means; we are not their ends. Ownership, or (to speak theologically) "derived owner-ship," properly understood, always increases obligation.

4.4. LAW AND THE PROTECTION OF THE WEAK

The third factor that has stimulated change is the recognition that law has a specific role in protecting the weak and the vulnerable. It is worth noting that the concern for the alleviation of animal suffering that emerged in the nineteenth century was part of a broader "humanitarian movement" equally concerned for the protection of children from abuse and cruelty, the abolition of slavery, the establishing of minimum working conditions, and the emancipation of women.[43] As Henry Salt, founder of the Humanitarian League (1894–1920), emphasised: "Humanitarianism must show that it is *not* 'bestarian,' and must aim at the redress of *all* needless suffering, human and animal alike."[44] Many of the key movers for animal protection—William Wilberforce, Lord Shaftesbury, and Fowell Buxton, to take only three examples—were prominent in these campaigns.[45] If one looks at the early debates concerning animal protection in Britain, in addition to the claim that cruelty is unjust, one sees the claim that cruelty also harms the perpetrator by diminishing his humanity. Consider, for example, the preamble to Lord Erskine's Cruelty to Animals Bill in 1809: "The abuse of that [human] dominion by cruel and oppressive treatment of such animals, is not only highly unjust and immoral, but most pernicious in its example, having an evident tendency to harden the heart against the natural feelings of humanity."[46]

From this starting point, we have continued to welcome a range of legislative measures that grant specific protection to those who are easily abused and exploited. The notion then that there is a legitimate social or public interest in limiting animal suffering has a long provenance. There is a benevolent motivation behind socially progressive legislation that some, perhaps even many, would hold to be the proper function of law, namely, to defend the weak and defenceless.

But the case for including animals within this legislative advance is even stronger today. It is buttressed by the increasing empirical evidence of a link between abuse and cruelty to animals and other forms of violence, notably against women and children. In the past, the connection, if any, was largely rhetorical. Early reformers sensed that there must be a connection and assumed that it was so. Today, however, there is a range of heavyweight publications that map the relationships between animal abuse and antisocial behaviour. To take just one example, Frank R. Ascione and Phil Arkow, in their collection *Child Abuse, Domestic Violence, and Animal Abuse* (the result of a multidisciplinary symposium of people professionally concerned with social work, child protection, domestic violence, and animal protection), maintain: "Violence directed against animals is often a coercion device and an early indicator of violence that may escalate in range and severity against other victims."[47] This does not mean, of course, that all those who abuse animals will subsequently perpetrate anti-social or violent behaviour. There is no simple cause and effect. Rather, cruelty to animals seems to be one of a cluster of potential or actual characteristics held in common by those who commit violent or seriously anti-social acts. It is worth noting that mental health professionals and top law enforcement officials in the United States consider cruelty to animals a warning sign. The American Psychiatric Association, for example, identifies animal cruelty as one of the diagnostic criteria for conduct disorders, and the Federal Bureau of Investigation uses reports of animal cruelty in analysing the threat of suspected and known criminals. Doubtless, much has yet to be done to explore and document that connection, but that there is a link is increasingly difficult to deny. It is an increasingly viable assumption that a world in which abuse to animals goes unchecked is bound to be a less morally safe world for human beings.

Such awareness should inform, inter alia, legislative attempts to limit the infliction of suffering on animals. The need for reform extends not only to the protection of domestic species, but also to "managed" species subject to commerce and exploitation. As already noted, the institutionalised use of animals in modern farming has become a major area of concern. And it seems that an increasing number of people want to move towards a society in which commercial institutions do not routinely and habitually abuse animals. A 1995 UK opinion poll on animal welfare found majorities against training animals for circuses (61%), exporting veal calves to the Continent (68%), hunting foxes for recreation (72%), keeping battery hens (72%), and trapping animals for fur (76%).[48]

4.5. ABSENCE OF MORAL JUSTIFICATION

We now need to address more precisely the moral issue involved in fur farming. Some people hold that the infliction of suffering on animals can never be morally justifiable.[49] This position deserves much more consideration than is usually given to it. The moral considerations already outlined indicate that there are good rational grounds for supposing that certain kinds of activity, directed against vulnerable subjects, are so morally outrageous that they ought never to be countenanced, whatever the circumstances. The infliction of prolonged suffering on captive creatures is, from this perspective, intrinsically objectionable. Circumstances, benefits, or compensating factors may limit the offence, but they can never make the practice morally licit.

Others hold that suffering can sometimes, perhaps rarely, be justified if it can be shown to be necessary, or if there is sufficient benefit, and if the end result cannot be achieved by other means.[50] For the latter, the issue turns on whether there is sufficient moral necessity, or benefit, involved in fur farming to justify its continuance.

In ethical terms, to show that something is necessary requires more than a simple appeal to what is fashionable or desirable.[51] Human wants do not by themselves constitute moral necessity.[52] It has to be shown that the good procured is essential and that no alternative means are available. When viewed from this perspective, it can be seen immediately that fur farming fails the basic moral test. The wearing of fur, while conceivably pleasant, fashionable, or even desirable, cannot reasonably be defined as essential. Fur is a luxury item. When weighed in terms of a cost-benefit analysis, the case fails, and spectacularly so. It is obviously unjustifiable to inflict suffering on animals for non-essential, indeed trivial, ends. In that sense, Elliot Morley was right to insist that animals should not be "bred for such destruction in the absence of sufficient justification."[53]

Unsurprisingly, perhaps, supporters of fur farming fail to address the central moral issue and frequently provide exaggerated claims for the "necessity" of fur. For example, Richard D. North accepts that fur is a luxury item *and* still defends it.[54] He maintains, "There is a powerful case to be made for the idea that the need for luxury is one of the most fundamental human urges, as it is one of the most powerful well-springs of activity in the whole animal kingdom."[55] He continues:

> Biologists have long understood a Darwinian explanation for the apparent excesses of display indulged in by animals such as the peacock. Sexual attractiveness that involves a conspicuous and costly display demonstrates a male's ability to satisfy to an extraordinary degree the capacity to fulfil his basic needs.[56]

Even allowing for the correctness of North's interpretation of animal behaviour, no human being has a "basic need" for adornment articles, such as fur coats or fashion accessories. Even if they could be shown to be a component in fulfilling sexual desire, the case would still have to be made that such wants (as distinct from needs) could not be met through alternative means. To say the least, the argument is frivolous in the context of animal suffering.

4.6. ANSWERS TO OBJECTIONS

Before we conclude this chapter, there are six objections in favour of fur farming that should be briefly addressed.

The first objection to the elimination of fur farming is that it is consistent with commonly held religious notions that animals have a subordinate place to humans and that they are made for human use. This objection deserves some scrutiny. While it is true that Judaism, Christianity, and Islam have supported instrumentalist attitudes to animals, and are therefore complicit in justifying exploitation, it should be noted that none of them (save for individual voices within the traditions) have ever supposed that our use of animals should be illimitable or without moral constraint. Moreover, there are positive resources within each tradition for a re-evaluation of our treatment of animals.[57]

As is well known, Judaism pioneered the biblically grounded principle of *tsaar baalei hayyim* (literally, consideration for "the pain of living creatures") against cruelty to animals.[58] Jewish scholars, such as the eighteenth-century legalist Ezekiel Landau, ruled that hunting for pleasure or killing for adornment articles, such as fur, is forbidden:

> We find in the *Torah* the sport of hunting imputed to no one but to such fierce characters as Nimrod and Esau, never to any of the patriarchs or to their descendents. The customary blessing, "Thou shalt outlive," offered to one donning a new garment, is . . . omitted altogether in the case of a fur coat. Such a blessing might make it appear that the killing of animals is not only condoned but actually desirable, which is contrary to the verse in Psalms "And his tender mercies are over all his works." . . . I cannot comprehend how a Jew could even dream of killing animals merely for the pleasure of hunting, when he has no immediate need for the bodies of the creatures.[59]

Islam, too, has a tradition of concern for animals, epitomised in the saying of the Prophet Muhammad "Kindness to any living creature will be rewarded."[60] The Prophet explicitly rejected cruel practices in his own day involving horses and birds. Islamic scholar Neal Robinson summarises the position of animals in Islam as follows: "According to the Qu'ran, all animals and birds belong to communities [of like creatures] and give praise to God. Hence the Prophet ordered his followers to be merciful even when slaughtering animals for food or killing dangerous species."[61]

Within Christianity, arguably one of the most anthropocentric of all world religions, there are growing signs of a vocal opposition to animal abuse, and especially the killing of animals for fur. It is often overlooked that, at the beginning of the most recent phase of the movement for animal protection, the archbishop of Canterbury, Donald Coggan, on accepting the presidency of the RSPCA, declared: "Animals, as part of God's creation, have rights which must be respected. It behoves us always to be sensitive to their needs and to the reality of their pain."[62]

Coggan was one of forty-one Anglican bishops, including three archbishops, who in 1992 signed a statement refusing to buy or wear fur themselves on moral and theological grounds. The signatories included Richard Holloway (primus of Scotland), Alwyn Rice Jones (archbishop of Wales), and Rowan Williams (then bishop of Monmouth, now archbishop of Canterbury).[63]

The idea that religious authorities can be uncritically utilised in this debate in defence of fur farming should therefore be jettisoned. That doesn't, of course, excuse these traditions of their insensitivity generally to animals, but the simple appeal to the high place of humanity in creation does not (or, rather, should not) by itself justify abuse. Indeed, there are grounds within almost all religious traditions to oppose the utilisation of animals for trivial purposes, such as luxury or adornment. These grounds include the intrinsic value of sentient creatures made by God; the responsibility of humans as stewards and guardians of God's creation; and, not least of all, a near-unanimous rejection of the deliberate infliction of suffering as an abuse of our power over animals. It is worth noting that the modern movement for the protection of animals owes a great deal to the Christian and Jewish founders, Arthur Broome and Lewis Gompertz, of the world's first national animal welfare society, the Society for the Prevention of Cruelty to Animals (later to become the RSPCA), which was founded in 1824.[64]

The second objection is that banning fur farming is a denial of individual freedom. In that sense, the statement is self-evidently true. The legal prohibition of any practice does, of course, limit individual freedom. But what has to be shown, morally, is that the outlawing of fur farming constitutes an unwarranted or unjustifiable invasion of individual liberty. It should be pointed out that, right from the outset, animal protectionists have had to suffer the use of this argument to prevent the prohibition of even the grossest acts of cruelty. For example, commenting on the failure of the first bill that attempted to outlaw bull-baiting in 1800, *The Times* was adamant that the attempt was misconceived since "whatever meddles with private personal disposition of a man's time or property is tyranny direct."[65]

The current attempt to cast animal protectionists in the guise of anti–civil libertarians misses the moral point that liberty to inflict suffering for trivial ends, even and especially to animals, violates civilised values and renders weaker humans vulnerable as well. For if the argument is logically sound, there are no good reasons for stopping at animals. Properly understood, there cannot be a civil right to be cruel.

The third argument is that banning fur farming is inconsistent when there are greater cruelties that need to be addressed. Whether there are greater cruelties than the infliction of prolonged suffering on wild animals is debatable. But, even allowing for that, the argument has a poor pedigree.

The same was also said, inter alia, about those who opposed bear-baiting.[66] For example, Richard Martin's attempt to bring in a bill "to prevent bear-baiting and other cruel practices" in 1824 was met with (what had even then become) the usual objection from consistency:

> Now, if the [honourable] gentleman [Richard Martin] laid down the general principle, that no pain should be inflicted on animals, beyond such as was necessary in putting them to death for the support of man, his legislation would be consistent; but he was certainly not fair in selecting partial instances to legislate on, in which the members of the House, the parties legislating, did not happen to be interested [hear!]. . . . Let them abolish fox-hunting and partridge shooting, and they might then abolish bear-baiting. . . . Who could say that hawking was less cruel than bear-baiting or fishing? Nay, fishing added treachery to cruelty. . . . Fishing was a cruel fraud [practised] on innocent and [defenceless] animals.[67]

If one takes the view that all welfare legislation for humans or animals has to be rigorously consistent (in the sense of encompassing all possible abuses) before any single law is enacted, one would have had to logically oppose the enactment of all socially progressive legislation for animals in Britain since 1800. The fact is that, out of necessity, animal protection legislation has to be a gradual, piecemeal affair, depending as it does on popular, democratic support for its enactment. Each case has to be judged on its merits, the relevant arguments advanced, and popular support marshalled. If, in this process, legislation is sometimes inconsistent, then it has to be recognised that all legislation—for both human and animal protection—depends upon public opinion, which is itself not always consistent.[68] In a democratic society, the risk of inconsistency has to be acknowledged. The alternative (in the case of humans as well as animals) is not even to begin the process because of the inevitable risk of inconsistency.

The fourth objection is that responsibility for animal welfare should rest with the European Commission rather than member states. It should be noted that this objection is not endorsed by the relevant commissioner, David Byrne. In a remarkably frank statement, he describes this attitude as "passing the buck" and continues:

> [S]peaking as the European Commissioner with responsibility for key areas of public concern, such as health and consumer protection and food safety, I am always prepared to accept my responsibilities. But, equally, I insist on ensuring that others should not hide behind others in evading their responsibilities.[69]

His reasoning deserves to be read at length:

> The public should be in a position where they can be confident that animals
> are treated humanely. And that their elected representatives and the public
> authorities take the issue seriously. But the question obviously arises, which
> authorities? Is it, for example, the role of the European Commission to ensure
> that animals are treated humanely? I will not duck the issue. The Commission
> ['s] role relates only to its legal powers and competence. *We cannot ensure*
> *that animals are humanely treated throughout the EU [European Union]. For*
> *a number of reasons—we do not have the resources, the powers or the*
> *legitimacy to do so.*[70]

And he underlines the point in even more stark language:

> *Again and again, often in the area of animal welfare, Member States are found*
> *to be at fault in not meeting acceptable standards. . . . I am growing increasingly*
> *weary at the repeated reports of my officials on continued non-respect of*
> *Community provisions on animal welfare.*[71]

Byrne's message is crystal clear. Not only may member states act, they
have a responsibility to do so. Under the 1999 protocol, they have a responsibility to "fully consider animal welfare" and the freedom to initiate appropriate legislation.[72] Far from expecting the commission to act, Byrne makes
clear that it has neither the resources nor the powers (or even, apparently,
"the legitimacy") to enforce existing regulations when they are inadequately
respected by some member states. In light of these frank admissions, the
case for member states to act positively on their own is overwhelming. To
wait for the EC to act on a Europe-wide basis is, in the words of Commissioner Byrne, to "pass the buck."[73]

The fifth objection is that the notion of public morality is misconceived,
even, in the colourful language of one Westminster MP, a "truly terrifying
concept."[74] But, as we have shown, the development of animal protection, as
well as the protection of weaker human subjects, has often entailed an
appeal to social values.[75] It should be accepted that morality cannot be
decided by opinion polls. Majorities are not always right, and popular
sensitivities can be misguided.[76] But such considerations should not blind
us to the fact that animal protection legislation in a democratic society has
always depended, as a last resort, on popular support.[77]

Neither is such an appreciation reprehensible. In a changing world with
(hopefully) developing moral sensitivities, it follows that the law should
reflect those changed moral perceptions. Opinion polls in the United King-

dom have indicated large majorities against not only animal circuses, the export of calves, sport hunting, battery hens, and trapping, but also fur farming, with 76% of the population supporting an outright ban.[78] The movement for the protection of animals needs that amount of public support in order to achieve, and justify, legislative change, at least in a democratic society. The law is the outward and visible sign of a changed or changing moral consensus.[79] Given such a long-standing consensus in a democratic society, those who wish to frustrate the majority view must provide convincing arguments for retaining the status quo.

The final objection is that changing the law, even if justifiable in terms of preventing abuses, should be used sparingly, especially when abolitionist legislation is proposed. This argument is generally sound. Obviously, not everything that the public dislikes should be made illegal. Consequently, arguments for prohibition or abolition have to be well made. But even if arguments for the prohibition of existing practices should be treated with caution, it does not follow that such arguments cannot be made, and reasonably so. Fur farming is an excellent case in point. Some systems of abuse cannot be reformed because, although their worst aspects may be ameliorated through regulation, they constitute such a moral offence that abolition is the only proper course of action.

4.7. CONCLUSION: NO ALTERNATIVE TO ABOLITION

Fur farming should be done away with, not only throughout the European Union, but also worldwide. Nothing morally essential would be lost and much would be gained from a ban on the practice. Our failure to pursue abolition would mean turning our backs on the long history of progressive anti-cruelty legislation. It would signal that we have, in effect, given up on the struggle to eliminate unjustifiable suffering in our society. It would constitute a worrying precedent that commercial concerns are immune from public moral sensibility. It would be to act in ignorance of the knowledge that we have acquired about the sentience and behavioural complexity of the other creatures with whom we share the earth. In short, any system of farming that inherently exposes animals to high levels of suffering for trivial ends cries out for abolitionist legislation. To their credit, some European countries have led the way; others should follow.

4.8. SUMMARY OF MAIN POINTS

1. Fur farming is virtually a worldwide phenomenon, and the associated practices vary little. Around 50 million mink and 7 million foxes are bred each year to meet the world demand for their skins. In addition to Europe, the United States, Canada, Russia, and China are the main fur farming countries in the world.

2. An increasing number of European countries, including Italy, Austria, Sweden, The Netherlands, and Croatia, have introduced or are in the process of introducing legislation to curtail or prohibit fur farming. In 2000, fur farming was outlawed in England and Wales on the ground of "public morality." Similar legislation has been passed in Scotland (4.1).

3. Concern for the right treatment of animals has a long legislative history. Society has a clear stake in safeguarding animals from acts of cruelty. Human beings benefit from living in a society where cruelty is actively discouraged (4.1).

4. The veterinary evidence shows that it is unreasonable to suppose that fur farming does not impose suffering on what are essentially wild animals kept in barren environments in which their behavioural needs are frustrated (4.2).

5. Growing ethical concern for animals has been reinforced by considerable intellectual work on the status of animals. There is an emerging consensus among ethicists for fundamental change (4.3).

6. Animals make a special moral claim upon us because, inter alia, they are morally innocent, unable to give or withhold their consent or vocalise their needs, and are vulnerable to human exploitation. Not least of all, managed animals are wholly dependent upon us and subject to our close control; we specifically *choose* to breed and rear them; otherwise, they would not exist. The moral rule of thumb is: the greater the power, the greater the responsibility (4.3).

7. Law has a proper role in defending the weak and the vulnerable, including animals and children, from exploitation (4.4).

8. There is increasing evidence of a link between the abuse of animals and other forms of violence, notably against women and children. It is an increasingly viable assumption that a world in which abuse of animals goes unchecked is bound to be a less morally safe world for human beings (4.4).

9. Those who regard the infliction of suffering on animals as intrinsically objectionable rightly oppose fur farming. In their view, there are certain acts against vulnerable subjects that are so morally outrageous that they can never be morally licit (4.5).

10. Fur farming is also unacceptable to those who hold that the infliction of suffering can sometimes be justified. Fur farming fails the basic test of moral necessity. It is wholly unjustifiable to subject animals to prolonged

suffering for trivial ends, such as fur coats or fashion accessories. Fur is a non-essential luxury item (4.5).

11. It is sometimes argued that fur farming is justifiable because it is consistent with religious notions that animals can be used for human benefit. But despite instrumentalist attitudes and complicity in animal abuse, Judaism, Christianity, and Islam have never held that our use of animals should be illimitable or without moral constraint (4.6).

12. The claim that banning fur farming is an infringement of legitimate freedom is untenable; many previous cruelties (now illegal) have been defended on that basis. Properly understood there can be no civil right to be cruel (4.6).

13. It is sometimes held that member states should wait for the European Commission to act on issues of animal welfare. In fact, under the 1999 protocol, member states already have the responsibility to "fully consider animal welfare" and the freedom to initiate appropriate legislation. One commissioner has publicly stated that some member states are failing to comply with even their existing responsibilities (4.6).

14. In a democratic society, the law should properly reflect our changed ethical perception of animals and, specifically, the public's long-standing opposition to fur farming (4.6).

15. There is an overwhelming case for the abolition of fur farming on ethical grounds. Any system of farming that inherently exposes animals to high levels of suffering for trivial ends cries out for abolitionist legislation (4.7).

5

Third Case

Commercial Sealing

Killing seals is a huge international business, taking some 900,000 seals annually.[1] The three largest seal hunts are Canada's commercial harp seal hunt which has landed more than a million seals during 2004–08 (the 2008 Total Allowable Catch (TAC) was set at 275,000); West Greenland's unregulated harp seal hunt, which currently lands some 90,000 animals each year (another 90,000 are killed but not landed); and Namibia's Cape fur seal hunt (the 2008 TAC was 80,000).

Official figures are not always known or available, but it is estimated that in recent years Canada has landed more than 330,000 seals (several species) annually. The Greenland seal hunt lands approximately 175,000 seals (several species) annually; tens of thousands of additional animals are killed but not landed each year. Russian seal hunts (also involving several species) may take up to 137,000 seals annually. In 2005, Norway began offering seal hunting as a tourist attraction and, in recent years some 18,000 seals (several species) have been killed in various seal hunts. An unknown number (probably in the thousands) of seals are shot in Scotland, United Kingdom, every year, but no records are kept of the numbers killed, nor is such documentation required.[2]

This chapter focuses on the Canadian seal hunt, also known as the "Atlantic hunt," because it is the largest marine mammal hunt in the world. But almost all the ethical considerations that follow also apply to seal hunting worldwide. The Canadian hunt has been the subject of criticism from the middle of the nineteenth century, but it is only since the 1960s that it has become a focus of international controversy. Criticism has focused on the annual, commercial hunt of harp seals in the Gulf of St. Lawrence. Both harp and hooded seals are killed in the course of the seal hunt, but harp seals made up about 99% of the seals killed during 2000–05. The three-year quota which ended in 2005 allowed 30,000 hooded and 975,000 harp seals to be killed. Figures indicate that a total of 317,672 harp seals were landed during 2005.[3] The 2008 TAC has only slightly reduced the notional number of allowed kills to 275,000.

On 17 March 2005, the Canadian minister of fisheries and oceans issued a statement titled "Canada's Seal Hunt: Beyond the Rhetoric." "Like the fishery," he argued, "the annual seal hunt is an important industry and a time-honoured tradition for people in Canada's coastal communities." Seals constitute "a valuable natural resource that provide[s] income in remote towns and villages where few other opportunities exist." He continued:

> Unfortunately, this industry and its importance to thousands of Canadians are often misunderstood and clouded by misleading rhetoric and sensational images that tell a selective, biased and often false story about the seal hunt. The tragic result is that this industry, and the people who rely on it for a living, are undeservedly cast in a negative light by a few powerful organizations putting their own agendas ahead of the truth.

In an attempt to "set the record straight," the minister made, inter alia, a number of claims:

1. The hunt is conducted in a "humane" way.
2. The hunting of "harp (whitecoat) and hooded (blueback) seal pups is strictly prohibited."
3. The hunt is "closely monitored and tightly regulated."
4. Coastal communities rely on the hunt "for their survival."[4]

This chapter interrogates these claims and examines whether the Canadian government's case withstands ethical and practical scrutiny.

5.1.   FIRST CLAIM: THE HUNT IS HUMANE

The minister maintains that to "prevent inhumane treatment, seals are killed quickly and according to strict regulations." He elaborated:

Canada's seal hunting methods have been studied and approved by the Royal Commission on Seals and Sealing, which found that the methods used in the seal hunt compare favourably to those used to hunt other wild animals, and those used to slaughter domestic animals—like cattle and poultry—for human consumption.[5]

Let us first focus on the methods of slaughter. According to the Marine Mammal Regulations (MMRs) that govern the hunt, the following may be used to kill ("dispatch") a seal:

(a) *a round club* made of hardwood that measures not less than 60 centimetres and not more than 1 metre in length and that, for at least half of its length, beginning at one end, measures not less than 5 centimetres and not more than 7.6 centimetres in diameter;

(b) *an instrument known as a hakapik,* consisting of a metal ferrule that weighs at least 340 grams with a slightly bent spike not more than 14 centimetres in length on one side of the ferrule and a blunt projection not more than 1.3 centimetres in length on the opposite side of the ferrule and that is attached to a wooden handle that measures not less than 105 centimetres and not more than 153 centimetres in length and not less than 3 centimetres and not more than 5.1 centimetres in diameter;

(c) *a rifle and bullets* that are not full metal–jacketed that produce a muzzle velocity of not less than 1,800 feet per second and a muzzle energy of not less than 1,100 foot pounds; or

(d) *a shotgun* of not less than 20 gauge and rifled slugs.[6]

The veterinary evidence showing the hunt is inhumane is from an independent, international team of five veterinary experts who studied the seal hunt in the Gulf of St. Lawrence in 2001 (hereafter "Burdon" or the Burdon Report). The panel included specialists in veterinary neurology and marine mammals and a past chair of the Canadian Veterinary Medical Association (CVMA). The veterinarians studied the hunt from the air and from the ground, viewed videotape evidence, and performed random post-mortems on seal carcasses abandoned on the ice floes. The postmortem examination of seventy-six seal carcasses revealed that, in thirteen (17%), there were no detectable lesions of the skull, leading to the conclusion that these seals had been skinned while conscious. In nineteen (25%) of the seal carcasses, there were minimal fractures, "including hairline or non-displaced fractures" to moderate fractures. The latter are insufficient to render the animals fully unconscious, although they may be associated with some decrease of conscious awareness. Taken together, these figures are the basis of the claim that up to 42% of the seventy-six seals may have been skinned while conscious. The remaining 58% of the carcasses indicated extensive fractures that would have been associated with some level of unconsciousness.

In addition, the Burdon Committee also examined the video footage obtained by the International Fund for Animal Welfare (IFAW) for the years 1998, 1999, and 2000. Their observations were as follows:

(a) The majority of hunters did not assess the level of consciousness prior to skinning or hooking; 79% did not perform the "blinking reflex" test (see pars. 2.17 and 2.18) "indicating that many of these seals could have been skinned or hooked alive."

(b) In "40 per cent of cases (32 per cent of the clubbed seals and 92 per cent of the shot seals) the hunter returned to strike the seal for a second time" with an "average time to second strike of 27 seconds." That means that the seals were alive and suffering at least until they were struck the second time, or until they received a blow that rendered them unconscious.

(c) Only 6% of the seals struck were bled immediately, and the "average time from initial strike to bleeding was 66 seconds." Even the seals in this small, rather privileged group, unless the first blow induced immediate unconsciousness, may still have been conscious—and experiencing pain to some degree—for more than one minute.

(d) Eighteen seals were observed being skinned, and "on average this occurred sixty seconds after the initial strike." It is "uncertain" how many had been bled or had "a level of consciousness checked to ensure that they were not skinned while conscious."

These facts reveal that the seals often experience a slow death preceded by suffering. The Burdon Report concluded that the hunt "is resulting in considerable and unacceptable suffering."[7]

Supporting the Burdon Report are two earlier studies, which also show that a high percentage of seal carcasses examined did not have enough cranial injury to guarantee the animals' unconsciousness when skinned. The Simpson Report in 1967 found that 56 of 154 examined skulls (36.4%) had not been fractured, and the Jordan Report in 1978 similarly found that 7 of 13 examined skulls (53.8%) had unfractured craniums.[8]

In the light of this, the question might not unnaturally be asked: on what grounds can the Canadian government claim that the hunt is "humane"? The answer is that it relies on a study by Dr. Pierre-Yves Daoust, a veterinarian from the Atlantic Veterinary College, and four other veterinarians, also of the same year (hereafter "Daoust" or the Daoust Report). The Daoust Report concluded that "the majority of seals taken during this hunt (at best, ninety-eight per cent in the work reported here) are killed in an acceptably humane manner."[9]

At first sight, the two sets of findings appear irreconcilable. As Dr. David Lavigne comments: "People who are concerned about the humaneness of Canada's commercial seal hunt are either left confused by the seemingly contradictory claims of experts, or are forced to choose between two apparently disparate opinions." But, as Lavigne points out, on closer examination it transpires that the confusion arises because of the *different criteria* adopted by each study:

> [Whereas the Burdon Report] addresses the question of whether seals were likely [to have been] conscious or unconscious at the time they were skinned, using post-mortem examination of skulls, in marked contrast, the figure cited from the Daoust et al.'s [R]eport represents *the number of seals clubbed or shot that were brought on board sealing vessels while still conscious.* That number ignores any and all animal suffering that occurs between the time animals are clubbed or shot until they eventually reach a sealing vessel, usually on the end of a hook or gaff.[10]

It is difficult to understand why the Daoust Report did not set out to assess the issue of consciousness immediately subsequent to the act of intended killing, especially since this has been the most canvassed issue in public debates. In addition to this extraordinary oversight, it is also difficult to account for some other aspects of the study.

The first relates to the fact that the sealers knew that they were being observed. Daoust conducted the study onboard a sealing vessel in the presence of DFO (Department of Fisheries and Oceans) enforcement officers; sealers knew not only that they were being observed, but also the uses to which such observations would be put. Daoust accepts that the presence of observers "may have incited sealers to hit the seals more vigorously."[11] If this is true, it would mean that fewer seals, or a smaller percentage, would be skinned alive when the hunters were being observed than would occur when the seals were hunted in the absence of observers. Even with observers, the numbers of seals skinned alive is unacceptable from a humane or moral point of view.

But the significance of observers goes further than this. As Lavigne points out, an observer's presence "has the potential to modify other sealing practices, including checking for a corneal reflex and bleeding animals immediately after clubbing."[12] Given such a potentiality, it is difficult to understand why Daoust did not utilise (as did the Burdon Report) the

method of conducting postmortem examinations of carcasses during unobserved periods of killing. In addition, Daoust appears to make no allowance
for the possibility of distortion of the usual practices due to observation. It
cannot be known whether the Daoust study reflects the usual method of
killing of seals when there is no observer.

Second, according to the MMRs, sealers should check that each seal is
unconscious before proceeding to hook or bleed it, and before killing
another. In reviewing the videotaped evidence provided by the IFAW
during the 2001 hunt, the Daoust Report accepts:

> Most hunters . . . failed to palpate the skull or check the corneal reflex before
> proceeding to hook or bleed the seal, or go to another seal. Some sealers
> claim that they can feel the collapse of the calvarium as they strike the seal.
> *Nonetheless, the presence of an incompletely crushed skull in 14% of seals killed*
> *with a hakapik and the occasional occurrence of live seals being hooked and*
> *brought on board should justify a more diligent adherence to either of these*
> *2 simple tests.*[13]

But this admission of the failure of sealers to secure unconsciousness in 14%
of videotaped cases means that the conclusion in the abstract of the Daoust
Report—namely, that 98% are killed "acceptably humanely"—is inaccurate
or misleading. While it may be true that Daoust found, according to its own
criteria, that the "majority of seals taken during *this* hunt" (that is, the one
observed) (*at best,* 98%) are killed in "an acceptably humane manner," it does
not follow, as claimed by the Canadian minister, that "virtually all harp
seals—*fully* 98 per cent—are killed in a humane manner."[14]

Third, and in the same vein, the Canadian minister referred to the
Daoust Report as the report "issued" by the CVMA, as if it were an official
report. This inference is bolstered by the reference in the abstract to the
report being compiled by "representatives of the Canadian Veterinary
Medical Association."[15] But, in fact, as the report itself indicates, "the
views expressed in this article are those of the authors and do not constitute
the official position of the CVMA." It is therefore misleading to suggest, as
Canadian government sources do, that "non-governmental associations
such as the Canadian Veterinary Medical Association have also found
that the large majority of seals taken during the seal hunt (ninety-eight
per cent) are killed in an acceptably humane manner" since no such
collective judgment has been made by the CVMA. In fact, the report
cited by the Canadian government actually says "*at best* ninety-eight per
cent" (that is, "up to"), which logically covers any eventuality from zero to
98%. The attempt here to inflate the significance of one report, while failing
to mention others, betokens partiality.

We need now to turn directly to the issue of humaneness. The Daoust Report notes that, since the prohibition on the commercial killing of white-coats (seal pups which begin to moult shortly after weaning at about twelve days) and bluebacks (young hooded seals, which do not shed their newborn coats until they are approximately fifteen months old), beaters (young harp seals, approximately three to four weeks old, that have completely shed their white coats) now constitute the bulk of the hunt. As Daoust acknowledges:

[These animals] are more wary than whitecoats and far more likely to move away and go into the water at the approach of sealers. Therefore, killing by fracturing the skull with a hakapik has become less practical, and sealers now often rely on shooting the animals with a rifle from their vessel.[16]

These observations have obvious relevance to assessing the relative humane-ness of the hunt, especially shooting.

We need to begin by offering a definition of "humane killing." The standard definition for vertebrates is the immediate inducing of uncon-sciousness, usually by means of the delivery of sufficient energy to the brain, which renders the animal insensible to pain. This definition is now accepted worldwide and is embodied in legislation in many countries. The UK government maintains, for example, in relation to whales:

[The] aim must, as with the slaughter of terrestrial animals, be to render a whale immediately insensible to pain, and for its subsequent death to occur without avoidable pain, stress, or suffering. It is accepted that this is unlikely to be achievable in 100% of cases, but we would not wish to define as acceptable anything that falls short of this standard.[17]

The question is: does seal hunting constitute "humane slaughter" as defined above, namely, the securing of immediate unconsciousness? In relation to the first method of killing, namely, clubbing, the answer is almost certainly negative. The reasons are both physiological and practical. As the Burdon Report observes, in theory a blow to the brain stem is the most efficient way of killing a mammal:

[But the] brain stem in mammals is the most highly protected part of the central nervous system. It is located ventrally within the calveria, beneath the cerebellum and overlying skull. Furthermore, in seals, flexion of the neck places a thick layer of blubber over the base of the skull. Therefore, the only target area available in a seal is the skull overlying the cerebral cortex. Delivering a blow to this area and the underlying cortex is a much less efficient way of rendering an animal unconscious.[18]

The salient point is that even a "large blow to the cerebral cortex is unlikely to result in immediate brain stem herniation" (that is, a rupture of the brain stem resulting in unconsciousness and/or death). Theoretically, it *could*, and *might* do so (given optimum conditions), but—and this is the crucial point—*it cannot be relied upon* as a method of delivering immediate unconsciousness. For this reason, the Burdon Report concludes that clubbing (and shooting) "should be viewed as stunning methods *only*, producing a *potentially* temporary loss of consciousness."[19]

The question therefore arises: can clubbing—even though it cannot be relied upon as a reliable method in most cases of securing unconsciousness—nevertheless be justified as a means of stunning prior to slaughter? It is at this point that we encounter the practical grounds for concluding that clubbing is not a humane method of killing. In order to secure anything like humane killing, two further procedures must be carried out on each individual animal. The first involves using one of two tests to determine consciousness: the so-called blinking reflex test or checking by palpation of the skull. Since it is very difficult to determine loss of consciousness through observation alone—because one cannot easily distinguish between voluntary and involuntary movement—the Burdon Report emphasises that it "must be assumed that all movement seen could be due to conscious voluntary muscle activity until the corneal reflex has been checked." Thus, the test must be performed *immediately* after clubbing and, if necessary, be followed by a further blow, or blows, to the head. Second, having determined stunning or temporary loss of consciousness, "death should be completed by exsanguination (bleeding out)." Burdon is clear that this action must be performed "before the hunter is able to move on to the next seal."[20]

Taken as a whole, there are a series of separate, practical steps that must be performed in order to secure humane slaughter or, more likely, to approximate it:

- The seal's brain stem must be clubbed with precise accuracy and with exactly the right amount of force in order to render the animal fully unconscious.
- In order to assess whether that has happened, one of the two tests (above) for determining consciousness must be performed.
- If that test indicates continuing consciousness, then the seal has to be clubbed again.
- Regardless of outward signs, the animal should be bled out immediately to ensure that consciousness is not regained.

It is important to emphasise that all these actions in relation to each seal need to be performed *before* the sealer moves on to another animal.

We have to consider how likely it is that sealers will faithfully and conscientiously perform these procedures *while they can see other seals slipping away from them into the water, and hence being unable to capture them, or in a context where other sealers and different sealing vessels will be competing for the same "resources."* Is it really likely that these procedures will be conscientiously followed when doing so may result in a loss of kills and therefore economic disadvantage?

To that question must be added other considerations. Sealers necessarily work in adverse conditions, that is, in freezing, often below-zero temperatures, on ice that is often unsteady or slippery, where one false move can result in a potentially life-threatening situation, for example, falling into freezing water and suffering hypothermia. Even in optimum conditions (when the animal is immobilised and the weather is good), it would be difficult to guarantee achieving the one blow that would render the animal immediately unconscious, but in adverse conditions, particularly when the sealers are tired or suffering from muscle fatigue, the chances are considerably reduced. The adverse factors may be summarised as follows:

- below-zero weather conditions;
- slippery, unstable, and unsteady ice;
- tiredness and/or muscle fatigue (because of the fast rate of clubbing);
- the target animal is frequently moving and trying to escape;
- the round club is sometimes covered with blood, which makes it slippery to hold and difficult to achieve a precise blow; and
- the need for the quick immobilisation of one seal in order to prevent another from escaping.

When these considerations are taken into account, it must be questioned whether the chances of humane slaughter in these circumstances can be anything other than remote. The point to be grasped is that these uncertainties should logically count *against* the use of animals in these circumstances. The more unlikely it is that anything like "humane slaughter" can be approximated, the stronger the moral argument against it.

We need now to turn to the second principal means of killing seals, namely, shooting. It is sometimes thought that shooting, perhaps because it appears more aesthetic than clubbing, must therefore be more humane, and it is true that an expert marksman can shoot a stationary target with great precision. But the word "stationary" here indicates the nature of the problem. The harp seal pups are moving targets. The pups, the ice they lie on, and the vessels from which the sealers shoot are all moving, making it extremely difficult for a sealer to kill a seal with one bullet. Sealers loathe shooting seals more than once, and the reason is straightforward enough: the main purchasing plant deducts $2 from the price of the pelt for every additional bullet hole. However understandable that rule may be from an economic perspective, it can only mean in practice that sealers have an economic incentive to leave wounded seals to suffer. Seals that are swimming are an even more difficult target, bobbing up here and there, and capable, especially when young, of swift movement. Even the ice is not static, since it moves up and down as well. These considerations mean that securing a shot to the head, and thus a "clean" kill, sufficient to induce instantaneous unconsciousness, is remote. It is much more likely that a seal would be shot somewhere in the body and wounded. In addition, there is the issue of recovering the wounded bodies from the water. Normally, this is done through gaffing or hooking and, unless the animals concerned are dead or wholly insensible, this procedure alone must induce considerable pain and suffering.

The Daoust Report maintains that, of the forty-seven carcasses it examined, thirty-five (74%) had been shot in the head "with the skull and brain completely destroyed." But this surprising finding needs to be placed against the report's admission: "At the Front in 1999, all seals examined by Daoust and Wong were shot from vessels or small speed boats, and most of them had been killed *by the time the observers arrived on site*."[21] This leaves open the possibility that such killings were not immediate, or that there might have been subsequent shots to the head after the seals were landed on the vessels. In either case, Daoust admits that 26% had *not* been killed by a shot to the head: "six (13%) animals had been shot in the neck, and three (6%) animals had been shot in the ventral region of the neck with destruction of soft tissues, including major blood vessels, but no bone fracture, and the remaining three (6%) animals had been shot in the thorax or abdomen." Apparently, one of the latter "was found alive by itself on an ice floe and was immediately killed with a hakapik by a DFO officer."[22]

The claim in the abstract of the report that the "large majority of seals taken during this hunt (at best, ninety-eight per cent in the work reported here) are killed in an acceptably humane manner" makes one wonder what meaning is being given to the words "*acceptably* humane manner." Acceptable to whom?—one might ask. A killing rate in which at least 26% do not die instantaneously, but suffer anything from a few seconds to minutes of considerable agony is not "acceptable" by conventional standards of slaughter. If such were the record of a veterinarian in professional practice, the individual would most likely be liable for prosecution under anti-cruelty legislation.

The Burdon Report says that any method for killing a seal that does not allow for the process of "stunning, checking and bleeding," as detailed above, "has an enormous potential to create suffering and is therefore unacceptable." It continues:

As this process cannot be consistently followed in open water, we consider that shooting seals in open water can never be humane. Any method of taking a seal which requires the seal to be recovered by gaffing or hooking before the process can be followed, can never be humane.[23]

Again, it is worth listing the practical considerations that militate against the possibility of shooting as a method of "humane slaughter." These include:

- below-zero weather conditions;
- unstable vantage point for shooting, that is, usually from a moving vessel, sometimes in uncertain waters;
- the quick movement of the seals when in water, and hence little time for preparation or precision with regard to aiming;
- the need for a consistently high level of marksmanship in order to secure a head shot;
- the need to recover the dead or wounded animal—sometimes at a distance—by gaffing or hooking;
- the inevitable time delay between shooting an animal and its recovery, a delay made worse by the fact that scores, even hundreds, of seals have to be recovered; and
- the inevitability of some wounded animals being left to die in open water.

The important point to be grasped—again—is that the unpredictability of these factors must logically count *against* the killing of animals in these circumstances. Unsurprisingly, the Burdon Report refers to the "tremendous lack of consistency in the treatment of each seal."[24] The point about "consistency" is not a trivial matter. The slaughter of large numbers of mammals requires uniformity and consistency in order to ensure the highest possible standards. Killing without uniformity and consistency means that animals are liable to suffering.

Here we go to the very heart of the problem: inconsistency, or arbitrariness, in the manner of death and the degree of suffering caused is an *inherent* feature of the Canadian seal hunt—inherent because it derives from the nature of the hunt itself, the methods of killing involved, and the uncertain circumstances in which the killing is pursued.

The minister maintains that the Royal Commission found that "the methods used in the seal hunt compare favourably to those used to hunt other wild animals, and those used to slaughter domestic animals—like cattle and poultry—for human consumption."[25] That view overlooks a number of important considerations. The first is that many wild animals in Canada are trapped for their fur in leghold traps that undoubtedly cause prolonged suffering—so much so that the use of such traps is illegal throughout the European Union (EU). Comparing the killing of seals with fur-bearing animals killed in traps is hardly a reliable indicator of humane treatment.

Second, the Daoust Report similarly refers to the slaughter of beef cattle in the United States, and notes how its putative 98% rate of "acceptably humane killing" for seals compares well with lesser percentages for cattle.[26] But one wonders why a *veterinary* report should want to engage in such special pleading since few would want to defend the variable and highly controversial cattle slaughter practices in the United States, as indicated by the research of, for example, Dr. Temple Grandin.[27] The comparison with poultry is even more revealing since laws in Canada relating to poultry transportation and slaughter are poorly enforced at the national level, and there are no laws regulating the treatment of birds at the farm level. Astonishingly, there are no national welfare laws for poultry in the United States.[28] Comparisons, in short, are being made with the worst, or even the non-existent.

Third, while conventional slaughter is often unsatisfactory and can render animals liable to suffering, it should be acknowledged that, despite the poor record of Canada (on poultry especially) and the United States (on cattle and poultry especially), many governments have worked progressively to improve slaughterhouse conditions since the 1980s, based on increasing evidence of animal sentience. The detailed and thorough report of the Farm Animal Welfare Council (hereafter FAWC) of the British government makes no less than 308 recommendations concerning slaughterhouse practices in relation to animal welfare.[29] This is not to imply, however, that conditions in Britain are ideal or anything approaching it; it is simply an example of how welfare standards in abattoirs can, if there is sufficient government support, be considerably improved in all countries.

While no one should be complacent about conventional slaughter—and all should recognise that slaughter at speed invariably compromises even the most effective methods—it is important in formulating comparisons to compare best with best or, rather, like with like. According to Dr. Ian Robinson, a British member of a 2001 international veterinary panel:

The Canadian Government insists that the seal hunt is an animal production industry like any other. They say that it might not be pretty, but basically, it is just like any abattoir except on the ice. But we found obvious levels of suffering which would not be tolerated in any other animal industry in the world.[30]

Fourth, the "basic principles" of conventional slaughter, as the FAWC insists, must involve "an effective process which induces immediate

unconsciousness and insensibility or an induction to a period of unconsciousness without distress, and [the] guarantee of non-recovery from the
process until death ensues."[31] It is precisely these basic principles that are
violated by the seal hunt: neither "immediate unconsciousness" nor "non-
recovery" can be "guaranteed" or even, in most cases, regarded as likely.
Both clubbing and shooting seals render the animals liable to high levels of
suffering and—other than in exceptional circumstances, when a blow or
shot renders the animals immediately unconscious—are inherently inhumane methods of killing.

We can say with confidence that clubbing and shooting render seals more
liable to suffering than is the case with conventional slaughter. That is the
only logical conclusion from the evidence. The Burdon Report, which
examined the widely divergent degrees of damage inflicted on the craniums
of dead seals, found that the "current methods and competency of clubbing
is significantly inaccurate in location, resulting in severe and unacceptable
suffering," and again, there is "utmost concern regarding the severe
suffering occurring in seals who have no lesions of the cranium, as well as
those having fractures felt not sufficient to render the seal unconscious."[32]
In other words, clubbed seals are subject to procedures, including handling,
dragging across the ice, bleeding out, and skinning, while they are still
conscious and capable of feeling pain.

5.2. SECOND CLAIM: SEAL PUPS ARE NOT KILLED

We now turn to the second claim that the hunting of "harp (whitecoat) and
hooded (blueback) seal pups is strictly prohibited." By itself, that might
imply that it is—or always has been—contrary to Canadian government
policy to allow the killing of whitecoats. Closer examination suggests otherwise. Pressure for change emanated not from inside government circles but
from outside them. In fact, it was the decision in 1983 by the European
Union to ban the import of products made from whitecoat harp and blueback hooded seal pups that led to a re-thinking of the issue. In 1987, the
Royal Commission recommended that the killing of these very young seal
pups be prohibited on the grounds that "the hunt is widely viewed as
abhorrent both in Canada and abroad."[33] In 1993, the MMRs were amended
to prohibit the trade in whitecoat and blueback seal pups in order to prevent
the killing of these seals.

At face value, these developments might suggest that seal pups are not
now killed as they once were. But, in fact, harp seal pups can be legally killed
as soon as they begin to shed their white coats, around twelve days after
birth. Hooded seals (which constitute only a small fraction of the number

hunted) can be killed when they shed their blueback pelts at about fourteen months of age. Products from the slaughter of whitecoat harp and blueback hooded seal pups are covered by the EU ban, but not others.

The Canadian government maintains, "Only weaned, self-reliant seals are hunted after they have been left by their mothers to fend for themselves.... The vast majority of harp seals are taken after more than 25 days of age."[34] In fact, according to the Canadian government's own official seal-landing reports, the majority of the seals killed between 2000 and 2005 have been less than one month of age, and a large percentage of those have been under twenty-five days old. Not only is the Canadian government's statement inaccurate, it obscures the fact that the seals that are killed are, biologically, very young animals. While it is true that pre-weaned, that is, nursing pups are not killed, it is untrue to say that seal pups are not killed. What is correct is that whitecoats and bluebacks are no longer killed. But, while all whitecoats and bluebacks are pups, all pups are not whitecoats and bluebacks. Moulting or moulted harp seal pups—ragged jackets and beaters, respectively—are, of course, pups. Just like dogs, any young seal (in the first three months of life, for example) is still a "pup," especially in a species that takes four to six years to reach sexual maturity and has a life expectancy of thirty years.

In the case of the overwhelmingly most hunted seal, namely, the harp, the advance is minimal. Two, ten, or fifteen more days of life is surely a welcome thing, but *morally speaking* it makes little or no difference whether seals are killed at twelve or twenty-five days old. Where seal pups are being sheltered by their mothers (and are more difficult to slaughter as a result), and where they are slaughtered in full view of them, it is possible that the mother seal endures an emotional trauma of some kind since she had been carefully nursing and caring for her young. But the moral objection to killing and inflicting suffering is not wholly altered by these considerations. It is certainly pathetic to slaughter young life, and it is a relevant moral consideration if the mother seals also suffer, but the distance of a few days alone does not render one form of sealing licit and another illicit. At best, the moral gravity of sealing may be slightly ameliorated in the former case, but nothing more.

The Royal Commission accepted the widespread abhorrence at killing weaning seal pups and maintained that the "resulting public protest cannot be effectively countered by any technical arguments about the facts of the issue."[35] This suggests that it judged that the protests were entirely governed by emotional considerations—so much so that rational considerations could not prevail against them. While it is true that issues relating to animals do arouse significant emotional responses (as do most of the important moral issues of our day), it is a mistake to suppose that concern for animals is simply a matter of emotion or—even worse—that moral judgments are simply emotional ones. There are solid rational grounds for extending moral solicitude to other species capable of suffering; indeed, it is morally inconsistent not to extend even the most basic considerations to similarly sentient species. This holds whatever age the sentient being may be.

In short, some people reading the minister's statement might erroneously conclude that seals are not killed at a very young age, whereas developments have caused the goalposts to be slightly moved, but little else. The changes in fact are largely cosmetic—no longer do we see red splashes of blood on white fur—but whatever the colour of the fur, the moral issue remains the same. That seal pups continue to be killed is abundantly clear by an analysis of the total allowable catch (TAC) and the landed catch (LC) since 1971. In 1971, the TAC was 245,000; of the LC, 210,579 were pups, and 20,387 were one year or more old, making a total of 230,966, of which 91% of the seals killed were pups. In 2005, the LC was 317,672, of which 98.5% were pups under two months of age. Apart from a brief drop in the numbers of seals killed, especially acute during 1985–1987 (due to the EU ban on seal imports), it is clear that, over a period of more than thirty years, the rate of killing has actually increased, and the overwhelming percentage of seals killed are still younger than a year old—no less than 97% in 2004, an increase of 6% over the 1971 figure.[36]

5.3. THIRD CLAIM: THE HUNT IS TIGHTLY REGULATED

The third claim is that the hunt is "closely monitored and tightly regulated." Even if more seal pups are killed, the argument is that there are now regulations in place that prevent suffering.

That a practice is tightly regulated does not, by itself, morally justify that activity. One could conceive, for example, that burglary might be regulated, according to certain codes (devised by burglars themselves), but that does not by itself make the practice justifiable. The impression is given that any cruelty that might take place is somehow an aberration or contrary to the rules, but what our analysis so far has made clear is that the methods of killing are themselves invariably inhumane. But the possibility should be faced: can the activity of sealing, however inhumane, be ameliorated by regulation?

The Burdon Report argued that, since the Canadian government "has indicated that sealing will continue indefinitely," certain steps should be taken to ensure that a more "reliable and consistent procedure" be adopted for killing which could "significantly reduce the present level of suffering."[37] The measures proposed include the process of stunning, checking, and exsanguination, as indicated above. The relevant MMRs are as follows:

28. (2) Every person who strikes a seal with a club or hakapik shall strike the seal
    on the forehead until its skull has been crushed and shall manually check
    the skull, or administer a blinking reflex test, to confirm that the seal is
    dead before proceeding to strike another seal.

   (3) If a firearm is used to *fish* [sic] for a seal, the person who shoots that seal
    or retrieves it shall administer a blinking reflex test as soon as possible
    after it is shot to confirm that it is dead.

   (4) Every person who administers a blinking reflex test on a seal that elicits
    a blink shall immediately strike the seal with a club or hakapik on
    the forehead until its skull has been crushed, and the blinking reflex test
    confirms that the seal is dead.

29. No person shall start to skin or bleed a seal until a blinking reflex test has been
    administered, and it confirms that the seal is dead.[38]

The Burdon Report held that these or similar procedures *could* ameliorate
the suffering caused. But it is worth noting that, at the same time, the report
was emphatic that "the existing regulations are neither respected nor enforced." What evidence is there that they are currently observed?

The MMRs (rightly) state that, if a sealer clubs a seal, he must ensure that
the seal is dead prior to moving on to the next. But if a sealer shoots a seal, he
has only to kill the seal "as soon as possible." This allows sealers to legally
immobilise many seals to prevent them from escaping by shooting at them
from boats, and only later going back to kill each one in turn. The point to
be grasped is that, as they exist today, the MMRs provide a legal framework
under which sealers can cause suffering to seals.

The Canadian government claims that "the hunt is closely monitored." It
is true that officers of the DFO monitor the commercial seal hunt in an
attempt to ensure that sealers adhere to the MMRs. But commercial sealing
in Canada is conducted by thousands of individuals on hundreds of small
vessels over hundreds of miles of open ocean. When hunting, sealers move
far away from the boats in many different directions on Ski-Doos, in small
boats (skiffs), and on foot. In 2003, the Charlottetown *Guardian* printed
DFO estimates of its expenditures on the monitoring of fisheries, and the
report showed that the monitoring of the seal hunt was second to last on the
department's list of priorities, receiving only 1.5% of its funds for petrol
hours.[39]

Moreover, in 2005, the DFO seal hunt co-ordinator for the Gulf of
St. Lawrence stated that his department assigns one enforcement officer
for every seven vessels (one officer to monitor seventy to eighty sealers, all
working in different areas). These officers gain access to the hunt by
helicopter and are easily identified by sealers when they approach. In the
Front (the area northeast of Newfoundland, where the bulk of the hunt is
conducted), enforcement officers are unable to gain access to the hunt by

helicopter because it occurs so far offshore, on very broken-up ice. Thus, the only way for enforcement officers to monitor the hunt is by travelling to the area on Coast Guard patrol vessels. These vessels are large icebreakers, and monitoring the activities of thousands of individual sealers on hundreds of small boats from such a vessel is practically impossible. According to the DFO, other observers do occasionally monitor the hunt from sealing vessels, but they do not have enforcement powers and appear to be monitoring for catch numbers rather than humane considerations. Also, given that each sealing vessel holds fewer than twelve crew members, sealing boat captains are loath to sacrifice berths. All these considerations tell against the claim that there is adequate, let alone "close," monitoring of the hunt.

Confirmation of the practical impossibility of regulating the hunt was provided, unwittingly, by a group seeking to prove the opposite. Another veterinary report—this time, the result of a working group composed of Dr. Daoust, senior author of the previous Daoust Report, and eight other veterinarians—was published in August 2005 (hereafter Daoust2). It aims to "minimize or eliminate animal suffering within the context of the hunt,"[40] but it acknowledges, inter alia, the following problems even within the existing system of regulation (many of which we have already noted):

- "Many sealers were trained to use three blows." Because of this, the group believes that the emphasis "should be placed not on the number of blows, but on achieving the destruction of the whole skull."[41] This admission is revealing since *repeated* blows cannot, by definition, be humane as recognised by the Burdon Report. By implication, it follows that the regulated hunting performed by "many" sealers is not humane.

- "The Group noted that many IFAW video clips show hunters who did not bleed animals after stunning and before hooking and skinning."[42] This means that Daoust2 accepts that some hooking or skinning while alive is possible, even likely. More to the point, *since this happens under existing regulations,* it follows that they are obviously not effective.

- The hunt "involves a large number of boats competing with each other to maximize their take of an open quota, over an extensive area, in a relatively short period of time."[43] The report recommends that the DFO implement "measures to reduce competitiveness and haste in the hunt." But what confidence can there be in a system and in the very same agency which has already failed to protect animals—especially when it is later acknowledged that the "DFO appears to lack sufficient dedicated capacity to monitor and enforce regulation of the hunt, especially at the Front"?[44]

- Daoust2 says: "DFO officers are often resident in the small communities that have social and economic links to the seal hunt. The Working Group believes that [the] DFO should consider bringing in officers from outside communities who are not faced with monitoring and potentially laying charges against friends and neighbours." Unsurprisingly, Daoust2 admits that "there may be an element of conflict in [the] DFO being both an advocate for the seal hunt and its regulator."[45] Quite so.

- The group recommends increased training and "professionalism" among sealers' organisations. But it noted that the training video "did not provide the trainees with a good sense of why and how this [the corneal reflex test] was carried out."[46] This admission is astonishing. It means that trainee sealers are not being provided with an adequate understanding of one of the two tests of consciousness. The report later says so explicitly: the group "does not believe that the corneal reflex, or more specially its absence, is well understood by those involved in the seal hunt."[47] Once grasped, the implications in terms of animal suffering are alarming. It means that sealers have been killing seals without an adequate understanding of how to judge whether they are unconscious prior to hooking and skinning. This makes a mockery of sections 28(2), (3), (4), and 29 in the MMRs as detailed above.
- But there is one further point that is even more disturbing: it is the explicit acceptance by the working group that the recommended three-step process (stunning, checking, and bleeding) cannot in practice be satisfactorily regulated and is, in any case, inevitably subject to delay. Daoust2 says that some members of the group judged that bleeding out should be a requirement of the MMRs, "making it an offence not to bleed a seal before hooking and skinning" (at present, the requirement is only to check for unconsciousness). But "other members" (presumably the majority view, since there is no recommendation on bleeding before skinning) felt that "*worker safety and the difficulties presented by the natural environment in which the hunt takes place were considerations that could make such a regulation difficult to apply, specifically in relation to hooking a seal.*"[48] Daoust2 comments that "*it may be difficult for hunters to accept the need to wait a period of time after cutting the axillary [sic] arteries, before hooking the seal to bring it back to the boat, or continuing with the skinning process.*"[49] It should be noted that the initial cuts required for bleeding are the same as those that are used for skinning. But—and this goes to the heart of the debate about the "humaneness" of the hunt—if bleeding out (which all veterinarians agree is essential in order to ensure non-recovery from what is in most cases likely to be only temporary unconsciousness) cannot be guaranteed, or even made subject to enforceable regulation, then it must logically follow that at least a proportion of seals are being subjected to gross cruelty by being skinned alive. The report says, "All members of the Working Group feel that sealers should make every effort to ensure that a seal is bled before hooking and skinning."[50] But making "every effort" and "guaranteeing" are different things.

It is alarming that a group of veterinarians should fail to grasp this—the most basic consideration of all—since however awful some slaughterhouse practices may be, there is none in the world that allows killing by being skinned alive. It really will not do for Daoust2 to say that sealing "*can be a* humane process";[51] self-evidently, if unconsciousness cannot be *guaranteed* before skinning, it cannot be.

The clinching evidence is provided by the Humane Society of the United States (HSUS) in the form of videotapes of the 2005 seal hunt, which show dramatically that the current regulations are not observed. They reveal, inter alia, seals that are knifed open without the blinking reflex or skull palpitation tests having been administered, repeated blows to the heads and bodies of many seals (including one case in which a seal received more than twenty blows), animals left unattended in obvious states of suffering, one trying to drag itself over the ice with blood streaming from its nostrils, and some hooked seals dragged over the ice while almost certainly conscious. As anticipated, when sealers find a group of seals, they hit out on all sides, trying to immobilise as many as possible before some escape. The video evidence demonstrates that the claim that the hunt is "tightly regulated" is empirically false.[52]

Dr. Mary Richardson, a Canadian expert in humane slaughter, a past chair of the Animal Welfare Committee of the Ontario Veterinary Medical Association, and a member of the Animal Care Review Board with the solicitor general of Ontario, reviewed the HSUS evidence and commented:

> Among other things, the videos show seals that have been battered with a club or hakapik, and then left, or hooked and dragged, or skinned while still alive. The tapes show many of the wounded seals are still conscious and struggling for prolonged periods, as evidenced by their voluntary movements (crawling, crying out, laboured breathing, rolling, etc.). In some scenes, seals with terrible head injuries are left in stockpiles of dead and dying animals, choking on their own blood and suffering tremendous pain—some for as long as 90 minutes. In others, sealers cut open seals that are clearly still conscious.
>
> These are not humane ways to die as defined by the criminal code of Canada. When clubbing seals, sealers are legally required to kill each animal and then ensure that it is in fact dead, before moving on to kill the next one. But the vast majority of times, the sealers do not take time to do this, which results in horrendous pain and suffering for the wounded animals.... The cruelty documented by the HSUS this year is not the extreme—it is the routine of the commercial seal hunt.[53]

At least three things are required for improvement through regulation. First, there need to be laws or legally backed regulations. Second, there needs to be adequate enforcement and, third, there has to be compliance. As is clear from the HSUS and IFAW videotapes over the years, many sealers do not comply with the regulations. Without compliance and enforcement, laws and regulations can have no impact at all.

In short, while in theory the worst aspects of the hunt could be ameliorated through strengthened regulations, logic and experience show that the enforcement of those regulations, let alone compliance, is a practical impossibility. Questions arising from this fact need to be weighed carefully. If more than thirty years of high-profile campaigning, expressions of international concern, videotape evidence, veterinary reports, an EU ban, and the promulgation of government-backed regulations have not been able to ameliorate the cruelty of sealing, what reasonable hope can there be for the observance of regulations in the future? In the words of the well-known axiom: "the best indicator of future action is past behaviour." Since the sealers depicted in the videotapes are, we may presume, mostly experienced sealers (those who, according to the rules, must instruct apprentices on how to hunt), what chance is there that they will teach practices fundamentally at variance with their own? How reasonable is it to suppose that such an entrenched, even culturally validated tradition, will be amenable to fundamental change? And, even more directly, how likely is it that such changes will take place when, in the overwhelming majority of cases, sealing is—and must inevitably remain—an essentially unobserved activity? These considerations suggest that the chances of regulations being more closely followed are as remote as the chances of humane killing by shooting and clubbing.

5.4. FOURTH CLAIM: HUNTING IS FOR SURVIVAL

The fourth claim is that Canadian coastal communities rely on the hunt "for their survival." This is certainly the nearest that the government comes to providing a moral justification for the hunt. The question is: can the claim for moral necessity be substantiated?

Attitudes towards the exploitation of animals are usually tempered by concerns for native peoples and their cultures. It is sometimes assumed that the use of animals by aboriginal peoples can be justified on the basis of subsistence and for cultural reasons. If "subsistence" is defined as "using wildlife locally for food, clothing, and shelter, and for making tools, rather than putting wildlife products into trade,"[54] then it *may* be that the moral test as detailed above can be met—at least in utilitarian terms. But the difficulty is that defenders of subsistence hunting are seldom satisfied with that definition, and invariably want to push it to include commercial trade. Indeed, as Lavigne notes, at the 1985 meeting of the Convention on International Trade in Endangered Species in Buenos Aires, "subsistence" hunting was redefined by Canada as "anything that turns an animal into 'hard cash.'"[55]

But while genuinely subsistence hunting may conceivably pass the test of necessity, it is impossible for *commercial* hunting to do so. And we must be clear that the annual seal hunt is a wholly commercial hunt. This can be demonstrated by the Canadian government's own figures, which detail the annual hunt as a "commercial quota," as distinct from "personal quotas" (killing of seals by residents adjacent to sealing areas throughout Newfoundland and Quebec), which include subsistence use by aboriginal peoples and by non-aboriginal coastal residents who reside north of 53°N latitude—the latter of which are able to hunt without a license.[56] Thus, even if we are persuaded that some subsistence sealing can be justified (and not all ethicists would be so persuaded, especially if there is suffering involved), we can be sure that such use is entirely distinct from the commercial Atlantic hunt.

The problem is compounded, however, because since the 1980s Canadian governments have strategically hidden non-aboriginal commercial wildlife slaughters behind a veil of native subsistence hunting. In order to combat the increasing unpopularity of fur, the industry and the Canadian government were advised as early as 1985 to utilise "contradictory emotional themes of interest to the same target publics, e.g., preservation of traditional indigenous cultures."[57] In fact, less than 2% of aboriginal people in Canada are involved in the commercial trapping of animals for fur. Yet, Canadian governments and the fur industry primarily defend the fur trade as vital to aboriginal cultures and economies. It is an effective, but entirely bogus, strategy and one that is used for the sealskin trade as well.

Canada's Inuit population continues to hunt small numbers of harp, although most of their seal hunting (arguably for subsistence purposes) concentrates on another seal species—the small northern ringed seal, *Phoca hispida*. However, it is non-native fishermen from Canada's east coast who almost entirely conduct the commercial hunt. Demographic considerations make the reason obvious. There is little aboriginal participation in Canada's commercial seal hunt off the coasts of Newfoundland and Labrador and in the Gulf of St. Lawrence. Early European settlers killed off the indigenous Beothuck population in Newfoundland—one of the earliest recorded examples of genocide. Consequently, there are few aboriginal people living in Newfoundland today. Although about one-third of Labrador's population is aboriginal, there are very few seals hunted commercially in the area. The statistics indicate that aboriginal people probably took less than 1% of the total harp seal kill in 2005.[58]

Information supplied by the Canadian government maintains that non-aboriginal coastal "sealers have noted that the income derived from sealing can represent 25–35 per cent of their total annual income." But the facts do not bear out this claim. More than 90% of sealers live in Newfoundland. They are actually fishermen, who participate in several fisheries throughout the year. The Newfoundland government estimates that about

4,000 fishermen participate in the seal hunt. According to government data and media reports, they make about 5% of their incomes from sealing and the rest from commercial fisheries, such as crab, shrimp, and lobster. Given the landed value of the seal hunt in Newfoundland and the average income of Newfoundland fishermen, if they actually earned 35% of their incomes from sealing, it follows that there would be less than 400 of them.

In reality, sealing is not a primary occupation on which people rely for their "survival"; rather, it is an economically marginal activity that could easily be replaced by the federal government. This point remains even if it is accepted that "employment opportunities are limited"[59] in coastal communities. But we must question that idea as well, given that Newfoundland's fishery is wealthier than it has ever been in history—earning well over $150 million more than it did prior to the collapse of northern cod stocks in 1992. This economic growth is because of the development of the shellfish industry, which in the early twenty-first century accounts for 80% of the value of Newfoundland's fishery, whereas sealing accounts for only 2%.[60] It is certainly possible that the hunt is economically useful to a small number of people who live in coastal communities, but to say more than that is to go beyond the evidence.

5.5. SEALS AS ECONOMIC COMMODITIES

It may be objected that, even if there is no strict necessity involved in hunting seals, it is nevertheless a profitable activity and one that the Canadian government should properly defend as important to its own national self-interest.

The problem with this view, however, is that it effectively reduces the status of seals to economic commodities. Indeed, the official government language used to describe the hunt consists of words such as "harvest" or "harvesting," "tools" (weapons of killing), "resource," "dispatch" (killing), "replacement yield." These words indicate a commodification of these marine mammals as if they were nothing more than lifeless or non-sentient resources here for us.

From the 1960s onwards, there have been various calls from fisheries' organisations and government officials to "cull" seals in order to protect fish stocks, especially cod.[61] That argument is now seldom, if ever, employed by the Canadian government. The reason is that further study has indicated that seals also help cod stocks by consuming several of their significant natural predators. Indeed, the government now rejects the idea that the hunt is a cull and explicitly states that it is "*not an attempt to assist in the recovery of groundfish stocks.*" The statement continues:

Seals eat cod, but seals also eat other fish that prey on cod. There are several factors contributing to the lack of recovery of Atlantic cod stocks such as fishing effort, the poor physical condition of the fish, poor growth, unfavourable ocean conditions and low stock productivity at current levels.

It is widely accepted in the scientific community that there are many uncertainties in the estimates of the amount of fish consumed by seals. Seals and cod exist in a complex ecosystem, which makes it difficult to find simple solutions to problems such as the recovery of cod stocks.[62]

This admission is significant because it has left the hunt without any justification, other than the purely economic—and that is pretty marginal at best. The government now claims that the hunt is "a sustainable, commercial viable *fishery* based on sound conservation principles."[63] Leaving aside the tendentious claims about "sustainability" and "conservation," we should note the use of the word "fishery" to describe the seal hunt. The comparison is revealing since fish have little or no legal protection and are treated wholly as a resource. Astonishingly, seals in Canada are legally classified as "fish." In fact, we know that fish are sensitive beings and there is—in at least some cases—empirical evidence that they are capable of experiencing pain and fear.[64] But to place seals in the same category as other beings perceived wholly in economic terms and treated as fungible, disposable items is a serious mistake.

Grasping this point takes us to the heart of the moral case against sealing. If seals were simply vegetables, that is, beings without sentience who could experience no pain, fear, or suffering and whose movements exhibited no complexity of awareness, then there would be no moral objection to using them and killing them. They might, like vegetables, have a kind of aesthetic value, but no one would think of mounting campaigns to protect them or worry about their rights. But seals do not belong to that category. On the contrary, seals are sentient and intelligent; they are highly developed social beings capable of experiencing intense pain and suffering. The mother seal, as is typical of mammals, is very protective of her young offspring and may well suffer at the death of an older pup even if the latter is on the verge of becoming independent. Studies show that many mammals react even when an unrelated animal is killed in their presence. It is because seals, like other mammals, are sentient (that is, they can experience both pain and pleasure) that it is right to say that they have—as individuals—"intrinsic" or "inherent" value. To use Kantian moral language, they are "ends in themselves" and not just "means to ends."

To categorise marine mammals as fish (which is taxonomically inexcusable) and therefore as commodities or resources represents an impoverished view of their status. The value of other sentient beings in the world does not rest (as in the cases of stones or cabbages) entirely or largely in their relationship to us and the uses to which we may put them. Instrumentalist views that see the value of animals as consisting entirely in their relationship to us are logically opposed to views that recognise and celebrate the intrinsic value of animals.

Now, it may be argued that instrumentalist views of animals still predominate in the world today and that the kind of attitude to marine mammals here espoused would have major implications for our use and treatment of animals in many areas of life. But what needs to be grasped is that attitudes to animals are changing, and changing fast. What the Canadian government does not seem to have recognised is that it needs to justify sealing in a new context of a growing ethical sensibility to animals. For example, the government argues that the "subsistence hunt is a valuable link to Canadian cultural heritage."[65] But, as we have seen, the commercial hunt can be easily distinguished from any putative subsistence needs, and the argument that a now otiose form of hunting links us with a past culture is flawed as a moral justification. By the same logic, the British ports of Bristol and Liverpool should continue trading in human slaves "as a valuable link to British cultural heritage" (which, after all, greatly benefited from the trade). Appeals to past cultural heritage cannot absolve us from having to justify traditional practices in a contemporary moral context.[66]

Furthermore, the appeals to sustainability and conservation really miss the mark in relation to considerations of animal protection. Since the 1960s, environmental organisations have, inter alia, expressed concern about the numbers killed and the survival of the species in the long term. Such concerns have intensified since TAC levels are exceeded and more animals are killed than landed. Also, the Canadian government's claim that the seal population stands at 5.2 million begs some questions.[67] But, however valid these concerns, they do not touch the issue of moral justification from the standpoint of animal protection. Governments of all shapes are increasingly, it seems, making the mistake of thinking that concerns for animals are entirely met by considerations of sustainability and conservation, whereas in fact animal protection extends to concern for *each individual animal* and not just to the species as a collective or as a whole. This blind spot is part of a deeper failure of perception—to see that individuals within a species, and not just the species itself, deserve our moral solicitude. Even more, it betokens a failure to see that there *are* individuals and not just species. Each and every individual within a mammalian species is unique—as unique as any individual human being with its own needs, preferences, and social affiliations. Language about seals as a "resource" is sub-ethical in this second sense: it utterly fails to see the value of each individual and to recognise the claim of each individual to moral consideration.

5.6. THE PROBLEM OF PARTISAN GOVERNMENTS

We need now to look at the role of the Canadian government in relation to sealing. As we have seen, the government has been pro-active in its support for the seal hunt. Although it claims that it no longer subsidises the hunt, it has clearly done so generously in the past.[68] And even though direct subsidies may be a thing of the past, the government still supports seal hunting in a variety of ways by, for example, providing icebreakers to take the sealers to the seals, sending delegations around the world to promote the hunt, and providing grants (or interest-free loans) to establish new processing plants—most recently to a few native people on the north shore of the St. Lawrence as part of its publicly declared intention to involve native people more prominently in the southern hunt.[69] The DFO, in its own words, still encourages the "fullest possible commercial use of seals."[70] It was not internal, but external, pressure that led the government to establish a Royal Commission which recommended the discontinuance of killing whitecoat seal pups. Such limited action as there has been for seal protection has taken place without, perhaps almost in spite of, the Canadian government.

This recognition should give us pause since it raises the much wider question of how governments should respond to issues of animal protection. There are worrying signs that other governments may follow the baleful example of Canada and view animals simply as economic resources, commodities, tools, or objects of sport, and use their power to side with commercial or vested interests. Examples of this include the British government's siding with pharmaceutical industries so as to facilitate more animal research in the United Kingdom, and the American government's tacit support for "hunter harassment" legislation that guarantees extraordinary rights to wildlife hunters in the United States. Unless the governments of the world understand their moral obligation to protect animals from cruelty, and set in place moderating measures to prevent (at least) the worst forms of exploitation, then the outlook for animal protection worldwide will be pretty bleak.

There is no evidence that the Canadian government has any grasp of why its defence of the hunt should attract international criticism. The minister says:

> It is especially disturbing that some organizations are seeking to damage a legitimate Canadian activity and Canada's reputation abroad in public-relations campaigns in order to raise money for their organizations .... these carefully orchestrated public-relations campaigns twist the facts of the seal hunt for the benefit of a few extremely powerful and well-funded organizations.[71]

Attributing unworthy motives is always an unattractive and suspect form of argument. Doubtless, there are extreme or unbalanced advocates on either side, but it is a calumny on animal protection organisations to maintain that their criticism of the seal hunt is motivated by the desire to raise money for their own organisations. It is a statement that neglects the fact that most of the organisations that campaign to end the seal hunt are charities—non-profits that spend the money they raise in carrying out their mandates. But the point is that these allegations avoid the main issue, which is the duty of the Canadian government to protect wildlife in its own country from cruel exploitation. This obligation is not, of course, the responsibility of just one government but of all.

We need to remember that wildlife—free-ranging animals—is not the property of any one country. Animal protection is an international concern involving, now more than ever, international expressions of solidarity. The days when any government could say "These animals are our national resource, and we will do what we like with them" are over. There is an urgent need for all governments to move beyond narrow national and economic interests and embrace systems of international protection for animals.[72]

In that regard, there are some small shafts of light. Perhaps the most significant of these was the agreement on animal welfare in the Amsterdam Treaty of the European Union in 1997. The protocol deserves to be read in full:

> The High Contracting Parties, desiring to ensure improved protection and respect for the welfare of animals as *sentient beings,* have agreed upon the following provision, which shall be annexed to the Treaty establishing the European Community[:] in formulating and implementing the Community's agricultural, transport, internal market and research policies, the Community and *the Member States shall pay full regard to the welfare requirements of animals,* while respecting the legislative or administrative provisions and customs of the Member States relating in particular to religious rites, cultural traditions and regional heritage.[73]

The protocol creates a clear legal obligation to pay full regard to the welfare requirements of animals and, for the first time, refers to them as "sentient beings" rather than as agricultural commodities. That apparently small change in wording indicates a sea change in attitude. While the treaty still provides no legal basis for the introduction of legislation specifically intended to improve the welfare of animals, it leaves member states free to introduce national legislation on issues of animal welfare as they see fit. The qualifying line in relation to "religious rites, cultural traditions and regional heritage" regrettably allows for possible derogations, although the "requirement is merely to 'respect' legislative or administrative provisions in these areas."[74] Despite this limitation, the Amsterdam Protocol is the first international agreement among governments on animal welfare which clearly accepts that animals are sentient beings and should be protected. It needs to become the first of many.

5.7. TRADE EMBARGOES ON SEAL PRODUCTS

The Amsterdam Protocol, then, requires all European countries to ensure animal protection. By the same token, it is also logical for EU member states to be able to restrict the importation of goods on the grounds of morally based concerns for animal welfare. Indeed, as we have seen, Article 30 of the EU regulations enables countries to take action on the grounds of "public morality," and that provision has already been invoked by the Westminster and Scotland parliaments as a justification for passing legislation against fur farming.[75]

In January 2004, the Belgian government also banned the import of seal products along with cat and dog fur. Belgium's announcement also included an order to begin labelling all fur, so that authorities can know what is on sale in Belgian shops and what is entering the country. The government no longer grants licenses to importers seeking to bring in cat or dog fur or sealskins. Both the bans and the labelling order went into effect immediately; the prohibitions are temporary, but the Belgian legislature is expected to replace the stop-gap measure with an even broader ban that would stop both imports and exports of cat and dog fur and sealskins.[76] The Belgian decision is groundbreaking because it is the first time that an EU member state has unilaterally banned seal products and has defended its decision on the grounds of public morality.

Likewise, under the GATT (General Agreement on Tariffs and Trade), there is an exception to its free trade policy, which states that embargoes may be put into place in order to "protect public morals." And it is on that basis that the existing embargo against the importation of harp seal products enshrined in the U.S. Marine Mammal Act of 1972 has been justified.

Both the WTO and the GATT are, of course, hugely controversial and may not stand the test of time. But as long as such agreements exist, they have the capacity to influence all international trading agreements in relation to animals and animal products. Their likely effect on animal protection is potentially massive and worldwide. The GATT could represent a serious setback for animal protection, and there are many in the animal protection community who fear that the role of the WTO could be utterly destructive of the limited, but significant, gains in international animal welfare.[77]

It is worth remembering that few people hold that free trade should be absolute. Even one of the pioneers of free trade philosophy, Henry George, maintained that the abolition of restrictions should exempt "those imposed in the interests of public health or morals."[78] But an obvious difficulty arises because, as Steve Charnovitz points out, "virtually anything can be characterized as a moral issue."[79] The question is whether a convincing case can be made on the basis of Article XX(a) in the GATT, which allows exemptions on the ground of "protecting public morality." Can a ban on seal products be justified on this basis?

The first possible ground is articulated by economist Richard N. Cooper, namely, that "the international community cannot and should not be able to force a country to purchase products the production of which offends the sensibilities of its citizenry."[80] The notion of "sensibilities" may appear, at first, too all-encompassing. But it is generally recognised that Muslim countries, for example, have the right to limit or prohibit the importation of alcohol, which offends not just Qur'anic injunctions, but also Muslim sensitivities more generally. Similarly, there are long-standing objections, both cultural and moral, to animal cruelty in many countries which, by the same token, should also be respected.

The second ground is that there are alternative measures "reasonably available"—a factor that has become prominent in previous adjudications of disputes. Currently, exported seal products include oil, skin, fur, and meat, but there are clearly reasonable alternatives to each of these. It would be difficult to claim that seals are a unique source of these products, which are unavailable elsewhere in the world.

The third ground is that countries could claim that they are not engaging in "unjustifiable discrimination" because they would be treating foreign products the same as domestic ones. The point has coherence in relation to animal cruelty laws. If a country exports products that contravene the host country's own legislation with regard to animal cruelty laws in general, and humane slaughter legislation in particular, then there is a prima facie case against allowing such imports. We have already seen that there are good grounds for supposing that the methods of slaughtering seals in Canada would not meet European standards of humane killing. A further question may be raised whether there is any "arbitrary or unjustifiable discrimination between countries where the same conditions prevail."[81] But it is clear—for example, in the case of the action by the Belgian government—that since all seal products, from whatever source, are susceptible to the same prohibition, that claim cannot reasonably be sustained.

The above are just some of the possible legal grounds under Article XX(a) of the GATT for excluding the importation of seal products. But there is a wider set of moral considerations here that should both inform adjudications about existing trade agreements and also influence future developments in this area. It is sometimes argued that we should not allow issues as seemingly minor as animal welfare to influence major trade agreements among the nations of the world. In fact, as Charnovitz points out, the adjudication panel of the WTO has never taken that view, and animal cruelty clearly, and rightly, falls "within the range of policies covered by article XX(a)."[82]

From an ethical perspective—which is far from being a minor or trivial matter—there is a range of considerations that relate to animals that buttress an even stronger legal claim that may be made on their behalf. We have already enumerated them. They include their inability to give or withhold consent, inability to vocalise their own interests, their moral innocence or blamelessness, and their vulnerability and defence-lessness.[83] Perhaps the most relevant of these considerations here is the recognition that animals cannot represent their own interests. Individuals who cannot adequately represent themselves have to depend upon benign moral representation. This consideration marks animals, along with vulnerable human subjects, notably infants and young children, as a special case. There are, therefore, strong grounds for extending to these beings special consideration when it comes to legal decisions that may affect or harm their own interests.

The capacity of the strong and the powerful to overlook the interests of the weak has been variously documented throughout human history, and nowhere is this clearer than in the two cases of children and animals. Unless active steps are taken to ensure that their interests are not overlooked, we can be almost certain that they will be. There is a moral challenge here to all those who espouse a free trade philosophy. Unless fundamental limits are observed, any libertarian trade system can easily turn into a means whereby the weak and the voiceless are further disenfranchised.

Charnovitz concludes his review by stating:

> Efforts will surely be made to limit the scope of XX(a) and like provisions to inwardly directed concerns. It will be argued that morality must stop at the border. In an increasingly interdependent global community, however, the linkages between morality and economic policy will become harder to overlook.

And he recalls the words of Lucia Ames Mead, "World righteousness and world economic welfare must be shown to be compatible."[84]

5.8. CONCLUDING ASSESSMENT

Some conclusions can be reached with confidence. First, the clubbing and shooting of seals are not humane methods of slaughter. The most reliable veterinary evidence points unmistakably in that direction. Basic principles of humane slaughter are violated by the hunt: neither "immediate unconsciousness" nor "non-recovery" can be "guaranteed" or even, in most cases, regarded as likely. Both clubbing and shooting seals render the animals liable to high levels of suffering and—other than in exceptional circumstances, when a blow or shot renders the animal immediately unconscious—are inherently inhumane methods of killing. Because of the physical environment in which it operates, and the way in which it must be conducted in order to be commercially viable, Canada's seal hunt is—and always will be—inhumane. And, if there is any doubt, the video footage makes abundantly clear that the suffering of the seals is considerable.

Second, regulations are not enforced, and neither are they enforceable. Grasping the commercial nature of the hunt is central to understanding why animal welfare is inevitably compromised. Commercial sealing is carried out by fishermen in hundreds of small boats, far offshore, amidst treacherous ice floes and hostile weather conditions. High fuel costs, dangerous work environments, and the proximity of opening dates for other commercial fisheries make it expensive and impractical for sealers to operate the seal hunt for extended periods of time. Moreover, sealing vessels compete against each other for quotas, killing as many animals as possible as quickly as possible. That is why, since the 1990s, the bulk of the commercial killing has occurred over just a few days each year.

Each year, apparent violations of Canada's Criminal Code and the MMRs are documented with minimal effort by animal protection groups, independent journalists, veterinarians, scientists, and parliamentarians. These violations include seals exhibiting responses to pain while being stabbed with hooks and dragged across ice floes, wounded seals left to suffer for prolonged periods of time, and conscious seals cut open and skinned. Video evidence of nearly 700 of these offences has been submitted to the DFO (the department charged with enforcing the MMRs) to no avail. Not a single charge has been laid in response, leading to the inevitable conclusion that the DFO lacks the will to enforce even its own regulations. That is one of the reasons that hopes that new or strengthened regulations will eliminate suffering are illusory. As Daoust2 unwittingly shows, enforcing and ensuring compliance with even the most basic regulation, namely, the three-step process (stunning, checking, and bleeding) are practically impossible.

Third, there is no adequate moral justification for the seal hunt. The infliction of suffering upon animals requires strong justification; indeed, there are some ethicists who would hold that the deliberate infliction of suffering on innocent and vulnerable beings can never be justified. In ethical terms, to show that something is necessary requires more than a simple appeal to human wants. It has to be shown (in utilitarian terms, at least) that the good procured is essential and that no alternative means are available. To point to economic advantage is insufficient as a moral justification, and neither can any claim for subsistence reasonably apply to the commercial Atlantic hunt.

We may debate those situations where animals pose some kind of threat or danger to the human species. But we should be clear that seals do not constitute—either directly or indirectly—*any* threat, ecological or otherwise. Neither do they constitute any health risk, nor is the reduction of their numbers required by notions of biodiversity. We have already noted that no reasonable claim against seals can be made in the interests of preserving fish stocks. Seals pose no general or particular adversity to the human species. They are not in any sense aggressors. To regard them, as some sealers do, as a nuisance species—"seal slugs," as they have been called—is without rational foundation. The hunt is thereby exposed as devoid of moral justification.

Fourth, to regard seals merely as economic commodities is an impoverished view of their status. Sealing is perceived by fishermen and the Canadian government as just another part of the fishery. This is reflected in the government department that manages it (the Department of Fisheries and Oceans), the individuals who conduct it (commercial fishermen), and the language used to describe it ("catching seals," "fishing for seals"). Taken as a whole, it appears that fishermen who hunt seals really believe that they are "fishing" and that the seals are deserving of as much, or as little, consideration as they would extend to any other ocean target. This historic understanding of seals as fish (that is, as beings perceived as non-sentient) may be the root cause of much inhumane behaviour. Moreover, as already noted, most sealers are fishermen from Canada's east coast. Many of them— because of misinformation disseminated over many years—have come to believe that seals caused the collapse of the northern cod stocks and are still impeding their recovery. Therefore, the very people killing the seals frequently view them as competitors for the fish and the reason that they personally suffer economic hardships. Such perspectives provide an environment in which there is an emotional incentive to mistreat the seals.

To regard hundreds of thousands of seals solely as resources to be harvested indicates a crudely instrumentalist understanding of animal life. Enlightened ethical thinking regards animals as sentient beings with their own inherent or intrinsic value. Such a view is at least implied in the EU Amsterdam Protocol of 1997. The Canadian government has simply failed to provide a convincing rationale for its advocacy of sealing in the light of changed ethical thinking.

Fifth, the Canadian government has become unreasonably partisan in its support for sealing. Government claims have been shown to be tendentious, misleading, or inaccurate. All governments, of course, want to support the economic well-being of the countries they serve, but each and every government should have a proper regard for animal welfare and exercise a moderating hand in relation to economic pressures that threaten to reduce the status of animals to mere commodities. It is clear that the Canadian government has not begun to exercise such a moderating hand. It has therefore set an unwelcome precedent for other governments, which could threaten the future prospects for animal protection worldwide. Moreover, governments should respect, if not always reflect, the views of their citizens, the majority of whom in Canada are opposed to the commercial seal hunt.[85]

Sixth, the Canadian government should act immediately to prohibit the commercial seal hunt. It is the responsibility of the Canadian government to protect its own wildlife from cruelty. The fact that governments can apparently act without accountability (even, it seems, to their own electorate) in matters relating to animal cruelty must be of concern to all right-thinking people everywhere. It cannot be sufficient to shrug off such culpability as though it were simply part and parcel of the round of politics with which we have become altogether too familiar. All governments are morally accountable for their support of cruelty.

Seventh, WTO adjudications must continue to allow concerns for animal welfare to constitute a moral exception to free trade. Free trade philosophy is still in a process of development. Despite some reversals, the GATT and the WTO accept in principle that there can be moral exceptions to free trade, and there is no rational ground for excluding concern for animals from that category. Indeed, we have shown that there are strong rational grounds for extending special moral solicitude to the innocent and the vulnerable, especially to children and animals, who are unable to represent themselves and who, necessarily, rely upon benign representation by others. The international community of animal advocates and all right-thinking citizens must speak up and insist that international trade regulations do not compromise the cause of animal protection.

Eighth, the moral case for trade bans against Canadian seal products is compelling. Animal protection is, and should be, a matter of international concern. We must look to governments to protect animals in their own countries, but when they fail to undertake this responsibility, then international pressure can and should be reasonably applied. Already, the United

States bans the import of seal products, and the government of Belgium has also done so—along with dog and cat fur. These actions should be welcomed and supported by the international community.

Although undoubtedly made more complex by the development of the GATT and the WTO, there is still ample scope for individual governments to take action on the grounds of public morality. We know from experience that trade embargoes work. When the European Union banned the import of seal products in 1983, it had an immediate effect on the number of seals killed, as the figures show: from 166,739 in 1982, to 57,889 in 1983, to 31,544 in 1984, to a record low of 19,035 in 1985.[86] In the absence of action by the Canadian government, trade bans are still the most effective means of preventing cruelty to seals.

Ninth, governments should initiate trade bans on seal products as a matter of urgency based on the moral imperative to prevent unjustifiable and prolonged suffering. We cannot avoid the evidence that seals are being skinned alive. While not true in all cases, reason and evidence indicate that a proportion, even a high proportion, will end up being subject to gross cruelty. The Canadian government says that the methods of killing seals are comparable with slaughter methods elsewhere. We know that this is not so. There is no country in the world that accepts a definition of humane slaughter that includes being skinned alive. The magnitude of the suffering involved—over a million harp seals were landed during 2004–08—is so great that international action is now essential.

5.9. SUMMARY OF MAIN POINTS

1. Killing seals is a huge international business, taking some 900,000 seals annually. The largest seal hunts are Canada's commercial harp seal hunt, West Greenland's unregulated seal hunt, and Namibia's Cape fur seal hunt. The Canadian seal hunt is the largest marine mammal hunt in the world, taking more than 330,000 seals (several species) annually.

2. In an attempt to justify the hunt, the Canadian minister of fisheries and oceans claims that the hunt is "humane." But a 2001 veterinary report concluded that the hunt results in "considerable and unacceptable suffering," detailing 42% of cases where there was not enough evidence of cranial injury to guarantee unconsciousness at the time of skinning, and 79% of cases where sealers did not check to ensure that the seals were dead prior to skinning them (5.1).

3. The Canadian government cites a report that 98% of seals were killed in an "acceptably humane" way. But any figure trying to show that the seals are killed humanely should calculate the time span between when they are

clubbed or shot and when they die or lose consciousness, not the time between when they are shot and when they reach the sealing vessel (5.1).

4. Basic principles of humane slaughter are violated by the hunt: neither "immediate unconsciousness" nor "non-recovery" can be "guaranteed" or even, in most cases, regarded as likely. Both clubbing and shooting seals render the animals liable to high levels of suffering and—other than in exceptional circumstances when a blow or shot renders the animal immediately unconscious—are inherently inhumane methods of killing (5.1).

5. The minister claims that the hunting of "harp (whitecoat) and hooded (blueback) seal pups is strictly prohibited." In fact, harp seals can be legally killed as soon as they begin to shed their white coats, at about twelve days after birth. Even though they have shed their white coats, they are still pups; the change is primarily cosmetic. Between 2000 and 2005, fully 96% of the harp seals killed have been under three months of age (5.2).

6. The minister claims that the hunt is "closely monitored and tightly regulated." But the videotape evidence of the 2005 seal hunt reveals, inter alia, that seals are knifed opened without the required blinking reflex or skull palpitation tests having been administered, that many seals receive repeated blows to the head and body (including one case in which a seal received more than twenty blows), that animals are left unattended in obvious states of suffering, including one trying to drag itself over the ice with blood streaming from its nostrils, and that some hooked seals are dragged over the ice while almost certainly conscious (5.3).

7. The minister claims that coastal communities rely on the hunt "for their survival." But while genuinely subsistence hunting *may* conceivably pass the test of necessity, it is impossible for commercial hunting to do so. And the annual Canadian seal hunt is a wholly commercial hunt and is classified by the government as a "commercial quota." Sealing is an economically marginal activity that could be easily replaced by the federal government (5.4).

8. The Canadian government regards seals as economic commodities. The official government language used to describe the hunt consists of words such as "harvest" or "harvesting," "tools," "resource," "dispatch," and "replacement yield," all of which indicate a commodification of these marine mammals as if they were nothing more than lifeless or non-sentient resources here for us to use (5.5).

9. The hunt is described as a "fishery." The comparison is revealing since fish have little or no legal protection and are treated wholly as a resource. To place seals in the same category as other beings perceived almost wholly in economic terms and treated as fungible, disposable items is a serious categorizing mistake. Seals are sentient and intelligent; they are highly developed social beings capable of experiencing intense pain and suffering (5.5).

10. The Canadian government is unreasonably partisan and bears immense responsibility for failing to protect its own wildlife from cruelty. Government claims have been shown to be tendentious, misleading, or inaccurate (5.5).

11. The Amsterdam Protocol requires all European countries to ensure animal protection. Article 30 of the EU regulations enables countries to take action on the grounds of "public morality," and the Belgian government has already banned seal products on this basis. Under the GATT and the WTO, there is an exception to free trade policy which states that embargoes may be put into place in order to "protect public morals," which has been understood historically as inclusive of animal welfare issues (5.6).

12. There are strong legal and moral grounds for including animals within the GATT/WTO exception. These moral grounds are based on important philosophical considerations: animals, like children, cannot adequately represent themselves, cannot vocalise their own needs, and depend upon benign representation. Moreover, they are also morally innocent, vulnerable, and defenceless. They need protection within international trade agreements (5.7).

13. The Canadian government should make the commercial seal hunt illegal. In the absence of action by Canada, other governments must act. Governments have to be made accountable by the international community for their support of cruelty. We know that trade bans work. When the European Union banned the import of seal products in 1983, it had an immediate effect on the number of seals killed, down from 166,739 in 1982, to a record low of 19,035 in 1985 (5.7).

14. Governments should initiate bans on seal products as a matter of urgency based on the moral imperative to prevent unnecessary and prolonged suffering. The commercial hunt is devoid of moral justification. There is no country in the world that accepts a definition of humane slaughter that includes being skinned alive (5.7).

Conclusion

Re-Establishing Animals and Children as a Common Cause, and Six Objections Considered

The argument of part I of this book was that concern for animal suffering, like concern for the suffering of young children, ought reasonably to arise from the following considerations: their inability to give or withhold their consent, their inability to verbalise or represent their interests, their inability to comprehend, their moral innocence or blamelessness, and, not least of all, their relative defencelessness and vulnerability. These considerations, and the sheer volume of animal suffering, are masked, minimised, or obfuscated by a range of powerful psychological and linguistic mechanisms that prevent us from directly confronting our treatment of animals as a moral issue. The argument of part II consisted of three practical critiques which show in detail how arguments that discount animal suffering, often embedded in official, public documents, are glaringly inadequate. Advocates of hunting with dogs, fur farming, and seal hunting are without moral excuse. This institutionalised cruelty should be abolished.

6.1. SINGER, INFANTS, AND ANIMALS

It may be helpful in this concluding chapter to show how my approach differs from the positions of other scholars, and one in particular—that taken by Peter Singer. Singer has made a seminal contribution to the field of animal ethics, and no one who has debated with him can deny his immense philosophical clarity and his courtesy (a factor sadly not always present in the writings of his many detractors). Indeed, since our first books on animals—his *Animal Liberation* and my *Animal Rights: A Christian Assessment*—were published in the same year in the United Kingdom,[1] I have observed with admiration both his philosophical development and his (rightly deserved) international acclaim as one of the intellectual leaders in the field of animal ethics. But, precisely because of his world renown, his position on ethics is now widely taken, even by those with some acquaintance with the field, to constitute "the pro-animal view." It is not in any disputatious spirit, but for the sake of clarity, that it is important to indicate some lines of divergence.

As previously explained,[2] the case for animals, at least historically, emerged within the broader context of the humanitarian movement in the nineteenth century where concern for suffering animals was included alongside, inter alia, concern for suffering children. The rationale is nowhere better expressed than by Anthony Ashley Cooper, the Third Earl of Shaftesbury (whose words I have often quoted elsewhere): "I was convinced that God had called me to devote whatever advantages he might have bestowed upon me to the cause of the weak, the helpless, both man and beast, and those who had none to help them."[3] That sense of pity for the weak, characterised as philanthropy or benevolence (sometimes in a disparaging sense), was actually the spur to both child and animal protection. What we now call the "animal rights movement" and the "movement for child rights" would have been impossible without the embodiment of that philanthropy in social organisation and, indeed, legislation.

It is, therefore, disappointing (although not unexpected) to find that Singer, while holding firmly to the "equal consideration of interests" view with regard to animals and humans, also thinks it is permissible to kill newborn babies up to a month old:

> Perhaps, like the ancient Greeks, we should have a ceremony a month after
> birth, at which the infant is admitted to the community. Before that time,
> infants would not be recognised as having the same right to life as older
> people. Such a date would still be early enough to ensure that the rights of all

those who are self-aware are fully protected, but it would be late enough to detect most cases of severe and irreparable disability.[4]

How does Singer come to this view? It arises because his support for the right to abortion (including late abortion) necessitates in turn the rejection of the view that killing innocents is always wrong:

> If I accept that it is justifiable for a woman to kill her foetus in the womb because she considers her family complete, or would rather have a child at a time that would better suit her career plans, or because a prenatal test has shown that her child will have Down's syndrome, I know that I cannot continue to hold conventional views about the sanctity of human life at other times and other states.[5]

And on what basis does Singer decide when it is all right to kill innocents? It is here that he specifically links the status of foetuses to that of animals:

> Surely what is important is the capacities or characteristics that a being has. It is doubtful if a foetus becomes conscious until quite late in pregnancy, well after the time at which abortions are usually performed; and even the presence of consciousness would only put a foetus at a level comparable to a rather simple non-human animal—not that of a dog, let alone a chimpanzee. If on the other hand it is self-awareness, rather than mere consciousness, that grounds a right to life, that does not arise in a human being until some time after birth.[6]

As a good and very consistent utilitarian, it is not surprising that Singer emphasises self-awareness and does not attribute any weight to innocence, for example. But there is a price to be paid for a utilitarian ethic, namely, that it undercuts the case for babies *and* animals. There are other (admittedly, non-utilitarian) considerations that should properly concern us, and these have been repeated throughout this book. But Singer gives no weight to them at all; they do not figure in any of his books as important moral considerations.

As an example, it is worth citing Singer's commentary (which he has subsequently defended) in *Pediatrics*, the journal of the American Academy of Pediatrics:

> If we compare a severely defective human infant with a nonhuman animal, a dog or a pig, for example, we will often find the nonhuman to have superior capacities, both actual and potential, for rationality, self-consciousness, communication and *anything else that can plausibly be considered morally significant*.[7]

Even if Singer's judgment about relative capacities is correct, his last sentence is wide of the mark. Innocence, vulnerability, and the capacity to give informed consent have been factors variously invoked in medical ethics over a long period. But since these factors cannot easily be shown by themselves to add to or decrease the amount of happiness, his utilitarian calculus does not take them into account.

There are three reasons for thinking that Singer's position is unfortunate, at least from a pro-animal perspective. In the first place, his argument wrenches pro-animal concerns from their historical trajectory. It cuts across decades of animal advocacy that have stressed the common vulnerability of both children and animals, and therefore the appropriateness of a common response. That moral link is now increasingly buttressed by an empirical link—one that shows that animal abuse is a precursor, even a predictor of serial murder and violence to children and other, weaker humans.[8] Now, Singer may reply: "So what? The historical linking of these two ideas may be mistaken. Most people may feel such and such, and most people may be mistaken. After all, ethics is not a popularity contest." It is true: ethics isn't a popularity contest and popular feelings can certainly be mistaken, but since Singer here argues against an enduring historical trajectory, he should at least state why the common considerations, such as innocence, vulnerability, and non-consent, should not have to be taken into account.

Second, strategically, Singer's approach—admittedly, unintentionally— fuels the popular but misguided notion that concern for animals is misanthropy or leads to the displacement of human rights. It gives the impression that the cause of sentient animals can be advanced by minimising our obligations to sentient humans. It therefore confirms the worst slander on animal advocates—that our cause represents not an expansion but a narrowing of human sympathy.

Now, as a utilitarian, Singer's overwhelming concern is with suffering, hence the emphasis on self-awareness (which he judges to be a prerequisite), and he is not opposed to painless killing as such. Whether mammals can be killed wholly painlessly is, of course, problematic, at least when contemplating the routinised, mechanised way in which most farm animals are nowadays killed. But even allowing for that possibility, it is difficult to endorse Singer's view that the killing of young innocents, human or animal, so long as they are not self-aware, does them no harm. The individual concerned is robbed of his or her future, and the robbery is the same whether or not the being in question can verbalise or understand the robbery; it has still taken place.

Third, Singer places in juxtaposition what is actually one of the strongest theoretical commonalities of ethical concern. Thus, the historic appeal to the common factors of the defencelessness and vulnerability of young children and animals is pushed aside in favour of (highly developed) self-awareness. The result is what I have elsewhere called "adultism" by which I mean taking "the model of relations between adult humans—free, self-conscious, rational beings—as the sole model of ethical interaction."[9] Ineluctably, these considerations favour adult or mature human beings, since they are most (adult) human-like. It is as if other beings acquire moral standing insofar as they get closer to being mature, human adults. This may be an improvement on naked "speciesism," but it comes at a cost to weaker (less self-aware but more vulnerable) human beings and most animals.

Known as one of the most important animal advocates in the world, Singer's thought is (fortunately or unfortunately) taken as a touchstone of progressive sensibility. When he advocates concern for self-aware animals and apparent unconcern for non-self-aware human babies, or at least places such concerns in juxtaposition, the world listens. The result is a tragic and public dichotomisation of moral concern—one that simultaneously bewilders animal advocates and provides ammunition to animal detractors.

6.2. REJECTING INSTITUTIONALISED SUFFERING

I now turn to briefly address six objections to my thesis.

The first is that I have chosen, by way of illustration, to concentrate on comparatively uncontroversial cases of animal suffering, affecting only a comparatively small number of animals, whereas there are other, more conflict-ridden areas, like animal testing.

Well, the three cases in this book are by no means uncontroversial and cumulatively affect millions of animals. While the total numbers killed by hunting with dogs in the United States and Europe are unknown, my modest estimate is around 150–200,000 a year. Commercial hunting in Canada accounts for around 300,000 seals a year, and worldwide, the number hunted is nearer 900,000. And in the United States, Russia, China, and many parts of continental Europe, fur farming destroys approximately 57 million animals every year. Of course, these numbers are not huge, if we compare them with, say, the millions, if not billions, of farm animals slaughtered every year. But the issue isn't just about numbers. Even just *one* case of institutionalised cruelty should be enough to arouse our moral concern.

Hunting, fur farming, and sealing are examples of institutionalised, routinised killing involving high levels of suffering. While they represent some of the grossest uses of animals today, the important point is that they continue to be tolerated even with the flimsiest of excuses. If nothing else, my detailed analyses of these three cases have exposed the peccability of the justifications offered by the current political establishments. These cases constitute object lessons in how unseriously humans take their responsibilities to animals.

That doesn't mean, of course, that they should be the limit of our concern for suffering animals; on the contrary, all suffering inflicted on animals can and should be exposed to similar critiques. The only exception is when such suffering is for the *individual* animal's own benefit, for example, in veterinary treatment (which may sometimes entail a degree of pain).[10] What is not morally legitimate, in my view, is the infliction of suffering on some animals in order to benefit others (either humans or other animals), and in so doing to simply use them as means to an end, even a laudable one. Here, again, I must register my disagreement with Singer who, as a utilitarian, justifies some experimentation on animals: "if one, or even a dozen animals had to suffer experiments in order to save thousands, I would think it right and in accordance with equal consideration of interests that they should do so." He continues: "This, at any rate, is the answer a utilitarian must give."[11] By the same logic, it must also be right for one or even a dozen humans to suffer experimentation in the same way in order to benefit thousands of other humans. That, at any rate, must be the answer that a (logical) utilitarian must give. For some of us—unpersuaded that wholly utilitarian considerations should govern our treatment of animals or humans—we would be as disinclined to support painful experimentation on animals as we would be disinclined to support the torture of human subjects, no matter how "beneficial" the results might be in either case.

Utilitarians, like Singer, believe that some suffering of animals can be justified in certain circumstances (and, by extension, so can the suffering of human subjects) if the "benefits" outweigh the "costs." But to people who judge that utilitarian calculations cannot be entirely set aside, and that, consequentially at least, such calculations must be allowed some weight (and, therefore, some animal suffering can be justified), there is a counterargument. I am indebted here to a remarkable essay by Anthony Flew, titled "Torture: Could the Ends Justify the Means?"[12] The "Consequentialist," he says, may sometimes want to justify torture, if it can be shown that the consequences of torturing are preferable to not doing so, while the "Deontologist" would be opposed to torture in principle. There appears to be an unbridgeable gulf between these two positions. But, writes Flew:

> Suppose that we do have to accept and to live with the conclusion that our rejection of torture cannot be absolute and indefeasible. That conclusion still leaves us with all the room we need. For to say that the norm prescribing

torture is defeasible is to say only that there are conceivable conditions in
which that norm may or must be overridden by other considerations. It is not
to say that these conditions commonly, or indeed ever, occur in fact, although
I think myself that they do.[13]

Flew concludes that, while not every act of torture may be morally unjustifiable, torture should nevertheless be absolutely rejected "as an institutional,
legal or social practice":

> Without inconsistency we can, and surely should, insist that the rules and
> indeed the laws, must categorically and effectively proscribe torture. If and
> when the conceivable, but in practice extremely rare, exceptional case occurs,
> the case in which torture would be justified, then let it be against the law that it
> is done, if it is done. Let it be one of those acts of defiance which may
> occasionally even against the best of laws be morally licit or even imperative,
> but which may be legally punished nevertheless *pour decourager les autres.*[14]

There is an obvious counter-argument to Flew's position. It is that it is
unjust that the one who acts morally, or whose actions are imperative,
should be punished, since that person is not getting what he deserves.
Propounding injustice is not a way to teach ethics nor to dissuade people
from acting immorally. But such a discrepancy inevitably occurs once one
tries, as surely one must, to balance both moral imperatives and to secure a
legislative framework that embodies those very imperatives. Given that law
is a very rough and ready means of securing moral action or, rather,
ensuring that certain evils are prohibited, we have no choice but to accept
that there may be genuine exceptions to good law (which should still remain
illegal), rather than accept that law should never be enacted because it
cannot allow for every eventuality or serve every conceivable moral good.

Even if people disagree with me about the inherent wrongness of inflicting suffering, the world would be a better, certainly a safer, place if we at
least worked on the assumption that the infliction of suffering on all sentient
beings, both human and animal, should be regarded as morally unacceptable and proscribed by law. At least in the case of human torture, practi-
tioners have to work with the knowledge that their activities are
unacceptable in international law and most national law. In the same way,
we need to reject the *institutionalisation* of animal suffering.

The importance of the phenomenon of institutionalisation has already been
discussed in chapter 2,[15] but should be emphasised again here. One abiding
feature of human institutions is their self-perpetuating character. They maintain themselves in existence without having to ask fundamental questions
about their existence. If I may be personal for a moment, I have spent my

life in service to two kinds of institutions: the church and the university. In both cases, I have been struck by the astonishing capacity of these human forms of organisation to keep themselves going (and to command almost unqualified loyalty in so doing) no matter how situations change or how their original purpose is transmuted. Not all institutionalisation is wrong, of course—far from it. After all, many humans find that their deepest aspirations are met and fulfilled in service to such institutions. But when it comes to animals, their use and abuse in, for example, farming, commerce, or science acquire an institutional status that is also self-perpetuating. And when institutions are criticised, they usually excel at defending themselves and finding novel justifications for their existence.

Ethicists need to give far more attention to the ways in which people are confined (as well as fulfilled) by the institutions they serve. G. R. Dunstan writes of how the moralist "having seen his vision, or arrived at his position by moral reasoning, must weave his insight into the fabric of society by creating an institution in which to embody it."[16] Certainly, ethicists should direct their attention to institutional life and help by refining rules, procedures, and conventions, so that they embody the highest moral potential. But the problem with most institutions that directly affect animals is that they do the opposite—at least in relation to their subjugated animal subjects. That is why I have outlined in chapter 2 how even these animal-exploiting institutions can be adapted to serve moral ends, such as the pioneering of alternatives to animal experiments rather than perpetuating the status quo.

6.3. KILLING, RIGHTS, AND SUFFERING

> *The second objection is that I have not specifically considered the morality of killing as distinct from the issue of causing suffering, whereas much foundational pro-animal literature (including my own) has insisted that moral considerations should also properly apply to killing sentient beings.*

One of the earliest animal advocates in the modern period was the philosopher Ros Godlovitch, who co-edited the landmark book *Animals, Men and Morals* in 1971.[17] If anyone has a claim to be the intellectual founder of the modern animal movement, it is Godlovitch, and Singer acknowledges that the ideas in his book *Animal Liberation* owe much to her influence.[18] Well, Godlovitch has also influenced my thought—and one of her ideas is especially pertinent, namely, that it is inconsistent to value the suffering of an individual without also, at the same time, valuing its life. Her argument strikes me as unassailable:

Although it seems coherent, absurdities follow from holding that animal
suffering is to be avoided but denying that animal life has value. For if a man
were to consider it his duty to *prevent* animal suffering without holding that
animal life has value, then it would follow that he ought to exterminate
all animal life. It seems an inevitable fact that all sentient creatures suffer to a
greater or lesser extent at some points in their lives. Suffering is accepted as a
concomitant of living and, as such (except for extremely severe and prolonged
suffering) is considered worth tolerating. But it is considered worth tolerating
because a value is placed on *living.*[19]

But accepting that animal life has value, and that it should not be
destroyed without good reason, is not the same as accepting that it is always
wrong to kill. Godlovitch herself implies that, in the case of prolonged,
intense, and unrelievable suffering, euthanasia may be justified. Not all
suffering is one or all of these three, but some is. Thus, there are agonising
situations (known only too well to those who keep companion animals) in
which part of our responsibility to weaker, defenceless beings is deciding in
extremis whether their own interests are served by their continuing to live.
But such decisions are always agonising precisely because we need to be sure
in each and every case that it is the individual's best interests that are being
served—and not our own. Here animals, like infants and comatose adults,
pose a special difficulty for us because they cannot represent themselves nor
make choices for themselves. It is easier to justify assisted dying in the case
of humans who can articulate the intolerable nature of their suffering than it
is in the case of the vulnerable and the innocent (both animal and human)
who have no voice in the matter.[20]

But the moral issue cannot be avoided. In the case of humans or animals
undergoing prolonged, intense, and unrelievable suffering, we are faced with
a conflict between two duties: the first is the protection of innocent life, and
the second is the duty to alleviate suffering. Faced with that *direct* conflict,
the most compassionate response should be to give preference to the second
duty.

But this exception and another—self-defence—does not mean that killing
sentient beings is a light matter or that it should be regarded as generally
acceptable. Considerations of innocence and vulnerability mean that killing
animals, like killing infants, should arouse a special kind of hesitation and
reserve. Who are we, after all, to end their lives and make judgments about
their "best interests"? If it weren't for the fact that our very power over these
beings necessitates a fundamental responsibility for their welfare, it is surely
an area in which we would hardly wish to engage at all.

Killing animals, as Karl Barth once wrote, should never become a "normal" element in our thinking.[21] Killing animals specifically for food is an

example of where killing has outrun any range of justifiability, since we can live healthy and happy lives without any recourse to flesh products. And there is a justification for vegetarianism solely in relation to considerations of suffering. Even if it is held that killing animals for food may sometimes be justified, vegetarianism is still morally obligatory since so many systems of agriculture routinely inflict suffering on animals, not only in the business of slaughter but also in its attendant practices, such as confinement, handling, branding, transport, and rearing—and that list doesn't even include the painful, non-veterinary mutilations of farm animals, such as de-horning and castration. The thesis of this book, while highlighting the specific issue of suffering, does nothing to discourage respect for sentient life in general (quite the reverse) and vegetarianism in particular.

> *The third objection is that I have not specifically based my arguments on the rights of animals, whereas I have, like others, specifically utilised and defended rights-based arguments.*

It is indeed true that I believe animals, along with humans, have rights, and in my previous books I have argued at length in defence of a rights-based position.[22] I admit, however, that animal rights has had a bad press lately, not least of all because of its association in the public mind with militancy. As I suggested in my introduction, some animal rightists have become their own worst enemy in that regard, failing to see how violence as a tactic is morally self-contradictory.

That should not obscure, however, the strong intellectual case that can be made for rights discourse. This is best approached from a historical perspective. I have argued elsewhere:

> We need to be aware that the movement for extending solicitude to animals has gone through various stages and has been shaped by different ideas—what I call the "humanitarian," "welfare" and "justice" conceptions of moral obligation. First came the simple "humanitarian" appeal to prevent cruelty and exercise kindness. This conceptualisation resulted in the formation of the RSPCA and various humane organisations in the United States. Second, there was a more expansive notion of animal "welfare," which went beyond a simple focus on cruelty and was concerned with suffering and well-being in the widest sense. And third, there has been the inclusion of animals within the sphere of "justice"—of which the language of direct duties and rights has become the most obvious expression.

And I added: "Although these notions still overlap and jostle together (and it is by no means clear that one should wholly obliterate the older ones), it should be evident that there is a progression of ideas from one to another."[23] Seen from this perspective, rights language provides two principal advantages. The first is the formal inclusion of animals within the domain of justice—a domain from which, historically, they have been excluded. Rights talk moves the discussion away from feelings and sympathy to what is objectively owed to animals as a matter of justice. This represents an improvement on previous appeals to care based purely on emotion, which is typified in the expression "animal lover" (as if concern for animals were simply an emotional or a food preference, such as liking ice cream).

The main objection to the person who proclaims herself an animal lover is that, while we do not condemn, belittle, or deny the justification of an emotional feeling, such feelings are purely subjective, so that if X loves her dog, she might then believe that someone else should not hurt the dog, but if Y does not love a stray cat, he might then judge it right to disregard its interests. Rights language introduces a kind of objectivity or near-universality that is missing from a language that deals only with emotions, which may or may not be experienced by others.

The second advantage of rights language is that it focuses more precisely the issue of moral limits; indeed, pre-eminently, such language *is* the language of strict limits. That is its function: to set limits and establish boundaries. It has the capacity to flag up transgressions and say: "Hey, wait; something is being overlooked here." Now, in practice of course, very few, if any, animal rightists or human rightists believe that all rights are absolute. Save for the more or less absolute obligation not to intentionally cause suffering, most rightists accept that rights can be overridden by competing duties as, for example, the right to live can (and, I believe, should) sometimes be overridden by the duty not to allow prolonged or unrelievable suffering. Thus, animal rights is parasitic on the notion of duty: rights translate into strong or strict duties that should only be overridden in exceptional circumstances. Of course, it is because rights talk betokens strong limits that it is so often disliked. I have myself (only half-jestingly) described animal rightists as animal welfareists who mean it.

Despite these two (and other) advantages, there are obviously limitations as well. From a theological perspective, rights language can be seen to be incompatible with the notion that creation is grace. Some Christians, especially cognizant of this thought, prefer to have no truck with any kind of rights language (despite the championing of human rights by church and synodical resolutions). That is a position that surely deserves respect. But it certainly won't do for Christians (as they sometimes do) to speak with near-certainty about the rights of humans and then quibble about the language when it comes to animals. To resolve this difficulty, I have suggested that we speak of the "theos-rights" of animals, based on the right of the Creator to have what is created treated with respect.[24] From a theological perspective, what is at stake is how we recognise God's *own right* in the creatures she has made: when "we speak of animal rights, we conceptualise what is objectively owed to animals as a matter of justice by virtue of their Creator's right."[25]

Nevertheless, despite this strong case (only touched upon here) and my necessary theological qualification, I have always made it clear that rights language is not the only possible kind of legitimate moral discourse in relation to animals. Rights talk should not obliterate other kinds of language, such as generosity, love, respect, and care—all of which have their place. It is a mistake to think that rights language is, as it were, the philosopher's stone in terms of correct argumentation, so that no argument can be valid unless it somehow issues in rights claims. The considerations at the heart of this book are complementary to a rights perspective. One might say, for example, that the innocent and the vulnerable have a right to be spared intentional suffering. But while defensible and sometimes desirable, rights language (for humans or animals) is not always essential.

All moralists (and I include myself in these strictures) ought to realise that no one ethical theory can do justice to the range and complexity of our obligations to both humans and animals. Whenever I give tutorials in ethics, I never cease to be struck by the limited adequacy of *all* ethical theories. How one wishes that one had a single unified theory that met every conceivable circumstance. That said, and modesty apart, any theory that includes the considerations outlined in this book cannot go far wrong, whatever the eventual terminology used.

The fourth objection is that I have made no attempt to quantify suffering or offer a cost-benefit analysis of the kind now provided by, for example, defenders of animal experimentation.[26]

The simple answer is that I have not done so because I have no faith in such (inevitably anthropocentric) calculations. Every position has its limits, and the limit of my position (and also, I believe, its strength) is that it does not engage with utilitarian calculations about how much suffering can be traded against "benefit" X, Y, or Z. The inevitable result of such calculation is permissive, i.e., it allows some forms of suffering. This is not a process in which any decent non-utilitarian ethicist should engage—in relation to either the suffering of infants or the suffering of animals. One of the great demerits of utilitarianism is its explicit acceptance that every act—no matter how infamous or horrible— can be calculated against some greater good, so that (inevitably) no act is ever seen as always wrong in itself. While utilitarianism has undoubtedly advanced the cause of animals because it (notionally, at least) takes all suffering into account, and while, according to its classical exponents, it would not permit many of the cruelties we now commonly accept, its weakness is that it has mushroomed a range of attempts to bargain away some suffering, and so has limited the moral significance of suffering itself.

That such calculations are not truly impartial can easily be seen from the fact that almost all utilitarians (and Singer here may be an exception) do not truly treat considerations of suffering equally—that is, they invariably privilege human suffering—so utilitarian calculations invariably centre on how much suffering we are right in inflicting on animals rather than humans. Moreover, the calculus is often so partial that almost never do utilitarians ask the central question, namely: does animal abuse ever really benefit us? As I have tried to show elsewhere,[27] there is a range of considerations, such as desensitisation, loss of empathy, and denial, which should always tell against the abuse of animals (simply because they harm "us"), but which in practice are hardly ever even included within the calculus.

But even if the calculus were less obviously biased than it is, my view is that ethicists need to turn the corner on this kind of procedure. As we have seen in the debates over the torture of suspected criminals, humans (and especially their institutions) are terribly good at finding rationalisations for even obviously degrading and inhuman acts, such as "water-boarding," which undoubtedly cause suffering.[28] What I have learned from years of exposure to arguments justifying animal suffering is that this intellectual well is never dry. Ever more sophisticated arguments, with greater and greater nuance, can be devised in defence of the indefensible, so even breathtakingly obvious acts of barbarity can acquire an appearance of intellectual respectability. Unfashionable as it may be in a culture that rejects any kind of impermeable moral line, the thesis of this book is that the line should be drawn at the intentional infliction of suffering on innocent and vulnerable subjects.

Of course, the question will inevitably be asked: what is it about the intentional infliction of suffering on innocents (even more than the intentional killing of innocents) that ought properly to engender this absolute or near-absolute response? The answer lies in the logic implicitly accepted with regard to the morality of euthanasia. Although Godlovitch is right that it is inconsistent to value suffering without also valuing life itself, it is also sometimes right to accept that considerations of suffering should take precedence over life itself. Prolonged suffering negates life, and the very worthwhileness of it. We know from experience and testimony that this is true of human beings, and it seems reasonable to suppose that it is true of all sentient beings. We may judge it especially true of those who are incapable of comprehension (who do not know why they suffer, for what purpose, or for how long), who cannot direct their suffering to moral or rational ends, and who are, in any case, utterly blameless. Suffering of this kind, both for humans and animals, is the worst of all.

The fifth objection is that there is an implicit, sometimes explicit, theological appeal in some of my arguments, which makes my thesis available only to those who are religious or who share the same theological perspective.

Since I am a theologian as well as an ethicist, it is natural that I should be partial to some theological arguments. To support my thesis, I have touched on some of them, and one in particular. If one believes that the crucified Christ is the most accurate picture of God the world has ever seen (as I do),[29] then it follows that those who are sensitive to the suffering of the crucified ought to be moved by the Christ-like suffering of innocent creatures. Here is the Christological argument at the heart of this book. The cross does not validate suffering, but the reverse; it is God's identification with innocent suffering. In the powerful words of Jürgen Moltmann: "God has made the suffering of the world his own in the Cross of his Son."[30] Moreover, it is not only an identification with innocent suffering, but also a vindication. For if the cross does provide us with a true picture of what God is like, it follows that God is a redeeming presence in all creaturely experiences of suffering. All innocent suffering will be transformed. As Moltmann has it: "God does not desire to be glorified without his liberated creation."[31] The failure of most Christians to see this truth should not unduly bother us. Familiarity with holy things can often engender blindness, and churches are, for all their merits, institutions that embody, perhaps more than most, the will to perpetuate themselves. In this process, they can easily lose sight of the purpose for which they came into being and, in so doing, frustrate the Spirit. But insights are not lost forever because the churches are institutionally slow, even sometimes moribund. Those outside the churches often, paradoxically, have a clearer sense of what the gospel involves than do regular worshippers. We should not be surprised at this, since insight is not confined, as some appear to think, by confessional boundaries.

I look forward to the time when the churches come to celebrate and honour the work of animal protection as an imperative arising from their belief in the Creator and in the gospel of the crucified. After all, similarly remarkable things have happened, for example, the growing consensus among churches that the environment should be cared for and protected as a Christian duty—an astonishing turnaround when one considers the prevailing dualism in previous centuries, which expressly discouraged concern for "earthly" matters as distinct from "spiritual" ones.

However, the considerations set out in this book ought to commend themselves to those of no faith as well as those of faith, and even those who (often for good reasons) are anti-faith. One doesn't have to be religious to grasp the moral relevance of the considerations—such as consent, innocence, and vulnerability—which are at the core of this book.

The final objection is that I haven't outlined the full case for animals, which now increasingly accepts scientific evidence that they are, for example, rational to some degree and display greater capacities for cognition and self-awareness than previously supposed.

Well, the appeal (perhaps even the originality) of this book is the way in which it takes the usual differences (still widely accepted) about animals, and shows that they cannot bear the weight of the usual negative interpretations. It is an attempt to meet people where they are—and take them further. That is the purpose of this book. It doesn't ask people to begin with a concept of rights, nor does it ask people to revise the commonly held differences between animals and humans, nor does it depend upon some privileged access to new scientific findings. I fully accept that the case for animals may, and probably will, be buttressed by the further questioning of at least some of the differences that are now widely accepted. Be that as it may, accepting the existence of sentience (as previously defined), a robust case for animals can now be made even within the confines of our existing mental furniture. The case, even and especially dependent only on traditional formulations, is strong enough to deserve a hearing now, and should result in major changes to the way we treat animals.

6.4. COMMON VULNERABILITIES

"Of the making of many arguments," Stephen R. L. Clark once observed, "there is no end."[32] Doubtless, I have missed some important counter-arguments, or under- or over-stated some considerations. No one volume can fully answer the "why" issue which is the title of this book. Others could surely better amplify some of the philosophical, theological, and scientific considerations that inform this work, and I hope they will do so. But the important question (and the basis on which this book should be judged) is whether I am on the right track, specifically whether there is something special about the moral claims of innocent, non-consenting, non-comprehending, vulnerable sentient beings, both animals and humans. By "special" here, I do not mean something simply unusual or extraordinary (though such a claim is indeed both) but also that it is challenging in the sense of being a test of the capacities of adult moral reasoning. For, as is so often the case, those beings that cannot adequately represent themselves invariably find themselves at the margins of moral enquiry and therefore of moral concern.

Animals and infants, I contend, constitute such paradigmatic cases. If I have given so much space to animals, it is because they deserve it and because the sufferings they endure are so commonly dismissed. But if the case is valid and the considerations compelling, then we need a new orientation in our moral thinking. And that orientation should also benefit those weaker human subjects who are also routinely marginalised and have so few to advocate their cause. Thus, as I conceive it, the animal project (as it is now sometimes called) can be seen as part of a wider rediscovery of those considerations that should equally apply to vulnerable human subjects. The attempts (both old and new) to divide and rule, to set vulnerabilities *against* each other, is an intellectually self-defeating process, since the considerations that apply to both are so nearly identical, which is also why, historically, the causes of animals and children were held to be so intertwined. Rediscovering that commonality is a part of the ethical task that confronts us.

6.5. SUMMARY OF MAIN POINTS

1. Historically, the case for animals emerged within the broader context of the humanitarian movement in the nineteenth century where concern for suffering animals was included alongside, inter alia, concern for suffering children (6.1).

2. Peter Singer's utilitarian position (given his support for the right to late abortion) is that only self-aware infants (aged one month or more) should be included within the moral community. His failure to value moral innocence (and other considerations, such as vulnerability and the inabilities to consent or comprehend) undercuts the case for babies *and* animals (6.1).

3. Singer's position (1) flies in the face of the historic trajectory of concern for animals and children as constituting a common cause; (2) fuels the popular, but misguided, view that concern for animals is misanthropy or leads to the displacement of human rights; and (3) places in juxtaposition one of the strongest theoretical commonalities of ethical concern (6.1).

4. To the first objection that I have avoided more conflict-ridden areas, like animal testing, I argue that, even if people disagree with me about the inherent wrongness of inflicting suffering, the world would be a better, and certainly a safer, place if we worked on the assumption that the infliction of suffering on all sentient beings, both human and animal, should be regarded as morally unacceptable and proscribed by law. We need to reject the institutionalisation of animal suffering (6.2).

5. To the second objection that I minimise the issue of killing sentient beings, I reply that it is inconsistent to value suffering without also valuing life itself. Killing (while sometimes allowable, for example, in the cases of euthanasia and self-defence) requires strong moral justification (6.3).

6. To the third objection that I haven't utilised rights-based arguments (which I have previously enumerated), I argue that rights language is defensible, even sometimes desirable, but is not always essential. In any case, the considerations outlined in this book can also support a rights view (6.3).

7. To the fourth objection that I have not engaged in any cost-benefit analysis, I reply that such procedures are inevitably anthropocentric calculations that invariably benefit the human calculators. A moral line should be drawn at the intentional infliction of suffering on both vulnerable humans and animals (6.3).

8. To the fifth objection that the theological appeal of some of my arguments will make the thesis less accessible, I argue that the central considerations stand alone and do not require a faith-based perspective (6.3).

9. To the sixth objection that I haven't given an account of the full scientific evidence for animal cognition and self-awareness, I reply that the originality of this book consists in demonstrating that—*even accepting traditional views of difference*—animals deserve special moral solicitude (6.3).

10. Animals and infants constitute paradigmatic cases of innocence and vulnerability. The issue of animals cannot be divorced from a wider rediscovery of those considerations that should equally apply to vulnerable human subjects (6.4).

NOTES

1. John Hick suggests: "Pain is . . . a specific physical sensation. Suffering, however, is a mental state, which may be as complex as human life itself. The endurance of pain is sometimes, but not always or even usually, an ingredient of suffering"; *Evil and the God of Love* [1966] (London: Collins, Fontana, 1968), p. 354. The point is that the empirical evidence is such that animals must now be unambiguously classed as capable of not just "pain" but also "suffering." If Hick had taken this on board, we might have been spared his attempt to justify animal pain because it enables the evolution of human life; pp. 345–53.

2. Humphry Primatt, *The Duty of Mercy and the Sin of Cruelty to Brute Animals* [1776] (Edinburgh: T. Constable, 1834), reprinted in Andrew Linzey and Paul Barry Clarke (eds.), *Animal Rights: A Historical Anthology* (New York: Columbia University Press, 2005) (hereafter Linzey and Clarke, *Animal Rights*), pp. 124–25.

3. Primatt, *The Duty of Mercy*, in Linzey and Clarke, *Animal Rights*, p. 125.

4. Ibid.; my emphasis.

5. See Andrew Linzey, *Animal Theology* (London: SCM, and Chicago: University of Illinois Press, 1994) (hereafter Linzey, *Animal Theology*), p. 46.

6. Aristotle, "Politics," in William Ellis (trans.), *The Politics of Aristotle* (London: Dent, 1912), 1254b2–6b12; Linzey and Clarke, *Animal Rights*, pp. 56–58.

7. St. Thomas Aquinas, "Summa Theologiae," in Fathers of the English Dominican Province (trans.), *The Summa Theologiae of St. Thomas Aquinas*, 2nd ed. (London: Burns and Oates and Washbourne, 1922), question 26, first article; reprinted in Linzey and Clarke, *Animal Rights*, p. 61 (hereafter Aquinas, "Summa Theologiae," in Linzey and Clarke, *Animal Rights*). In context, St. Thomas considers whether man's dominion or mastery of creation was the result of Adam's disobedience to God or whether Adam was given this power at the beginning of creation. His answer is that "for his disobedience to God, man was punished by the disobedience of those creatures which should be naturally subject to him," but "in the state of innocence, before man had disobeyed, nothing disobeyed him that was naturally subject to him" whereas "[n]ow all animals are naturally subject to him" (pp. 60–61).

8. Aquinas, "Summa Theologiae," in Linzey and Clarke, *Animal Rights*, p. 61.

9. Aquinas citing Aristotle (*Politics* i.5), in Linzey and Clarke, *Animal Rights*, p. 61.

10. St. Thomas Aquinas, "Summa contra Gentiles," in Anton C. Pegis (trans.), *Basic Writings of St. Thomas Aquinas* (New York: Random House, 1945), vol. 2, pp. 220–24

(hereafter Aquinas, *Basic Writings*); Linzey and Clarke, *Animal Rights*, p. 10; my emphasis.

11. C. S. Lewis, *Present Concerns*, ed. Walter Hooper (New York: Harcourt Brace Jovanovich, 1986), p. 79; cited and discussed in Wesley A. Kort, *C. S. Lewis: Then and Now* (New York: Oxford University Press, 2001), p. 156. See also Andrew Linzey, "C. S. Lewis's theology of animals," *Anglican Theological Review* 80, no. 1, Winter 1998, pp. 60–81.

12. "If any passages of Holy Scripture seem to forbid us to be cruel to brute animals . . . this is either to remove man's thoughts from being cruel to other men . . . or because injury to an animal leads to the temporal hurt of man"; Aquinas, *Basic Writings*; Linzey and Clarke, *Animal Rights*, p. 10.

13. Primatt, *The Duty of Mercy*, in Linzey and Clarke, *Animal Rights*, p. 124.

14. See "Humans as the servant species," chap. 3 in Linzey, *Animal Theology*, pp. 45–61.

15. St. Augustine, *City of God*, trans. Marcus Dodd (Edinburgh: Clark, 1877), book 1, p. 32; Linzey and Clarke, *Animal Rights*, pp. 59–60.

16. Gillian Clark, "The fathers and the animals: the rule of reason?" in Andrew Linzey and Dorothy Yamamoto (eds.), *Animals on the Agenda: Questions about Animals for Theology and Ethics* (London: SCM, and Chicago: University of Illinois Press, 1998) (hereafter Linzey and Yamamoto, *Animals on the Agenda*), p. 68.

17. Aquinas, *Basic Writings*; Linzey and Clarke, *Animal Rights*, p. 7.

18. Obviously, there is something in dentistry that strikes a human chord of vulnerability since it is an example used by others, including Mark Rowlands, *Animals Like Us* (London: Verso, 2002), pp. 14–15.

19. For an explanation of this term, see Tom Regan, *The Case for Animal Rights* (Berkeley: University of California Press, 1983) (hereafter Regan, *The Case for Animal Rights*), pp. 96–99.

20. See Terry Waite, *Taken on Trust* (London: Hodder and Stoughton, 1993), which is a remarkable story of how a human being in conditions of captivity can nevertheless rise above the worst that other humans can do to him. Few humans, let alone animals, could write of such an experience:

> Living for years deprived of natural light, freedom of movement and companionship, I found that time took on new meaning. Now I can see that past, present and future are carried in the experience of the moment, and the exhortation of Christ to live for the day has assumed a new depth and resonance for me. We all suffer. Many individuals have suffered so much more than I have. I am truly happy to have discovered that suffering need not destroy; it can be creative. (p. xiii)

Such consolations elude animals if, as supposed, they have no rational comprehension.

21. Clark, "The fathers and the animals," in Linzey and Yamamoto, *Animals on the Agenda*, p. 68.

22. Thomas Hobbes, "De Homine" [1658], in Bernard Gert (trans.), *Man and Citizen* (London: Harvester, 1976) (hereafter Hobbes, "De Homine"), pp. 37f.; Linzey and Clarke, *Animal Rights*, p. 19.

23. Hobbes, "De Homine"; Linzey and Clarke, *Animal Rights*, p. 19.

24. Hobbes, "De Homine" Linzey and Clarke, *Animal Rights*, p. 19.

25. Hobbes, "De Homine"; Linzey and Clarke, *Animal Rights*, p. 20.

26. Michael P. T. Leahy, *Against Liberation: Putting Animals in Perspective* (London and New York: Routledge, 1991) (hereafter Leahy, *Against Liberation*), p. 139; original emphasis.

27. Michael P. T. Leahy, "Brute equivocation" [a reply to Andrew Linzey, "For animal rights," pp. 177–87], in Michael P. T. Leahy and Dan Cohn-Sherbok (eds.), *The Liberation Debate: Rights at Issue* (London and New York: Routledge, 1996) (hereafter Leahy and Cohn-Sherbok, *The Liberation Debate*), p. 200.

28. Leahy and Cohn-Sherbok, *The Liberation Debate*, p. 202.

29. Leahy, *Against Liberation*, chap. 5, "Ludwig Wittgenstein: language games and primitive beings."

30. Ibid., p. 266.

31. Hobbes, "De Homine"; Linzey and Clarke, *Animal Rights*, p. 20.

32. Peter Singer, cited in Leahy, *Against Liberation*, p. 262. The lines from Singer are from his review of Leahy's book in the *New York Review of Books*, April 1992, pp. 10–11.

33. Noam Chomsky, *Chronicles of Dissent: Interviews with David Barsamian* (Monroe, Me: Common Courage, and Stirling, Scotland: AK, 1992), p. 14.

34. See, for example, Michael A. Grodin and Leonard H. Glantz (eds.), *Children as Research Subjects: Science, Ethics and Law* (Oxford: Oxford University Press, 1994) (hereafter Grodin and Glantz, *Children as Research Subjects*); and Susan E. Lederer, *Subjected to Science: Human Experimentation in America before the Second World War* (Baltimore, Md.: Johns Hopkins University Press, 1995). The latter is particularly revealing because it shows the close relationship between human and animal experimentation. For further discussion, see also chap. 11, "Towards cruelty-free science," in Andrew Linzey, *Animal Gospel* (London: Hodder and Stoughton, and Louisville, Ky.: Westminster John Knox, 1998) (hereafter Linzey, *Animal Gospel*), pp. 92–98.

35. *The Proposed International Guidelines for Biochemical Research Involving Human Subjects* (a joint project of the World Health Organization and Council for Organizations of Medical Sciences) (Geneva: WHO, 1982), p. 22, par. 1f.

36. *Trials of War Criminals before the Nuremberg Military Tribunals under Control Council Law* (Washington, D.C.: U.S. Government Printing Office, 1949), vol. 2, no. 10, pp. 181f. (hereafter *Nuremberg Code*). I am grateful to Dr. J. M. Finnis for this reference and for note 35 above. Both are cited and discussed in Linzey, *Animal Theology*, p. 111. The Nuremberg Code and the Helsinki Declaration are also reproduced as appendices to Grodin and Glantz, *Children as Research Subjects*, pp. 218–23.

37. Regan, *The Case for Animal Rights*, p. 377; also in Linzey, *Animal Theology*, p. 111.

38. *Nuremberg Code*, p. 181.

39. Samuel Pufendorf, *The Law of Nature and Nations* [1688], trans. C. H. and W. A. Oldfather (New York: Oceana, 1931) (hereafter Pufendorf, *The Law of Nature*), vol. 2, pp. 180–83, 530–31; Linzey and Clarke, *Animal Rights*, pp. 116–17.

40. Pufendorf, *The Law of Nature*; Linzey and Clarke, *Animal Rights*, p. 117.

41. Pufendorf, *The Law of Nature*; Linzey and Clarke, *Animal Rights*, p. 118.

42. Pufendorf, *The Law of Nature*; Linzey and Clarke, *Animal Rights*, p. 119.

43. See discussion in Regan, *The Case for Animal Rights*, pp. 278ff.

44. C. S. Lewis, *The Problem of Pain* (London: Geoffrey Bles, 1940), p. 117.

45. St. Thomas distinguishes between "substances" and "intellectual substances." Humans share the former with animals, but "intellectual substances approach nearest to being always [existent], since they are incorruptible"; Aquinas, *Basic Writings*; Linzey and Clarke, *Animal Rights*, p. 9.

46. E. L. Mascall, *The Openness of Being: Natural Theology Today: The Gifford Lectures in the University of Edinburgh 1970–1971* (London: Darton, Longman and Todd, 1971), p. 257; see also pp. 264–66. Mascall was a professor of historical theology at King's College, London, and one of the leading British Thomists.

47. Paul Badham, "Do animals have immortal souls?" in Linzey and Yamamoto, *Animals on the Agenda* (hereafter Badham, "Do animals?"), p. 186.

48. Badham, "Do animals?" in Linzey and Yamamoto, *Animals on the Agenda*, pp. 186–87.

49. Ibid., p. 187. As an aside: the analysis bristles with difficulties from a theological perspective. How can one, logically, make earthly considerations the criteria for eternal life since, by definition, eternal life is God's own gift, irrespective of creaturely merits? Isn't a Creator God who is capable of making sentient beings also capable of making them immortal? How do we know precisely what spiritual capacities other-than-human creatures might have? And, in any case, why would God create beings in which he/she had no interest and who were destined to permanent non-existence? Badham lets in dolphins (possibly) because of reports that they "turn towards the sun in a characteristic way at sunrise and sunset" (p. 187), but the manifold and often highly complex capacities of animals are frequently hidden from humans and are presumably only known fully to their Creator. One needs more than a humanly devised system of detecting spiritual capacities before one can reasonably propose the permanent exclusion of other creatures from God's saving grace—if only for the reason that humans are themselves notoriously fallible. More than a little humility in the face of God's mysterious creation is called for. See Andrew Linzey, introduction to "Part three: disputed questions," in Linzey and Yamamoto, *Animals on the Agenda*, pp. 118–19, which takes issue with Badham's methodology.

50. See, for example, Arthur Peacocke and Grant Gillett (eds.), *Persons and Personality: A Contemporary Inquiry* (Oxford: Basil Blackwell, 1987), which utilises such an array of definitions, both theological and philosophical and some plainly contradictory, as to make one wonder whether the notion has any coherence.

51. I am grateful to Mark Rowlands for this argument.

52. Lewis, "Vivisection," first published as a pamphlet by the New England Anti-Vivisection Society [1947] and in Walter Hooper (ed.), *Undeceptions: Essays on Theology and Ethics* (London: Geoffrey Bles, 1952), pp. 182–86; also reprinted in Andrew Linzey and Tom Regan (eds.), *Animals and Christianity: A Book of Readings* (London: SPCK, and New York: Crossroad, 1989) (hereafter Lewis, "Vivisection"), p. 162.

53. Guunlaugur A. Jónsson, *The Image of God: Genesis 1:26–28 in a Century of Old Testament Research* (Lund: Almqvist & Wiksell International, 1988) (hereafter Jónsson, *The Image*).

54. Samuel Rolles Driver, *The Book of Genesis* (London: Methuen, 1922), p. 32; Jónsson, *The Image*, p. 41.

55. Samuel Rolles Driver, "The cosmology of Genesis," *Expositor*, 3rd ser., vol. 3, 1886, p. 32; Jónsson, *The Image*, p. 42.

56. Theodorus C. Vriezen, "La création de l'homme[o] d'après l'image de Dieu," *Oudtesamenentische Studien* 2, 1943, p. 99; Jónsson, *The Image*, p. 118. This view has not lacked modern apologists, for example, Christopher L. Fisher, who maintains: "As the one creature on Earth made in the image of [the] Creator, this picture of human uniqueness is not a surprise to theology, which has long recognized the *absolute divide* between humans and other creatures" (his emphasis), which, apparently, derives from a variety of physical and spiritual capacities ("Animals, humans and x-men: human uniqueness and the meaning of personhood," *Theology and Science* 3, no. 3, 2005, p. 307). This wholly exalted view of humankind is only "traditional" in that it was commonly held before the arrival of modern biblical scholarship on the meaning of the image, as exemplified by David Clines (see note 57 below).

57. David A. Clines, "The image of God in man," *Tyndale Bulletin* 19, 1968, p. 101; Jónsson, *The Image*, p. 222; emphases removed.

58. Jónsson, *The Image*, p. 219; my emphasis.

59. See Linzey, *Animal Theology*, pp. 45–61, where the case is developed at length.

60. Lewis, "Vivisection," p. 162.

61. I owe this phrase to Professor Dan Robinson of Georgetown University.

62. Albert Schweitzer, *Civilisation and Ethics*, trans. C. T. Campion (London: Allen & Unwin, 1923), p. 119.

63. I have critiqued Peter Singer's "equality of consideration" ethic in the second chapter ("The moral priority of the weak") of my *Animal Theology*, pp. 28–44, in which I argue for the generosity paradigm instead of the equality paradigm. See also discussion of the adequacy of Singer's view in my conclusion in this volume, pp. 152–55.

64. John Henry Newman, "The crucifixion," *Parochial and Plain Sermons*, 8 vols. (London: Rivingtons, 1868) (hereafter Newman, *Sermon*), vol. 2, p. 133. The sermon is also discussed in chap. 8, "The Christ-like innocence of animals," in Linzey, *Animal Gospel*, pp. 64–67.

65. Newman, *Sermon*, p. 135; original emphasis.

66. Ibid., p. 136.

67. Ibid., pp. 136–37; my emphasis. Newman's reference to an experiment pre-dates the controversy about vivisection that raged at Oxford in the late 1880s. Opponents of the newly emerging science of vivisection at that time included E. B. Nicholson, H. P. Liddon, E. A. Freeman, and Lewis Carroll (Charles L. Dodgson). In 1885, John Ruskin, the Slade Professor of Fine Art, resigned his post following the vote that endowed vivisection in the university (see letter in the *Pall Mall Gazette*, 21 April 1885). It is interesting to speculate about the "chance publication" to which Newman refers. One possibility is that such literature was brought to Newman's attention by

his younger brother, Professor William Francis Newman (1805–1897), a classicist and liberal religious thinker, who was also president of the Vegetarian Society of the United Kingdom from 1873 to 1884.

68. Newman, *Sermon*, p. 137.
69. Ibid., p. 138.
70. Ibid.

CHAPTER 2

1. Denys Turner, *Faith Seeking* (London: SCM, 2002), p. 61.
2. My comments are hardly original, of course; see Edward Leach's classic work, "Anthropological aspects of language: Animal categories and verbal abuse," in Eric Lenneberg (ed.), *New Directions in the Study of Language* (Cambridge, Mass.: MIT Press, 1966).
3. René Descartes, letter to Henry More, 5 February 1646, in Anthony Kenny (ed. and trans.), *Descartes: Philosophical Letters* (Oxford: Oxford University Press, 1970); extract in Tom Regan and Peter Singer (eds.), *Animal Rights and Human Obligations*, 2nd ed. (Englewood Cliffs, N.J.: Prentice Hall, 1989), p. 15. The argument is odd in many ways, not least the assertion that because dogs and cats do not adequately cover up their excrement, they must lack rational sense. In the light of global warming and environmental pollution, we might ask, how adequately have humans cleared up *their* mess?
4. For a discussion of the positive insights about animals within Judaism and Christianity, see Andrew Linzey and Dan Cohn-Sherbok, *After Noah: Animals and the Liberation of Theology* (London: Mowbray, 1987); for a discussion of animal-friendly saints, see pp. 91–116 in that work.
5. J. P. Mahaffy, *Descartes* (London: Blackwood, 1901), p. 118; cited and discussed in A. Richard Kingston, "Theodicy and animal welfare," *Theology* 70, no. 569, November 1967, pp. 482–88. Kingston's article is also reproduced in Andrew Linzey and Tom Regan (eds.), *Animals and Christianity: A Book of Readings* (London: SPCK, 1989) (hereafter Linzey and Regan, *Animals and Christianity*), pp. 71–78.
6. Joseph Rickaby, *Moral Philosophy* (London: Longmans, 1889), p. 249; also discussed in Kingston, "Theodicy," in Linzey and Regan, *Animals and Christianity*, p. 72.
7. Charles E. Raven, *The Creator Spirit: A Survey of Christian Doctrine in the Light of Biology, Psychology and Mysticism* (London: Hopkinson, 1926, 1927), p. 120; also discussed in Kingston, "Theodicy," in Linzey and Regan, *Animals and Christianity*, p. 77.
8. Bernard E. Rollin, "Animal pain," in Andrew Linzey (ed.), *Encyclopaedia of Global Concern for Animals*, forthcoming. I borrow these insights into pain and behaviourism from Rollin. See also Rollin, *The Unheeded Cry: Animal Consciousness, Animal Pain and Science* (Oxford: Oxford University Press, 1990) (hereafter Rollin, *Unheeded Cry*), a landmark book on scientific and philosophical attitudes to animal pain.
9. Ibid.

10. Ibid.

11. Konrad Lorenz, *On Aggression*, trans. M. Latzke (London: Methuen, 1966), p. 54; also cited and discussed in Stephen R. L. Clark, *The Moral Status of Animals* (Oxford: Clarendon, 1977), pp. 38–39.

12. Charles Darwin, *The Expression of Emotions in Man and Animals* [1872] (Chicago: University of Chicago Press, 1965) (reprinted from the authorised edition, New York and London: Appleton, n.d.). I am grateful to Priscilla Cohn for this reference.

13. Donald R. Griffin, *Animal Minds* (Chicago: University of Chicago Press, 1975), p. 251; see also Rollin, *Unheeded Cry*; and among the many articles: Margaret Rose and David Adams, "Evidence for pain and suffering in other animals," in Gill Langley (ed.), *Animal Experimentation: The Consensus Changes* (New York: Chapman and Hall, 1989); M. Zimmerman, "Behaviour investigations of pain in animals," in I. J. H. Duncan and V. Molony (eds.), *Assessing Pain in Farm Animals* (Luxembourg: Office for Official Publications of the European Community, 1986); C. J. Yierck and B. Y. Cooper, "Guidelines for assessing pain reactions and pain modulation in laboratory animal subjects," *Advances in Pain Research and Therapy* 6, 1984, pp. 305–22; and E. M. Wright, K. L. Marcella, and J. F. Woodson, "Animal pain: evaluation and control," *Lab Animal* 9, 1985, pp. 20–36.

14. David DeGrazia, *Taking Animals Seriously: Mental Life and Moral Status* (Cambridge: Cambridge University Press, 1996), p. 123. Chapters 4–7 survey and analyse the empirical evidence about animal consciousness and sentiency.

15. But see Paola Cavalieri, *The Animal Question*, with the foolish subtitle: *Why Non-human Animals Deserve Human Rights* (Oxford: Oxford University Press, 2001). Of course, Cavalieri is arguing for "an expanded theory of human rights" (pp. 137f.), but it is still an unfortunate example of a home goal by an animal advocate. Otherwise the book is an acute philosophical discussion which deserves the accolades it has received.

16. I borrow the phrase from J. A. T. Robinson, *Can We Trust the New Testament?* (London: Mowbray, 1977). Robinson detects four tendencies in approaches to the study of the New Testament: "the cynicism of the foolish," "the fundamentalism of the fearful," "the scepticism of the wise," and "the conservatism of the committed"; pp. 13–29. See the discussion in the introduction to Andrew Linzey and Peter J. Wexler (eds.), *Fundamentalism and Tolerance: An Agenda for Theology and Society* (London: Bellew, 1991), pp. vi–viii.

17. McLeod cited in Ronald Ferguson, *George McLeod: Founder of the Iona Community* (London: HarperCollins, 1990), p. 194.

18. Peter Roberts, "The experts say this is not cruel . . . ," in David Paterson and Richard D. Ryder (eds.), *Animals' Rights: A Symposium* (Fontwell, Sussex: Centaur, 1979), p. 131.

19. Thomas Nagel, "What is it like to be a bat?" (chap. 12), in his *Mortal Questions* (Cambridge: Cambridge University Press, 1979), pp. 164–80.

20. Committee of Inquiry into Hunting with Dogs, chaired by Lord Burns (London: HMSO, 1999), par. 6.49, p. 117.

21. Lord Burns, Debate on the Hunting Bill, *Hansard*, 12 March 2001, p. 533.

22. *Codes of Recommendations for the Welfare of Livestock: Report by the Farm Animal Welfare Advisory Committee* (London: MAFF, 1970), p. 5; discussed in Andrew Linzey, *Animal Rights: A Christian Assessment* (London: SCM, 1976) (hereafter Linzey, *Animal Rights*), pp. 65–66.

23. Colin Tudge, "Farmers in loco parentis," *New Scientist*, 18 October 1965; cited and discussed in Linzey, *Animal Rights*, p. 2; my emphasis.

24. John Napier, "Introductory address," in *Stress in Farm Animals*, proceedings of a joint symposium held by the Society for Veterinary Ethology and the RSPCA, *British Veterinary Journal*, no. 130, 1974, p. 85; also discussed in Linzey, *Animal Rights*, p. 64.

25. "Trout trauma puts anglers on the hook?" news release, Royal Society, 29 April 2003, p. 1. For the full research, see Lynne U. Sneddon, Victor A. Braithwaite, and Michael J. Gentle, "Do fish have nociceptors: evidence for the evolution of a vertebrate sensory system," *Biological Sciences* 270, no. 1520, June 2003.

26. See, for example, the previous work by Verheijen at the University of Utrecht discussed by John Webster, *Animal Welfare: A Cool Look at Eden* (Oxford: Blackwell, 1994), p. 224.

27. Ross Clark, "We should ignore this codswollop [sic] hook, line, and sinker," *The Times*, 1 May 2003 (hereafter Clark, "We should ignore"). The same dismissive attitude is taken by fisherman Keith Elliot, who assures us that "the research was a load of tosh," in "Fishing lines: make-up? my face needs a miracle," *Independent*, 4 May 2003.

28. Clark, "We should ignore."

29. Lorenz, *On Aggression*, also cited and discussed in Miriam Rothschild, *Animals and Man: The Romanes Lectures* (Oxford: Clarendon, 1986), p. 52; my emphasis.

30. Peter Carruthers, *The Animals Issue: Moral Theory in Practice* (Cambridge: Cambridge University Press, 1992) (hereafter Carruthers, *Animals Issue*), p. 171.

31. Ibid., p. 193.

32. I am grateful to Mark Rowlands for this paragraph of elucidation; see his "Consciousness and higher-order thoughts," *Mind and Language* 16, no. 3, 2001, pp. 290–310, and his *The Nature of Consciousness* (Cambridge: Cambridge University Press, 2001), chap. 4.

33. Carruthers, *Animals Issue*, p. xi.

34. Ibid.

35. Peter Carruthers, "Sympathy and subjectivity," *Australasian Journal of Philosophy* 77, 1999, available at http://www.philosophy.umd.edu/Faculty/pcarruthers/Sympathy-and-subjectivity.htm.

36. W. A. Whitehouse, *The Authority of Grace: Essays in Response to Karl Barth*, ed. Ann Loades (Edinburgh: Clark, 1981), p. 205.

37. Ibid., p. 210.

38. The effect of this experience was such that it is mentioned in many of my writings. See, for example, Andrew Linzey, *Animal Gospel* (London: Hodder and Stoughton, and Louisville, Ky.: Westminster John Knox, 1999), pp. 45–46.

39. Ruth Harrison, *Animal Machines* (London: Vincent Stuart, 1964). Harrison often said that she would write a follow-up book called *Since Animal Machines*, but she was always too busy working practically for farm animal welfare to complete it.

Perhaps, one day, someone will write it for her, or sympathetic academics will produce a collection in her honour.

40. Tom Regan, *The Case for Animal Rights* (London: Routledge and Kegan Paul, 1983), pp. 243–48; original emphasis. See also the discussion in Andrew Linzey, *Christianity and the Rights of Animals* (London: SPCK, 1987), pp. 82ff.

41. Andrew Linzey, foreword to Stephen H. Webb, *On God and Dogs: A Christian Theology of Compassion for Animals* (New York: Oxford University Press, 1998), p. xi.

42. While promulgated in 1979, the drafting of the convention was not completed until ten years later. The UN General Assembly adopted the Convention on the Rights of the Child on 20 November 1989. See Cynthia Price Cohen, "United Nations Convention on the Rights of the Child: developing international norms to create a new world for children," in Kathleen Alaimo and Brian Klug (eds.), *Children as Equals: Exploring the Rights of the Child* (New York: University Press of America, 2002), pp. 51ff.

43. See Peter Lee-Wright, *Child Slaves* (London: Earthscan, 1990), which is based on his television programme of the same title, an altogether disturbing insight into how children are utilised as cheap labour from India to Mexico.

44. *Concise Oxford Dictionary* (1963), p. 619.

45. See his classic essay "Politics and the English language," in George Orwell, *Inside the Whale and Other Essays* (Harmondsworth: Penguin, 1962), pp. 143–57.

46. Noam Chomsky, *Chronicles of Dissent: Interviews with David Barsamian* (Monroe, Maine: Common Courage, and Stirling, Scotland: AK, 1992) (hereafter Chomsky, *Chronicles*), p. 22. See also Chomsky, *Understanding Power: The Indispensable Chomsky*, ed. Peter R. Mitchell and John Schoeffel (London: Vintage, 2003), including his comments on vegetarianism and animal rights, pp. 356–58.

47. Chomsky, *Chronicles*, pp. 11–12.

48. Ibid., p. 12.

49. See, for example, Robert Sharpe, *The Cruel Deception: The Use of Animals in Medical Research* (Wellingborough, Northamptonshire: Thorsons, 1988); C. Ray Greek and Jean Swingle Greek, *Sacred Cows and Golden Geese: The Human Cost of Experiments on Animals* (New York: Continuum, 2000), and also their *Specious Science: Why Experiments on Animals Harm Humans* (New York: Continuum, 2003). Despite the popular titles, the authors are medically qualified and provide detailed critiques of the scientific shortcomings of using animals in testing.

50. Chomsky, *Chronicles*, p. 131.

51. Taken from work by the one *Sunday Times* journalist, Steve Connor, who courageously researched the issue: "Giant sheep clones worry scientists," *The Sunday Times*, 10 March 1996, pp. 1–2. See the subsequent research report, K. H. S. Campbell, J. McWhir, W. A. Ritchie, and I. Wilmut, "Sheep cloned by nuclear transfer from a cultured cell line," *Nature* 380, 1996, pp. 64–66, and my critique, Andrew Linzey, "Ethical and theological objections to animal cloning," *Bulletin of Medical Ethics*, no. 131, September 1977, pp. 18–22; also reprinted in Linzey, *Animal Gospel*, pp. 121–29, from which the paragraph in the text is largely borrowed.

52. "The propaganda system," in Chomsky, *Chronicles*, pp. 61–74.

53. Two important works on the legal front are Gary L. Francione, *Animals, Property and the Law* (Philadelphia, Pa.: Temple University Press, 1995), and Steven M. Wise, *Rattling the Cage: Towards Legal Rights for Animals* (London: Profile, 2000).

54. John Laumer, "Booming organic food market in UK," available at www.treehugger. com/files/2005/06booming_organic.php.

55. "Meat-free products boost premier," *BBC News*, available at http://newsvote.bbc.co. uk/mpapps/pagetools/print/news.bbc.co.uk/1/hi/business/5251920.

56. For my critique of animal-unfriendly conservationists with specific reference to ruddy ducks and squirrels, see Andrew Linzey, "So near and yet so far: animal theology and ecological theology," in Roger S. Gottlieb (ed.), *Oxford Handbook of Religion and Ecology* (New York: Oxford University Press, 2006), pp. 348–61.

57. See, for example, Linzey and Clarke, *Animal Rights*; Linzey and Regan, *Animals and Christianity*; Susan J. Armstrong and Richard G. Botzler (eds.), *The Animal Ethics Reader* (London: Routledge, 2003); Steve F. Sapontzis (ed.), *Food for Thought: The Debate over Eating Meat* (Amherst, N.Y.: Prometheus, 2004); Tom Regan and Peter Singer (eds.), *Animal Rights and Human Obligations*, 2nd ed. (Englewood Cliffs, N.J.: Prentice Hall, 1989); James P. Sterba (ed.), *Earth Ethics: Introductory Readings on Animal Rights and Environmental Ethics*, 2nd ed. (Upper Saddle River, N.J.: Prentice Hall, 2000); and Donald VanDeVeer and Christine Pierce (eds.), *The Environmental Ethics and Policy Book: Philosophy, Ecology, Economics* (Belmont, Calif.: Wadsworth, 1994).

58. See Lloyd Spencer's excellent web site, *Material on Walter Benjamin*, available at www.leedstrinity.ac.uk/deprt/media/staffIs/Wbenjamin/WBindexhtm.

59. Andrew Linzey and Jacky Turner, "Bioethics: making animals matter," *Biologist* 45, no. 5, November 1998, pp. 209–11.

CHAPTER 3

1. See the BBC Web site, http://news.bbc.co.uk/1/hi/uk/428122.stm (accessed 7 September 2008).

2. See http://www.mfha.com/memb.htm (accessed 7 September 2008).

3. See http://www.mfha.com/abfo.htm (accessed 7 September 2008). For an account of the growing popularity of fox-hunting in the U.S, see Michael Markarian, "Tally ho, dude! foxhunting in America," *Animals' Agenda* 19, no. 6, November–December 1999, pp. 22–27.

4. See http://www.fresco.ie/imfha/history2.htm (accessed 7 September 2008).

5. See http://www.defra.gov.uk/rural/hunting/inquiry/evidence/frenchhuntingpacks.htm (accessed 7 September 2008).

6. See, for example, http://www.howtobooks.co.uk/abroad/france/hunting.asp and http://www.hunting-france.com.

7. Recommendations in *Report on Cruelty to Wild Animals*, chaired by Scott Henderson (London: HMSO, 1951), cmd 8266. See http://news.bbc.co.uk/1/hi/ uk_politics/1846577.stm. There is also an outline of the history at: http://www.ifaw.

org/ifaw_international/join_campaigns/national_regional_efforts/ifaw_in_action_
united_kingdom/the_ban_on_hunting_with_dogs/background/a_history_of_the_
campaign.php.

8. *Report of the Committee of Inquiry into Hunting with Dogs in England and Wales,* chaired by Lord Burns (London: HMSO, June 2000) (referred to in the notes and text as "Burns").

9. Letter from the Committee of Inquiry to the then secretary of state for the Home Office, 9 June 2000, reproduced at beginning of Burns, p. 1.

10. Essential reading should include Keith Thomas, *Man and the Natural World: Changing Attitudes to Nature, 1600–1800* (London: Allen Lane, 1983), especially chaps. 1–4; James Turner, *Reckoning with the Beast: Animals, Pain and Humanity in the Victorian Mind* (Baltimore, Md.: Johns Hopkins University Press, 1980); Richard D. Ryder, *Animal Revolution: The Struggle against Speciesism* (Oxford: Blackwell, 1989); and Hilda Kean, *Animal Rights: Political and Social Change in Britain since 1800* (London: Reaktion, 1998).

11. Perhaps the best single guide to contemporary thought is Marc Bekoff with Carron A. Meaney (eds.), *Encyclopedia of Animal Rights and Animal Welfare* (Westport, Conn.: Greenwood, 1998). For guides to the literature, see, for example, Charles R. Magel, *Keyguide to Information Sources in Animal Rights* (London: Mansell, 1989); and John M. Kistler, *Animal Rights: A Subject Guide, Bibliography, and Internet Companion* (Westport, Conn.: Greenwood, 2000).

12. Burns, par. 6.12, p. 109; my emphasis.

13. Burns, par. 6.9, p. 108.

14. See Richard Sorabji, *Animal Minds and Human Morals: The Origins of the Western Debate* (London: Duckworth, 1993), which is an excellent guide to an extensive discussion of the status of animals by predominantly Greek philosophers.

15. For extracts from the works of all these thinkers and others, see Andrew Linzey and Paul Barry Clarke (eds.), *Animal Rights: A Historical Anthology* (New York: Columbia University Press, 2005) (hereafter Linzey and Clarke, *Animal Rights*).

16. Burns, par. 6.31, p. 112.

17. Burns, par. 6.33, p. 113.

18. Burns, par. 6.11, p. 109.

19. Burns, par. 6.42, p. 115; my emphasis. On the question of evidence, it is perhaps worth noting that Professor John Webster maintains that, from a veterinary perspective, "the genetic similarity between the dog and the fox is so close that we must assume that they have a similar capacity to suffer fear, pain and exhaustion. It is thus no more nor less cruel to hunt a fox than it would be to hunt a dog," John Webster, *Animal Welfare: A Cool Eye towards Eden* (Oxford: Blackwell Science, 1995), p. 221. I reminded Webster of his own words since he (unaccountably) appeared for the Middle Way Group (that supports the licensing of hunting) at the public hearings on hunting in September 2002. See http://www.defra.gov.uk/rural/hunting/huntinghearingsschedule.htm.

20. Burns, par. 6.46, p. 116.

21. Burns, par. 6.49, p. 117, my emphasis.

22. Ibid.

23. Ibid.

24. *Concise Oxford Dictionary* (1963), p. 245.

25. Lord Burns, Debate on the Hunting Bill, *Hansard*, 12 March 2001, p. 533; see also previous discussion in chap. 2 of this volume.

26. Burns, par. 6.49, p. 117.

27. Burns, par. 6.67, p. 120.

28. See Farm Animal Welfare Council, *Report on the Welfare of Livestock when Slaughtered by Religious Methods* (London: HMSO, 1985), pp. 19f., and its more recent *Report on the Welfare of Farmed Animals at Slaughter or Killing, Part 1: Red Meat Animals* (London: DEFRA, 2003), which concluded that "a separate study of brain response indicated responses for up to 60 seconds" after shehita slaughter, and again concluded that "slaughter without pre-stunning is unacceptable and that the Government should repeal the current exemption [in UK law]" pp. 16, 35.

29. Burns, par. 6.68, p. 120.

30. Burns, par. 5.22, p. 86.

31. Burns, par. 27, p. 10; my emphasis.

32. Burns, par. 5.11, p. 84; my emphasis.

33. Burns, par. 3.75, p. 67; my emphasis.

34. Burns, par. 5.94, p. 102; my emphasis.

35. Burns, par. 5.93, p. 101.

36. Burns, pars. 7.27–29, p. 130.

37. Burns, par. 7.18, p. 127.

38. Burns, par. 9.27, p. 150.

39. Burns, par. 829, p. 140.

40. Ann Mallalieu, "Hunting is our music," in Brian MacArthur (ed.), *The Penguin Book of Twentieth-Century Protest* (London: Penguin, 1999), p. 468; my emphasis.

41. Burns, par. 9.40, p. 153.

42. Immanuel Kant, *Lectures on Ethics: Duties towards Animals and Other Spirits* [1780–1781], trans. Louise Infield (New York: Harper and Row, 1963), pp. 239–41; extract in Linzey and Clarke, *Animal Rights*, pp. 126–27.

43. St. Thomas Aquinas, "Summa contra Gentiles," in Anton C. Pegis (trans.), *Basic Writings of St. Thomas Aquinas* (New York: Random House, 1945), vol. 2, pp. 220–24; extract in Linzey and Clarke, *Animal Rights*, p. 10.

44. Jeremy Bentham, "An introduction to the principles of morals and legislation" [1789], in his *A Fragment on Government and an Introduction to the Principles of Morals and Legislation*, ed. Wilfred Harrison [1823] (Oxford: Blackwell, 1948), pp. 411–12; extract in Linzey and Clarke, *Animal Rights*, p. 136, original emphasis.

45. John Stuart Mill cited and discussed in James Rachels, *The Elements of Moral Philosophy*, 3rd ed. (Boston: McGraw-Hill, 1999), pp. 97–98; my emphasis.

46. Ibid., p. 103, my emphasis.

47. Peter Singer, *Animal Liberation*, 2nd ed. (New York: Random House, 1990), p. 234.

48. John Locke, "Some thoughts concerning education" [1693], in *The Works of John Locke in Ten Volumes*, 10th ed. (London, 1801), vol. 9, pp. 112–15; extract in Linzey and Clarke, *Animal Rights*, pp. 119–20.

49. Burns, par. 10.11, p. 159.

50. Burns, par. 35, p. 12; my emphasis.

51. Burns, par. 3.56, p. 62; my emphasis.

52. Burns, par. 3.75, p. 67; my emphasis.

53. Burns, par. 42, p. 83; my emphasis.

54. Burns, par. 5.37, p. 90; my emphasis.

55. Burns, par. 5.37, p. 91; my emphasis.

56. Burns, par. 5.43, p. 91; my emphasis.

57. Burns, par. 5.36, p. 89; my emphasis.

58. Burns, par. 5.48, p. 92; my emphasis.

59. Burns, par. 5.89, p. 101; my emphasis.

60. Burns, par. 5.117, p. 106; my emphasis.

61. Burns, par. 5.43, p. 91.

62. Burns, par. 5.12, p. 84.

63. Burns, par. 5.16, p. 85.

64. Burns, par. 5.17, p. 85.

65. Burns, chap. 5, pp. 81–105, and especially the "cautionary notes," pp. 81–82.

66. Burns, par. 2, second bullet point, p. 82.

67. Rory Putman, *The Natural History of Deer* (Ithaca, N.Y.: Cornell University Press, 1988), pp. 171–72.

68. Burns, par. 7, seventh bullet point p. 82.

69. Burns, par. 9.49, p. 544.

70. Alun Michael, Standing Committee on the Hunting Bill, 14 January 2003, available at www.publications.parliament.uk.

71. Jane Ridley, *Fox Hunting* (London: Collins, 1990), p. 1. See also pp. 14f. for details of how foxes have been preserved for hunting from the earliest times. For my review, see Andrew Linzey, "Hotly in pursuit," *Church Times*, 29 November 1991.

CHAPTER 4

1. Figures taken from Fur Commission USA press release, October 23, 2008, available at http://www.furcommission.com/news/newsF11a.htm (accessed February 8, 2009). See also http://www.respectforanimals.co.uk/home.php/facts/more/fur_factory-farming (accessed September 6, 2008). See also "Fur no longer on fashion's menu," *Taipei Times*, November 10, 2005, p. 13, available at http://www.taipeitimes.com/News/feat/archives/2005/11/10/2003279614, which notes that there are still twenty fur farms operating in Russia; and "Mink farming in the United States," *Fur Commission USA*, November 2005, p. 1, available at www.furcommission.com/resource/Re-sources/MFIUS.pdf, which notes that the United States ranks fourth in the world in fur production. Mink make up nearly the entirety of all fur-farmed animals in the United States, and data over several decades are available from the USDA at http://usda.mannlib.cornell.edu/MannUsda/viewDocumentInfo.do?documentID=1106. For a U.S. government report on the state of the U.S. fur industry, mainly with an

eye to trade, see http://hotdocs.usitc.gov/docs/pubs/industry_trade_summaries/ pub3666.pdf.

2. *Sandy Parker Reports*, Weekly International Fur News, 15 October, 2007, Vol. 31 Issue 32, p. 3.

3. See "Wild Fur," British Fur Trade Association website, available at http://www. britishfur.co.uk/main/fur-farmed_or_wild/Wild_Fur.

4. For details of the other "target" animals trapped, including raccoons, beavers, wolves, bobcats, lynx, and coyotes, see "Trapping on National Wildlife Refuges" on the website of Born Free in association with the Animal Protection Institute, available at http://www.bornfreeusa.org/facts.php?p=62&more=1. I am grateful to Richard Deville and Nicki Brooks of Respect for Animals for their invaluable help with this reference and 1–3 above.

5. Bont voor Dieren, "Factory farming: mink farming," available at http://www.bont-voordieren.nl/english/dutch.php?action=minkfarming (accessed 18 March 2006); see also "Why is it wrong to wear fur?" *Animal Defenders International*, available at http://www.ad-international.org/fur/go.php?ssi=19, which discusses the state of international fur farming.

6. Information from Respect for Animals, available at http://www.respectforanimals. co.uk/home.php/facts/more/fur_factory-farming (accessed 6 September 2008).

7. "[T]he only method of euthanasia approved for mink by FCUSA is bottled gas, either pure carbon monoxide or carbon dioxide." See http://www.furcommission.com/ resource/Resources/MFIUS.pdf (accessed 6 September 2008).

8. See http://www.hsus.org/furfree/news/new_york_bans_anal_electrocution.html (accessed 6 September 2008). Video evidence of anal electrocution practiced in the United States has been collected by both the HSUS (Humane Society of the United States) and PETA (People for the Ethical Treatment of Animals): http://video.hsus. org/?fr_story=8c91084c49ccc01e5a0f32c613c0c2c87bd62ff3&rf=bm; http://www.petatv .com/tvpopup/video.asp?video=furfarm&Player=flv.

   For a pro-fur discussion of U.S. killing methods (which bewails the likely costs to fur production of animal welfare regulation), see J. E. Oldfield of Oregon State University, http://ars.sdstate.edu/animaliss/furfarm.html (accessed 6 September 2008). I am grateful to Pierre Grzybowski of the HSUS for the references to the U.S. situation.

9. For the shocking video evidence, see http://www.peta.org/feat/ChineseFurFarms/ index.asp (accessed 6 September 2008).

10. Bont voor Dieren, "Curtain falling for fur farming in Europe," available at http:// www.bontvoordieren.nl/english/index.php?action=farming (hereafter "Curtain falling"); Clemens Purtscher, *Peltztierhaltung und Pelzhandel in Österreich—Rechtliche Reglungen und Handlungsbedarf* (Universität Wien, 2000), p. 116, available at http:// www.infurmation.com/pdf/purtscoo.pdf. For details of the Austrian legislative provisions, see Kärntner Tierschutzverordnung, Anlage 3, Zu §§ 10 bis 15. See an analysis of this law at Purtscher, *Peltztierhaltung und Pelzhandel*, pp. 61–62, available at http://www.infurmation.com/pdf/purtscoo.pdf. The following is an example of legislation banning mink farming in one of the Austrian states: Wiener Tierschutz- und Tierhaltegesetz: Änderung. Artikel 1, 5 § 15a. Landesgesetzblatt für Wien, 1996, Stück

46, p. 259, available at http://www.wien.gv.at/recht/landesrecht-wien/landesgesetz-blatt/jahrgang/1996/pdf/lg1996046.pdf.

11. Bont voor Dieren, "Curtain falling."

12. See "The Dutch situation," available at http://www.bontvoordieren.nl/english/index. php?action=farming. The full text announcing the change in the Dutch Animal Health and Welfare Law can be found at Besluit van 10 December 1997, houdende uitvoering van artikel 34, eerste lid, van de Gezondheids—en welzijnswet voor dieren (Besluit aanwijzing voor productie te houden dieren), Staatsblad 1998, p. 51. The history of events leading up to the proposed mink breeding ban can be found at http://www.bontvoordieren.nl/english/dutch.php?action=minkfarming; and http://www. bontvoordieren.nl/english/dutch.php?action=discussion.

13. Animal Protection Institute, "Bill to restrict fur farming in Sweden on the horizon," *API News: The Fur Trade Today—10/03/05*, available at http://www.api4animals.org/news?p=218&more=1 (accessed 18 March 2006); Asa Lexmon, *Sweden Livestock and Products: Animal Welfare Legislation in Sweden 2005* (Washington, D.C.: USDA Foreign Agricultural Service 2005), p. 5, available at http://www.fas.usda.gov/gain-files/200510/146131334.pdf.

14. Bont voor Dieren, "Curtain falling"; see also Decreto Legislativo 146/2001 ("Attuazione della direttiva 98/58/CE relativa alla protezione degli animali negli allevamenti"), pubblicato nella Gazzetta Ufficiale n. 95 del 24 aprile 2001, D. LGS 146/2001 (enforcement of Dir. 98/58/CE regarding the protection of animals in farms).

15. Bont voor Dieren, "Curtain falling." I am grateful to Dr. Joanna Swabe, senior policy adviser of Bont voor Dieren, for the references.

16. "Croatia bans fur farming," available at http://www.respectforanimals.co.uk/home. php (accessed 13 January 2007).

17. Fur Farming (Prohibition) Act, 2000, chap. 33, § 1 (Eng.), available at http://www. opsi.gov.uk/ACTS/acts2000/20000033.htm.

18. Fur Farming (Prohibition) Act, 2002, asp 10, § 1 (Scot.), available at http://www.opsi. gov.uk/legislation/scotland/acts2002/20020010.htm.

19. Elliot Morley, "Oral answers to questions: fur farming (prohibition) bill," *Hansard*, 15 May 2000, col. 40 (hereafter Morley, "Oral answers to questions"), available at http:// www.publications.parliament.uk/pa/cm199900/cmhansrd/vo000515/debindx/00515-x.htm.

20. Ibid., col. 76; my emphasis.

21. Sir William Pulteney moved the first bill against bull-baiting on 2 April 1800. For the debate, see *Hansard* 35, 1800, pp. 202–13, cited and discussed in James Turner, *Reckoning with the Beast: Animals, Pain and Humanity in the Victorian Mind* (Baltimore, Md.: Johns Hopkins University Press, 1980) (hereafter Turner, *Reckoning with the Beast*), pp. 15, 148.

22. The volume of law, most of it relating to disputed practices, is steadily growing. See, for example, Kevin Dolan, *Laboratory Animal Law* (Oxford: Blackwell Science, 2001), which provides an overview of the legal obligations to animals used in research; Mike Radford, *Animal Law in Britain: Regulation and Responsibility* (Oxford: Oxford University Press, 2001) (hereafter Radford, *Animal Law in Britain*), which provides an overview of substantive animal law and policy in Britain; and

David B. Wilkins, *Animal Welfare in Europe: European Legislation and Concerns* (The Netherlands: Kluwer Law International, 1997), which provides an overview of animal-related law in Europe.

23. See Andrew Linzey, "John Wesley: an early prophet of animal rights," *Methodist Recorder*, 10 April 2003:

> Methodists were accused of being one of the two most subversive groups in the country in a parliamentary debate. To general approval, one member of parliament claimed that Methodism aimed at nothing less than the destruction of "the old English character, by the abolition of all rural sports." One recent Methodist sermon was singled out because of its preposterous suggestion that cruel sports would "render mankind cruel." In Methodism, he argued, "everything joyous was to be prohibited, to prepare the people for the reception of their fanatical doctrines" (p. 15).

That debate was on 24 May 1802, and it concerned the proposed abolition of bull-baiting. The speaker was the notorious Tory MP William Wyndham, who opposed virtually every one of the ten bills opposing bull-baiting—right up to its abolition in 1839 (p. 15).

24. See, for example, Simon Brooman and Debbie Legge, *Law Relating to Animals* (London: Cavendish, 1997), pp. 46–47, which discusses the pioneering Protection of Animals Act, 1911, in the United Kingdom, which was, in turn, a revision of the 1849 Cruelty to Animals Act. The 1911 act made it an offence to "cruelly beat, kick, ill-treat, over-drive, over-load, torture, infuriate or terrify any animal." It also broadly excluded wild animals, laboratory animals, and animals used for food. The 2006 UK Animal Welfare Bill amends the 1911 act to impose, inter alia, a "duty of care" on all who manage domestic animals and animals under human control, see http://www.opsi.gov.uk/ACTS/acts2006/pdf/ukpga_20060045_en.pdf.

25. Edward Carpenter et al., *Animals and Ethics: A Report of the Working Party Convened by Edward Carpenter* (London: Watkins, 1980), pp. 16–17. The working party included Dr. Michael Brambell, Professor Kenneth Carpenter, David Coffey, Ruth Harrison, Professor Sydney Jennings, and Professor W. H. Thorpe. These principles, which followed the Brambell Committee's recommendations (*Report of the Technical Committee to Enquire into the Welfare of Animals Kept under Intensive Livestock Husbandry Systems* [London: HMSO, 1965], cmnd. 2836), inspired the Five Freedoms that have been adopted as (sadly, only voluntary) welfare guidelines by the Department for Environment, Food and Rural Affairs (DEFRA) of the UK government. See DEFRA, "Food and drink—freedom foods," available at http://www.defra.gov.uk/foodrin/poultry/assurance.htm (last modified 8 August 2003), which explains the Five Freedoms and their voluntary nature.

26. Tom Regan, *The Case for Animal Rights* (London: Routledge and Kegan Paul, 1983) (hereafter Regan, *The Case for Animal Rights*), pp. 96–99.

27. See, for example, Richard D. North, *Fur and Freedom: In Defence of the Fur Trade* (London: Institute of Economic Affairs, 2000) (hereafter North, *Fur and Freedom*), p. 39, which argues that fur farming is no worse than regular animal farming.

28. "Farm Animal Welfare Council disapproves of mink and fox farming," press notice, FAWC, 4 April 1989.

29. Ibid., p. 1.

30. Letter from Professor C. R. W. Spedding, chair of the Farm Animal Welfare Council, to the parliamentary secretary, Ministry of Agriculture, Fisheries, and Food, 31 March 1989.

31. A. J. Nimon and D. M. Broom, "The welfare of farmed mink (*Mustela vison*) in relation to housing and management: a review," *Animal Welfare* 8, 1999, pp. 205, 222; see also C. M. Vinke, "Some comments on the review of Nimon and Broom on the welfare of farmed mink," *Animal Welfare* 10, 2001, p. 315 (questioning the relevance and basis for concluding that mink are not domesticated and therefore have the same needs as wild animals); and A. J. Nimon and D. M. Broom, "Response to Vinke's short communication: comments on mink needs and welfare indicators," *Animal Welfare* 10, 2001, p. 325.

32. A. J. Nimon and D. M. Broom, "The welfare of farmed foxes *Vulpes vulpes* and *Alopex lagopus* in relation to housing and management: a review," *Animal Welfare* 10, 2001, pp. 223, 241–42.

33. Scientific Committee on Animal Health and Animal Welfare, *The Welfare of Animals Kept for Fur Production* (European Commission: Health and Consumer Protection Directorate-General, 2001), pp. 185–86 (hereafter Scientific Committee on Animal Health, *The Welfare of Animals*), available at http://www.europa.eu.int/comm/food/animal/welfare/international/index_en.htm.

34. Scientific Committee on Animal Health, *The Welfare of Animals*, pp. 71, 84–88.

35. Ibid., p. 185.

36. Press release, Scientific Committee on Animal Health and Animal Welfare, "New report recommends improved conditions in fur farms," 19 December 2001.

37. See http://www.respectforanimals.co.uk/home.php/facts/more/fur_factory-farming (accessed 13 January 2007).

38. David DeGrazia, *Taking Animals Seriously: Mental Life and Moral Status* (Cambridge: Cambridge University Press, 1996), p. 284.

39. See, for example, Marc Bekoff and Carron A. Meaney (eds.), *Encyclopedia of Animal Rights and Animal Welfare* (Westport, Conn.: Greenwood, 1998), which comprises a broad range of ethical and philosophical positions urging reform of the status quo.

40. Immanuel Kant, *Metaphysics of Morals* [1797], trans. John Ladd (New York: Bobbs-Merrill, 1965) (hereafter Kant, *Metaphysics*), pp. 345–46; extract in Andrew Linzey and Paul Barry Clarke (eds.), *Animal Rights: A Historical Anthology* (New York: Columbia University Press, 2005) (hereafter Linzey and Clarke, *Animal Rights*), p. 79.

41. Kant, *Metaphysics*, pp. 345–46; Linzey and Clarke, *Animal Rights*, p. 79.

42. Ibid.

43. See Hilda Kean, *Animal Rights: Political and Social Change in Britain since 1800* (London: Reaktion, 1998) (hereafter Kean, *Animal Rights*), pp. 136, 143.

44. George Hendrik, *Henry Salt: Humanitarian Reformer and Man of Letters* (Chicago: University of Illinois Press, 1977), p. 193 (emphasis in original) (quoting a reprint of

Henry Salt's play *A Lover of Animals*, which was originally published in the *Vegetarian Review*, February 1895).

45. Kean, *Animal Rights*, pp. 56–57, describes the roles of these individuals in the animal protection movement.

46. Lord Erskine, "Second reading of the bill for preventing malicious and wanton cruelty to animals," *Hansard*, House of Lords, 15 May 1809, p. 277, available at http://www.animalrightshistory.org/ers_lord-erskine/1809-erskine-speech.htm, which discusses those two rationales. The author is grateful to Dr. Chien-hui Li, previously of Wolfson College, Cambridge, for this reference.

47. Frank R. Ascione and Phil Arkow (eds.), *Child Abuse, Domestic Violence, and Animal Abuse* (West Lafayette, Ind.: Purdue University Press, 1999), p. xvii; see also Phil Arkow, "Animal abuse, child abuse and domestic violence—compelling connections," *Guardian* (publication of the Women's Humane Society) 30, no. 1, Spring 1998; Arkow, "The relationships between animal abuse and other forms of family violence," *Family Violence and Sexual Assault Bulletin* 12, nos. 1–2, 1996; Howard Davidson, "On the horizon: what lawyers and judges should know about the link between child abuse and animal cruelty," *American Bar Association Child Law Practice*, 17, no. 4, June 1998; A. William Ritter, Jr., "The cycle of violence often begins with violence toward animals," *Prosecutor* 30, no. 31, January–February 1996; Jared Squires, "The link between animal cruelty and human violence: children caught in the middle," *Kentucky Children's Rights Journal* 8, no. 2, Winter 2000—all of which discuss the link between animal abuse and violence against women and children. The author is grateful to Phil Arkow for these references and for his pioneering work. See also Paul Wilson and Gareth Norris, "Relationship between criminal behavior and mental illness in young adults: conduct disorder, cruelty to animals and young adult serious violence," *Psychiatry, Psychology and Law* 10, no. 1, April 2003, which suggests that cruelty to animals, as one component of conduct disorder, is a significant indicator of subsequent anti-social behaviour. See also Andrew Linzey (ed.), *The Link between Animal Abuse and Human Violence* (forthcoming).

48. Market Opinion and Research International (MORI), "Poll on animal welfare," *Daily Telegraph*, 8 August 1995; cited and discussed in Andrew Linzey, *Animal Gospel: Christian Faith as if Animals Mattered* (Louisville, Ky.: Westminster John Knox, 1998), pp. 163–64.

49. See, for example, Regan, *The Case for Animal Rights*, pp. 286–87, discussing such a view.

50. That is the position of Peter Singer, for example. Although often associated with "animal rights," his position is wholly utilitarian. Peter Singer, *Practical Ethics* (Cambridge: Cambridge University Press, 1979), p. 58.

51. See Richard A. Posner, "Animal rights: legal, philosophical, and pragmatic perspectives," in Cass R. Sunstein and Martha Nussbaum (eds.), *Animal Rights: Current Debates and New Directions* (New York: Oxford University Press, 2004) (hereafter Sunstein and Nussbaum, *Animal Rights*), pp. 51, 59, which discusses Singer's approach.

52. Gary L. Francione, "Animals—property or persons?" in Sunstein and Nussbaum, *Animal Rights*, pp. 108, 115–16, which describes how hunting, fur production, and the testing of cosmetics on animals cause suffering that is ultimately unnecessary.

53. Morley, "Oral answers to questions," col. 76. It is perhaps worth adding that even those who argue against animal rights are sometimes equivocal about fur. Michael P. T. Leahy, for example, confesses that "[f]urs are a far tougher nut to justify unless one is thinking of primitive peoples who depend upon them for staying alive"; Leahy, *Against Liberation: Putting Animals in Perspective* (London: Routledge, 1994, rev. paperback ed.), p. 266.

54. North, *Fur and Freedom*, pp. 12, 18, 22–23.

55. Ibid., p. 23.

56. Ibid.

57. See, for example, Andrew Linzey and Dan Cohn-Sherbok, *After Noah: Animals and the Liberation of Theology* (New York: Continuum, 1997) (hereafter Linzey and Cohn-Sherbok, *After Noah*), pp. 35–59, 62–69, which examines Jewish and Christian limits on the use of animals and provides an account of the resources within the Jewish and Christian traditions for a positive view of animals; Neal Robinson (ed. and trans.), *The Sayings of Muhammad* (London: Duckworth, 1991) (hereafter Robinson, *The Sayings of Muhammad*), pp. 48–49, which discusses the sayings of the Prophet Muhammad on animals; and Richard C. Foltz, *Animals in Islamic Tradition and Muslim Cultures* (Oxford: One World, 2006).

58. Linzey and Cohn-Sherbok, *After Noah*, p. 30, explores the origin and meaning of this principle.

59. Elijah Judah Schochet, *Animal Life in Jewish Tradition: Attitudes and Relationships* (Tel Aviv: KTAV, 1984), p. 19; cited and discussed in Linzey and Cohn-Sherbok, *After Noah*, pp. 53–54.

60. Robinson, *The Sayings of Muhammad*, pp. 48–49.

61. Ibid., p. 48; Qur'anic verses 6.38 and 24.41.

62. Archbishop Donald Coggan, "Presidential message to the annual general meeting of the RSPCA," reprinted in Andrew Linzey, *Christianity and the Rights of Animals* (New York: Crossroad, 1987), appendix: "Church statements on animals 1956–1986."

63. Andrew Linzey (ed.), *Bishops Say No to Fur: Cruelty and Christian Conscience* (Nottingham: Lynx, 1992), foreword by Alwyn Rice Jones, archbishop of Wales.

64. Arthur Broome, an Anglican priest, called the first meeting to inaugurate the society and also wrote the first prospectus. Andrew Linzey, *Animal Theology* (London: SCM, and Chicago: University of Illinois Press, 1994), pp. 19, 36. In 1832, the society issued a declaration that stated, "the proceedings of this Society are entirely based on the Christian Faith and on Christian Principles"; *RSPCA Minute Book*, no. 1, pp. 38, 40–41, discussed in Turner, *Reckoning with the Beast*, pp. 15, 148. The author is grateful to Olive Martyn, the librarian of the RSPCA, for this reference. Broome's work was immensely sacrificial. He gave up his London church to work full time (unpaid) for the society as its first secretary and ended up in prison because of the society's debts. Radford, *Animal Law in Britain*, p. 42; see also Turner, *Reckoning with the Beast*, p. 15 (for the lines from the prospectus, information about Broome, and discussion of the complex relationship between the two men and the society).

65. Editorial, *The Times*, 25 April 1800; cited and discussed in A. W. Moss, *The Valiant Crusade: The History of the R.S.P.C.A.* (London: Cassell, 1961) (hereafter Moss, *The Valiant Crusade*), p. 14.

66. Robert Peel, "Speech: on Martin's bill," House of Commons, 11 February 1824, *Hansard*, cols. 131–32 (hereafter Peel, "Speech: on Martin's bill"). Richard Martin also attempted to pass several animal welfare bills against, inter alia, bull-baiting and dog-fighting in the 1820s; see Moss, *The Valiant Crusade*, pp. 17–18.

67. Peel, "Speech: on Martin's bill," cols. 131–32.

68. See, for example, "Public opinion," in Seymour Martin Lipset (ed.), *The Encyclopedia of Democracy* (New York: Congressional Quarterly, 1995), pp. 1012, 1027–38, on how public opinion is an important influence on politics and is an important means of evaluating the effectiveness of a democracy.

69. Address by Commissioner David Byrne to the Conference of Ethics and Animal Welfare in Stockholm, 29 May 2001.

70. Ibid.; my emphasis.

71. Ibid.; my emphasis.

72. Ibid.

73. Ibid.

74. Andrew Hunter, "Oral answers to questions: fur farming (prohibition) bill," *Hansard*, col. 64, 15 May 2000, available at http://www.publications.parliament.uk/pa/cm199900/cmhansrd/vo000515/debindx/00515-x.htm. The comment was in response to Elliot Morley's remarks about morality.

75. For an insightful discussion, see Sunstein, "Introduction: what are animal rights?" in Sunstein and Nussbaum, *Animal Rights*, pp. 3, 8, which describes how the balancing of human and animal interests hinges on the issue of values.

76. See, for example, Steven M. Wise, "Animal rights, one step at a time," in Sunstein and Nussbaum, *Animal Rights*, pp. 19, 21–22, which discusses popular support for slavery in British history and the similarities to animal rights.

77. See Sunstein, "Introduction," in Sunstein and Nussbaum, *Animal Rights*, p. 8.

78. Market Opinion and Research International, "Attitudes towards fur," available at http://www.mori.com/polls/1997/fur.shtml (accessed 16 March 2006).

79. See, for example, Lynne L. Dallas, *Law and Public Policy: A Socioeconomic Approach* (New York: Carolina Academic, 2005), p. 193, which discusses how law reflects changes in public perception.

CHAPTER 5

1. All of the figures provided here are derived from the Scientific Opinion of the Panel on Animal Health and Welfare on a request from the Commission on the Animal Welfare Aspects of the killing and skinning of seals, *The EFSA Journal* (2007) 610, 1–123. Available at: http://www.efsa.europa.eu/EFSA/efsa_locale-1178620753812_1178671319178.htm. I am grateful to Dr David Lavigne for this reference.

2. See http://advocatesforanimals.com/index.php/active-campaigns/look-out-for-seals.html.

3. The official source International Council for the Exploration of the Sea (ICES/ NAFD) is provided in www.ifaw.org/ifaw/dimages/custom/2_Publications/Seals/ sealsandsealing2005.pdf. See appendix 1, "Quotas and landed catches of harp seals in Canada," p. 16. I refer to "landed catches" because they are what the government reports after the hunt, i.e., the number of animals recorded as landed on sealing vessels or at the dockside—a count of pelts accumulated. But, of course, more animals are killed than are landed. Some are clubbed or shot and not recovered ("struck and lost") and are therefore never landed. Scientists attempt to estimate the total kill by correcting landed catch statistics by accounting for animals struck and lost. They also attempt to account for seals taken incidentally in, for example, commercial fisheries. The total kill figures are used in population models to estimate local population size, replacement yields, and the like. So, when referring to the numbers "killed" in the hunt, one needs to use the estimated kill and not the landed catch statistics, which underestimate the numbers of animals actually killed. I am obliged to Dr. David Lavigne for this important qualification, which reinforces concern about the huge total number of kills as a result of the hunt.

4. "Canada's seal hunt: beyond the rhetoric," commentary by the minister of fisheries and oceans, Canada, 17 March 2005, pp. 1–2; see also www.dfo-mpo.gc.ca/media/ statem/2005/20050317_e.htm (accessed 13 May 2005) (hereafter Minister's Statement).

5. Minister's Statement.

6. Section 28 of the Marine Mammal Regulations (hereafter MMRs); my emphasis. See http://laws.justice.gc.ca/en/F-14/SOR-93-56/118970.html#rid-119056. These are the legal weapons. In practice, illegal weapons are also used. These include gaffs (long wooden poles with boathooks on the ends), handmade hakapiks that are not the regulation size and weight, and shotguns and rifles of inadequate gauge. All of this has been documented in video evidence and is found in direct testimony from sealers obtained through freedom of information laws in Canada; see http://www.gan.ca/ campaigns/seal+hunt/factsheets/sealers+testimony.en.html (accessed 13 May 2005).

7. R. L. Burdon, J. Gripper, J. A. Longair, I. Robinson, and D. Ruehlmann, *Veterinary Report, Canadian Commercial Seal Hunt, Prince Edward Island, March 2001*; for classifications of consciousness, see p. 7; for observations from video footage, see p. 9; and for conclusion, see pp. 1, 13; see also http://www.ifaw.org/ifaw/dfiles/file_95.pdf (accessed 16 May 2005), pp. 1–36 (hereafter Burdon Report).

8. See E. Simpson, "Seal hunting in the Gulf of St. Lawrence," *Nature* 214, 1967, p. 1274; and W. J. Jordan, "The killing of the harp seal pups, 1978," report following an investigation, 7–12 March 1978, in the Magdalen Islands during the annual seal hunt (London: RSPCA, April 1978), see especially pp. 3–7.

9. Pierre-Yves Daoust, A. Crook, T. K. Bollinger, K. G. Cambell, and J. Wong, "Animal welfare and the harp seal hunt in Atlantic Canada," *Canadian Veterinary Journal* 43, no. 9, September 2002, pp. 687–94; see also http://www.pubmedcentral.nih.gov/ articlerender.fcgi?tool=pmcentrez&artid=339547, pp. 1–13 (accessed 13 May 2005) (hereafter Daoust Report). The reference is to the abstract, which is p. 687 in the original, and p. 1 on the Internet. Subsequent page references are to the Internet version.

10. David M. Lavigne, "Canada's commercial seal hunt is not 'acceptably humane'" (hereafter Lavigne's Analysis), IFAW, January 2005, p. 1; my emphasis.

11. Daoust Report, p. 8; Lavigne's Analysis, p. 2.

12. Lavigne's Analysis, p. 2.

13. Daoust Report, p. 10; my emphasis.

14. Minister's Statement, p. 2; my emphasis.

15. Ibid.; see also Lavigne's Analysis, p. 1.

16. Daoust Report, p. 2.

17. As shown by the correspondence between the High North Alliance and the UK commissioner to the International Whaling Commission, concerning the UK position on humane killing standards, 21 March 1995, available at http://www.highnorth. no/Library/Ethics/th-uk-po.htm. The only exception allowed to this rule is religious slaughter, which has been opposed by the government's Farm Animal Welfare Council for this reason; see note 29 below.

18. Burdon Report, p. 4.

19. Ibid.; my emphasis.

20. Ibid., p. 5.

21. Daoust Report, p. 6; my emphasis.

22. Ibid., p. 7.

23. Burdon Report, p. 1.

24. Ibid.

25. Minister's Statement, pp. 1–2.

26. Daoust Report, p. 10.

27. Temple Grandin, "Welfare of cattle during slaughter and the prevention of non-ambulatory (downer) cattle," *Journal of the American Veterinary Association* 219, 2001, pp. 1377–82.

28. See Karen Davis, "Birds used in food production," in Andrew Linzey (ed.), *Encyclopaedia of Global Concern for Animals*, forthcoming.

29. *Report on the Welfare of Farmed Animals at Slaughter or Killing, Part 1: Red Meat Animals* (London: FAWC, June 2003) (hereafter FAWC *Report*), especially pp. 54–63.

30. Ian Robinson cited at http://www.ifaw.org/ifaw/general/default.aspx?oid=82078 (accessed 17 May 2005).

31. FAWC *Report*, par. 8, p. 2.

32. Burdon Report, p. 8.

33. A. H. Malouf, *Seals and Sealing in Canada: Report of the Royal Commission*, 3 vols. (Ottawa: Supply and Services Canada, 1987) (hereafter *Royal Commission*), vol. 1, recommendation 2, p. 40.

34. Fisheries and Aquaculture Management, Department of Fisheries and Oceans, Canada, "Atlantic Canada seal hunt: myths and realities," available at www.dfo-mpo.gc.ca/seal-phoque/myth_e.htm (accessed 13 May 2005), pp. 1–2 (hereafter "Myths and realities").

35. *Royal Commission*, p. 38.

36. These data are compiled from official kill reports from Canada's Department of Fisheries and Oceans. Source for the 1971 quota is Department of Fisheries and

Oceans, *The Atlantic Seal Hunt: A Canadian Perspective*, pp. 1–24. In 2006, 345,344 kills were of seals one year or less out of a total catch of 354,344, see Sheryl Fink, *Seals and Sealing 2007* (Guelph: ON, Canada: International Fund for Animal Welfare), Appendix II, p. 16.

37. Burdon Report, p. 1.
38. MMRs; my emphasis.
39. *Guardian* (Charlottetown), 20 January 2003, p. A4.
40. Charles Craguel, Alice Crook, Pierre-Yves Daoust, J. Lawrence Dunn, Stéphane Lair, Alan Longair, Joost Philippa, Andrew Routh, and Alison Tuttle, *A Report of the Independent Veterinarians' Working Group on the Canadian Harp Seal Hunt: Improving Humane Practice in the Canadian Harp Seal Hunt* (prepared by B. L. Smith Groupwork, August 2005), p. 2. There are some welcome recommendations in the report, notably that "a seal should not be shot in the water, or in any circumstances when it is possible the carcass cannot be recovered" (p. 2), which should logically exclude all shooting from boats. Also, the recommendation that "confirmation of irreversible loss of consciousness or death should be done by checking by palpation that the skull is crushed rather than checking the absence of corneal (blink) reflex" (p. 2) is probably sound given the widespread ignorance of the importance of the other test. But there are a number of disquieting aspects to the report. First, the group met with sealers, industry representatives, government managers, and scientists for a day and then spent two days "in camera" to formulate their recommendations (p. 2). We are told that four representatives of the sealing industry "made presentations on the industry, past, present, and future, as well as hunting methods," and that "information was provided about the social and economic importance of the seal hunt to coastal communities" (p. 6). The group apparently viewed "video clips" from IFAW, but met no animal welfare professionals, scientists, or humane officials nor heard the detailed moral critique that can be made of sealing. This does not suggest an even-handed approach to the issue. Second, the group concluded, "if carried [out] by a trained and skilled individual, a three-step method of stunning, checking, and bleeding seals can result in rapid, irreversible loss of consciousness, and death, and thus can be a humane process" (p. 2). The word "if" is doing a lot of work in this sentence. It is precisely because the "ifs" cannot be relied upon that the process cannot be claimed as "humane." Moreover, the standard definition of humane killing has been revised here; it departs from the FAWC definition, mandated by the British government, which requires "immediate unconsciousness and insensibility, or an induction to a period of unconsciousness without distress and [the] guarantee of non-recovery from this process until death ensues" (see pp. 126–27 of this book). There is an obvious difference between a "rapid" and "instantaneous" unconsciousness. It is difficult to avoid the conclusion that the group revised the definition for its own ends. Third, the group claims that "perception of the seal hunt seems to be based largely on emotion" (p. 5), which suggests that the group does not know the difference between emotional and ethical considerations. Again: "Campaigns and rhetoric that play to emotion at the expense of understanding and communication of factual information will neither increase the use of humane methods nor reduce animal suffering" (p. 6), which (again) conveniently overlooks the ethical issue and presents one side of the argument in a pejorative way. All

becomes clear, however, when we reach the end of the paragraph: "It is not the Group's intent to enter into the discussion about whether or not there should be a hunt" (p. 6)— in other words, it doesn't intend to actually address the central issue about moral justifiability. Ethicists have learned to be wary of reports that make prescriptions while not actually or adequately addressing the moral issue.

41. Ibid., p. 8.
42. Ibid., p. 10.
43. Ibid., p. 11.
44. Ibid., p. 14.
45. Ibid.
46. Ibid., p. 15.
47. Ibid., p. 16.
48. Ibid., p. 10; my emphasis.
49. Ibid.
50. Ibid.
51. Ibid., p. 2; my emphasis. The confusion is evident from the wording of the report: the "summary" says that bleeding is "an important element" (p. 3), whereas it is later described as "essential" (p. 7).
52. The *2005 Seal Hunt Footage*, 23 minutes, was compiled and distributed by the HSUS. The video evidence is important because without it, it is possible to entertain a sanitised version of the hunt in which scrupulous care is taken to avoid suffering. In fact, the 2005 footage shows that, even while being filmed, the sealers adopted a remarkably cavalier attitude both to the suffering of the seals and to the legal regulations.
53. Mary Richardson, "The horror of the seal hunt," *National Post*, 9 June 2005, p. A20.
54. David M. Lavigne, Victor B. Scheffer, and Stephen R. Kellert, "The evolution of North American attitudes toward marine mammals," in J. R. Twiss, Jr., and R. R. Reeves (eds.), *Conservation and Management of Marine Mammals* (Washington, D.C.: Smithsonian Institution Press, 1999) (hereafter Lavigne et al., "Evolution of North American attitudes"), p. 37. See also D. M. Lavigne, "Canada's leghold leg-pull," guest editorial, *BBC Wildlife*, March 1989, p. 133, and Lavigne, "Rights and wrongs: should indigenous peoples have different 'rights' to hunt wildlife, including endangered species, and to trade in wildlife products?" "Taking Issue," *BBC Wildlife*, November 1997, pp. 36–37, 40.
55. Lavigne et al., "Evolution of North American attitudes," p. 37.
56. Fisheries and Aquaculture Management, Department of Fisheries and Oceans, Canada, "Frequently asked questions about Canada's seal hunt," available at www.dfo-mpo.gc.ca/seal-phoque/faq_e.htm (accessed 13 May 2005), p. 2 (hereafter FAQ).
57. "Defence of the fur trade," a discussion paper prepared by the Department of External Affairs, Canada, May 1985, p. 9. I am grateful to Lavigne for this reference. See also the discussion in Andrew Linzey, *Animal Gospel* (Louisville, Ky.: Westminster John Knox, 1998), pp. 116–22.
58. The figure is arrived at by the following calculations. The Canadian government states in the Atlantic Seal Hunt 2003–2005 Management Plan, section 6.6.1 (Equitable Allocation):

DFO continues to be supportive of Aboriginal efforts to hunt seals commercially. This plan provides an allocation for Labrador sealers to hunt harp seals commercially. There is also an allocation for harp seals for the Canadian Arctic, as sealing for this species has been limited in recent years.

According to the official DFO kill report in 2005, no harp seals were taken in the Arctic, while 7,594 were killed in Labrador. Seal kill reports are not recorded by ethnicity of the sealers. Thus, to determine how many seals were killed by aboriginal people in Canada's commercial seal hunt, we have had to make some demographic assumptions. Approximately one-third of the population of Labrador is of aboriginal ethnicity. In the absence of data from the DFO, it is reasonable to assume that one-third of commercial sealers operating in the Labrador area are aboriginal and also that one-third of the seals killed in Labrador are taken by aboriginal sealers. If these assumptions are correct, of the 7,594 seals killed in 2005 in the Labrador quota, 2,531 would have been killed by aboriginal sealers. This would account for eight-tenths of 1% of the total 2005 commercial kill of harp seals of 317,672. I am grateful to Rebecca Aldworth for this information.

59. FAQ, p. 5.
60. Landed fishery values, 1998–2003, are from Newfoundland's Department of Fisheries and Aquaculture. Newfoundland's inflation data are from the government of Newfoundland; see www.economics.gov.nf.ca/mnInflation.asp (accessed 13 May 2005).
61. In fact, government officials were still making the same claim as late as 1996. See, for example, "Government scientists say seals eat vast amounts of cod and are hampering their recovery," in Deborah Mackenzie, "Seals to the slaughter," *New Scientist*, 16 March 1996, p. 36.
62. FAQ, p. 6; my emphasis.
63. "Myths and realities," p. 3; my emphasis. The Burdon Report also makes a similar point, p. 12.
64. See, for example, research by Lynne U. Sneddon, Victor A. Braithwaite, and Michael J. Gentle, "Do fish have nociceptors: evidence for the evolution of a vertebrate sensory system," *Biological Sciences* 270, no. 1520, June 2003; and previous work by Verheijen at the University of Utrecht, which is discussed by John Webster, *Animal Welfare: A Cool Look at Eden* (Oxford: Blackwell, 1994), p. 224.
65. "Myths and realities," p. 4.
66. The argument from "tradition" is not, properly speaking, an ethical argument at all, just an appeal to the status quo. In England, we have become only too familiar with it as a defence of hunting with hounds, but its speciousness has been finally exposed and hunting is now (thankfully) banned.
67. See FAQ, p. 1, which refers to a "1999 peer-reviewed study" which came to this figure, but no further information is given. The figure, unsurprisingly, is disputed. For the federal government's view, see www.dfo-mpo.gc.ca, and for management reports, http://www.dfo-mpo.gc.ca/seal-phoque/report-rapport_e.htm. For the *Report of the Eminent Panel on Seal Management* (which included at least one person involved in the seal industry), see www.dfo-mpo.gc.ca/seal-phoque/reports-rapports/expert/repsm-rgegp_e.htm, and for contrary views, see the critique by Greenpeace at www.greeenpeace.org/raw/content/international/press/reports/canadian-seal-hunt-

no-managem.pdf and the Web site of the International Marine Mammal Association at www.imma.org (all accessed 16 May 2005).

68. According to the Canadian government, "All subsidies ceased in 2001"; "Myths and realities," p. 4.

69. See, for example, "DFO continues to be supportive of Aboriginal efforts to hunt seals commercially," *Royal Commission,* p. 20, par. 6.6.1.

70. FAQ, p. 2.

71. Minister's Statement, p. 2.

72. I make the case in my "Other eyes and other worlds," the introduction to the *Encyclopaedia of Global Concern for Animals,* forthcoming, which is a guide to international animal protection. What became clear in editing the *Encyclopaedia* was that countries which are guilty of disrespecting human rights mostly disrespect animal rights as well.

73. My emphasis. The full text of the treaty can be found at http://www.europarl.eu.int/topics/treaty/section2_en.htm#chap8 (accessed 20 May 2005).

74. The view of the Eurogroup for Animal Welfare can be found at http://www.eurocbc.org/page673.html; see also its own Web site, http://www.eurogroupanimalwelfare.org.

75. See chap. 4, in this volume.

76. See the news release of the HSUS, available at http://www.hsus.org/about_us/humane_society_international_hsi/hsi_europe/belgium_joins_the_ranks_of_eu_countries_to_ban_dog_and_cat_fur.html. In addition, there has been a long history of (unsuccessful) British attempts to restrict or ban the import of seal products. In 1980, a trade order was promulgated to require the labelling of all sealskin imports into the United Kingdom, but it sadly failed to make progress; see Trade Descriptions (Sealskin Goods) (Information) Order, 1980, no. 1150. In 2003, the minister for trade and investment was pressed to take action, but maintained, "The view of the WTO, which has to make a decision unanimously, is that it is not prepared to allow animal welfare issues to be a criterion for stopping trade in particular kinds of products"; *Hansard,* 4 November 2003, col. 222WH. As we show, there are grounds for disputing that view, since some animal welfare issues properly come under the heading of moral exceptions. The claim that "the EU is attempting to impose its ethical views on other countries" (ibid.) is also untenable. See also the question to the secretary of state for foreign and commonwealth affairs about making known British opposition to the seal hunt, in *Hansard,* 24 January 2005, col. 151W. Since Belgium has taken the lead, it is now appropriate for other EU member states, including the United Kingdom, to follow, especially since the principle about morality and animal welfare issues has already been conceded. As we have seen, five EU member states (Belgium, France, Italy, Greece, and Denmark) have already outlawed trade in dog and cat fur.

77. See, for example, the concerns expressed by the RSPCA at http://www.rspca.org.uk/servlet/ContentServer?pagename=RSPCA/Campaigns/WTOrules (accessed 20 January 2007); also see the excellent letter from Caroline Lucas, MEP for South East England, to Commissioner Mariann Fischer Boel on the WTO and animal welfare, available at http:www.carolinelucasmep.org.uk/interests/pdf/Boel_AnimalsWTO_Qn_Jun05.pdf (accessed 20 January 2007).

78. Henry George, *Protection or Free Trade* [1886] (New York: Schalkenbach Foundation, 1991), p. 286; cited and discussed in Steve Charnovitz, "The moral exception in trade policy," *Virginia Journal of International Law* 38, no. 689, Summer 1998, pp. 21–22, also available at www.worldtradelaw.net/articles/charnovitzmoral.pdf (accessed 13 May 2005) (hereafter Charnovitz, "The moral exception"). I am indebted to Charnovitz for his insightful and important paper on which I have drawn freely. See also Charnovitz, "GATT and the environment: examining the issues," *International Environmental Affairs* 4, no. 3, 1991, pp. 203–33, available at www.ciesin.org/docs/008-061/008-061.html. There is a useful discussion for and against embargoes at http://darwin.bio.uci.edu/~sustain/issueguides/Embargoes. On the continuing debate about the responsibilities of multinationals, see, for example, John B. Cobb, Jr., "Can corporations assume responsibility for the environment?" available at http://www.religion-online.org/showarticle.asp?title=261 (all accessed 13 May 2005).

79. Charnovitz, "The moral exception," p. 21.

80. Richard N. Cooper, *Environment and Resource Policies for the World Economy* (New York: Brookings Institute, 1994), p. 30, cited in Charnovitz, "The moral exception," p. 21.

81. Charnovitz, "The moral exception," p. 22.

82. Ibid., p. 24.

83. See these considerations discussed in chap. 1, pp. 34–36.

84. Lucia Ames Mead, *Law or War* [1928] (New York: Garland, 1971), p. 86, cited as the concluding line of Charnovitz, "The moral exception," p. 28. Charnovitz also rightly refers to Kant's statement that "[t]he peoples of the earth have thus entered in varying degrees into a universal community, and it has developed to the point where a violation of rights in one part of the world is felt everywhere"; Immanuel Kant, "Perpetual peace: a philosophical sketch," in Hans Reiss (ed.), *Kant's Political Writings* (Cambridge: Cambridge University Press, 1979), pars. 107–8, p. 93, and in Charnovitz, "The moral exception," pp. 48–49. But Kant's point, if valid, can also be extended to include animals. Animals also form part of the "universal community—if not through choice then certainly by *our* choice because we have adopted them into our moral universe. Animals have thus acquired moral significance because of the ways humans relate to them and treat them. We might say, then, that "the peoples of the earth have thus entered in varying degrees into a universal community, of which animals form a part, and it has developed to such a point where a violation of rights—to either humans or animals—in one part of the world is felt everywhere." Put more simply, the abuse of animals anywhere, like the abuse of humans, ought to concern us all everywhere.

85. Polling by the Angus Reid Group in 1997 (now operated by Ipsos Canada) showed that only four in ten (39%) of Canadians support the seal hunt, see http://www.ipsos-na.com/news/pressrelease.cfm?id=3889. The Canadian government says that "results of the [2000] survey indicate that, after being presented with arguments for and against the hunt, 53% of Canadians support the seal hunt"; *Royal Commission*, p. 20, par. 6.5.4. But the "arguments for" invariably include the claim that sealing is "humane"—which is precisely what cannot be assumed.

86. All figures from DFO sources, reproduced in "Appendix II, Allowable catches and reported kills of harp seals in Canada," Sheryl Fink, *Seals and Sealing in Canada 2007*

(Guelph: ON, Canada: IFAW, 2007), p. 16. I am grateful to Dr. David Lavigne for this reference.

Chapter 6

1. Peter Singer, *Animal Liberation: A New Ethics for Our Treatment of Animals* (London: Jonathan Cape, 1976); Andrew Linzey, *Animal Rights: A Christian Assessment* (London: SCM, 1976).
2. See pp. 105–6.
3. Lord Shaftesbury, letter, 30 April 1881, cited and discussed in Andrew Linzey, *Animal Theology* (London: SCM, and Chicago: University of Illinois Press, 1994), pp. 36–37.
4. Peter Singer, "Killing babies isn't always wrong," *Spectator*, 16 September 1995, p. 22. In this article, Singer summarises his view, which is developed at length in his *Rethinking Life and Death: The Collapse of Our Traditional Ethics* (Oxford: Oxford University Press, 1994) (hereafter *Rethinking Life and Death*). In context, Singer is contrasting his view with Pope John Paul II's encyclical *Evangelium Vitae* (London: Catholic Truth Society, 1995), which defends the sacredness of all innocent human life and which attempts to provide a consistent ethic of life from a Catholic perspective. For a discussion from a Catholic viewpoint sympathetic to animals, based on the papal encyclical, see John Berkman, "Is the consistent ethic of life consistent without a concern for animals?" in Andrew Linzey and Dorothy Yamamoto (eds.), *Animals on the Agenda: Questions about Animals for Theology and Ethics* (London: SCM, and Chicago: University of Illinois Press, 1998), pp. 237–47.
5. Singer, "Killing babies," p. 20.
6. Ibid., p. 22.
7. Singer, "Sanctity of life or quality of life?" *Pediatrics* 72, July 1983, pp. 128–29; cited and discussed in Singer, *Rethinking Life and Death*, p. 201; emphasis added.
8. The link with serial murder, for example, is now so strong that Jack Levin and Arnold Arluke conclude that there is a predictive link with those who torture cats and dogs in a hands-on manner; see "Reducing the link's false positive problem" and other important contributions in Andrew Linzey (ed.), *The Link between Animal Abuse and Human Violence* (Brighton: Sussex Academic Press, forthcoming).
9. Linzey, *Animal Theology*, p. 38; see pp. 28–44 for my earlier critique of Singer.
10. I owe this important distinction to Tom Regan. See his *The Case for Animal Rights* (London: Routledge and Kegan Paul, 1983).
11. Singer, *Practical Ethics* (Cambridge: Cambridge University Press, 1979), p. 58.
12. Anthony Flew, "Torture: could the ends justify the means?" *Crucible* (journal of the Board for Social Responsibility of the Church of England), January 1974; I have also discussed Flew's views in Linzey, *Animal Rights*, pp. 55–57.
13. Flew, "Torture," p. 22.
14. Ibid., p. 23.
15. See pp. 57–70.
16. G. R. Dunstan, *The Artifice of Ethics* (London: SCM, 1974), p. 4.

17. Stanley Godlovitch, Roslind Godlovitch, and John Harris (eds.), *Animals, Men and Morals: An Enquiry into the Maltreatment of Non-Humans* (London: Gollancz, 1971).

18. Singer, *Animal Liberation*, p. xv.

19. R. Godlovitch, "Animals and morals," in Godlovitch et al., *Animals, Men and Morals*, p. 168; emphasis in original.

20. For my defence of assisted dying, see Andrew Linzey, "Assisted dying: a critique of the theological objections," *Bulletin of Medical Ethics*, no. 214, April–May 2006, pp. 21–25.

21. Karl Barth, *Church Dogmatics*, ed. G. W. Bromiley and T. F. Torrance (Edinburgh: Clark, 1961), vol. 2, no. 4, p. 354. Interestingly, among theologians, Barth devotes more space to the status of animals than any other, and his discussion of killing animals, while flawed, is the most extensive. See Andrew Linzey, "The neglected creature: the doctrine of the non-human and its relationship with the human in the thought of Karl Barth," unpublished Ph.D. diss., University of London, 1986.

22. See Linzey, *Christianity and the Rights of Animals* (London: SPCK, and New York: Crossroad, 1987), especially chap. 5; and, more recently, *Animal Theology*, chap. 1.

23. Linzey, "Beyond caricature," preface to Andrew Linzey and Paul Barry Clarke (eds.), *Animal Rights: A Historical Anthology* (New York: Columbia University Press, 2004), pp. xxviii–xxix.

24. Linzey, *Christianity and the Rights of Animals*, chap. 5, "The theos-rights of animals."

25. Ibid., p. 97.

26. See, for example, *Review of the Cost-Benefit Assessment in the Use of Animals in Research* (London: Animal Procedures Committee, 2003), which attempts to explain in elaborate detail how much "cost" (i.e., harm) can be inflicted on animals in relation to putative "benefits." The Animal Procedures Committee is the UK government's advisory committee on animal experiments.

27. See "Does animal abuse really benefit us?" in Andrew Linzey (ed.), *The Link between Animal Abuse and Human Violence* (forthcoming).

28. See, for example, "Waterboarding is torture," available at http://www.americanprogress.org/issues/2008/02/waterboarding_pulse.html; and the commendable Web site of the National Religious Campaign against Torture: http://www.nrcat.org/index.php (both accessed 8 September 2008).

29. The line is borrowed from John Austin Baker, *The Foolishness of God* (London: Darton, Longman and Todd, 1970), p. 406; see also my *Animal Gospel: Christian Faith as if Animals Mattered* (Louisville, Ky.: Westminster John Knox, 2000), p. 47.

30. Jürgen Moltmann, *The Crucified God* (London: SCM, 1974), p. 277.

31. Jürgen Moltmann, *The Church in the Power of the Spirit*, 2nd ed. (London: SCM, 1992), p. 60. This line and the one sourced in note 30 above are cited and discussed in the impressive work of Paul S. Fiddes, *The Creative Suffering of God* (Oxford: Clarendon, 1988), pp. 4, 85. They also form part of my meditative liturgy, "A vigil for all suffering creatures," in Andrew Linzey, *Animal Rites: Liturgies of Animal Care* (London: SCM, and Cleveland, Ohio: Pilgrim, 1999), pp. 91–100.

32. Stephen R. L. Clark, *The Moral Status of Animals* (Oxford: Clarendon, 1977), p. 182.

INDEX

abortion, 153–4
adultism, 155
aloga zôa, 18
American Academy of Pediatrics, 153
American Psychiatric Association, 106
Amsterdam Treaty; protocol on animal
    welfare, 140–1, 146, 149
Animal Care Review Board (Ontario), 133
Animal Liberation, 152, 158
Animal Machines, 56
animals (*see also* cruelty to animals, suf-
    fering of animals)
  behavioural needs of, 100–1
  captivity of, 17, 106
  consciousness of, 53–5
  control of, 88–93
  in courses in higher education, 67–8,
    72
  definition of, 10
  as devoid of the divine image, 12, 28–9,
    41, 173n
  gastrocentric view of, 56
  as God's creatures, 108–9
  intrinsic value of, 56, 71, 93, 109, 137–8,
    145–6
  as linguistically deficient, 11, 18–22, 41,
    45
  linguistic denigration of, 44–5, 70, and
    their advocates, 48, 70
  moral innocence of, 23, 35, 42, 113, 159
  as naturally slaves, 11–5, 40
  as non-persons, 26–7, 172n
  as non-rational beings, 11, 16–8, 41
  as not moral agents, 11, 22–5, 41
  requiring the protection of law, 105–6,
    109–110, 183–4n
  rights of, 160–2, 167, 175n

as soulless, 12, 25–7, 41, 45–6
as a special moral case, 36–7, 42, 103–4,
    113, *see* Conclusion passim.
unable to give or withhold consent,
    20–22, 34, 42, 113
unable to represent their own
    interests, 35, 42, 113
as vulnerable and defenceless, 35–6, 42,
    103–4, 113
welfare, definition of, 80
Animal Rights: A Christian Assessment,
    152
Animals, Men and Morals, 158
anthropomorphism, 47, 51–3, 71
Aquinas, St Thomas, 80
  on animals naturally subject, 12–5, 14–5
  on animal souls, 25, 172n
  on cruelty, 170n
  functionalist teleology of, 12–5, 29
  on dominion, 169n
  on killing animals, 13
Argentina, fur production in, 97
Aristotle: 80
  functionalist teleology of, 12–5
  influence on Aquinas, 25
  intellectual hierarchy in, 12–3
Arkow, Phil, 105
Ascione, Frank R., 105
Atlantic Veterinary College, 118
Australia, hunting with dogs in, 75
Austria, regulations on fur farming, 99,
    113, 182n
Augustine, St, 16

Badham, Paul, 25–7, 172n
Baltic States, The, fur production in, 97–8

Banks, Tony, 77
Barth, Karl, 28, 159, 197n
behaviourism, 46–7, 49, 70
Belarus, fur production in, 97
bear-baiting, 66, 110
Belgium
    ban on fur products, 141, 142,
        147, 194n
    hunting with dogs in, 75
Benjamin, Walter, 68
Bentham, Jeremy, 62, 80, 86
Berkeley, George, 80
Birkbeck College, London, 69
Blair, Tony 77
Blue Cross, 45
Book of Common Prayer, 44
Bovine Spongiform Encephalopathy
    (BSE), 69
British Fur Trade Association, 98
Broom, D. M., 102, 185n
Broome, Arthur, 109, 187n
Brunner, Emile, 28
bull-baiting, 66, 94, 100, 109
bull-fighting, 68
Burdon Report on sealing, 117–9, 121–2,
    124–5, 127, 129–31
Burns, Lord, 51
Burns Report, 4, 51, 77–96
Buxton, Fowell, 105
Byrne, David, 110–11

Canada (see also Department of Fisheries
    and Oceans (DFO), Marine
    Mammal; Regulations (MMRs),
    Royal Commission on Seals and
    Sealing, sealing)
    commercial sealing in, see ch. 5
        passim
    estimates of seals killed, 115–6, 155
    fur production in, 97–8, 113
    government defence of sealing, 5,
        116–7, 139–141, 128, 130, 135, 136–7,
        139–41, 146, 147–9
    humaneness of seal hunt, 117–127,
        142, 147–9
    hunting with dogs, 75
    killing of seal pups, 127–9, 148
    regulation of hunt, 129–134, 148
    sealing for survival, 134–6, 148

seals as economic commodities, 136–9,
    148
trade embargoes on seal products,
    141–4, 149
Canadian Veterinary Medical
    Association (CMVA), 117, 120
Cambridge, 46, 102
Carruthers, Peter, 53–5
Cartesianism, 45–6, 49, 53, 55, 70
Charnovitz, Steve, 142–4, 195n
Child Abuse, Domestic Violence and
    Animal Abuse, 105, 186n
children
    with animals as special cases 36–7, see
        Conclusion passim
    child labour, 58, 177n
    cruelty to, 57–8
    commonality of ethical concern with
        animals, 154–5, 165–6
    common vulnerability with animals,
        35–6, 40
    and infants as a test case, 30–4
    moral status of, 5
    suffering of, 26–7
    UN Convention on the Rights of the
        Child, 32, 58, 177n
China
    control of Internet, 65
    fur production in, 97–8, 113, 155
    methods of killing of fur bearing ani-
        mals, 98, 182n
Chomsky, Noam
    analysis by, 4, 44, 72
    on Indian gravestone inscription,
        20–1
    on the propaganda system, 59, 63–5
    on vegetarianism and animal rights,
        177n
Christianity, see Christology and theology
Christology
    and Christ-like suffering of animals,
        38–40, 42, 164
    and reinterpretation of human power,
        15, 29
    sensitivity to the Crucified should
        sensitise us to all innocent suffering,
        42, 164
circuses, 68, 106, 112
Clark, Gillian, 16, 18

Clark, Stephen R. L., 165
Clines, David A., 28–9
cock-fighting, 66
Coggan, Donald, 108
conservation, 68, 178n
consequentialism (*see also* utilitarianism), 62, 156–8
consumer choice, 66–7, 70, 72
Convention on International Trade in Endangered Species, 134
Cooper, Anthony Ashley (Lord Shaftesbury), 105, 152
Cooper, Richard N., 142
Countryside Alliance, 85
Croatia, Animal Protection Act of, 99, 113
cruel sports (*see also* hunting and coursing), 66, 68, 82, 84–8, 90–1, 94, 100, 109–110, 179n
cruelty to animals (*see also* suffering of animals, and cruel sports): 14, 39, 51, 57–8, 66, 82, 147, 151
   defended as a civil liberty, 109, 114
   definition of, 83, 95–6, 100
   deprivation and, 101–3
   early parliamentary opposition to, 110
   as an indicator of anti-social behaviour, 87–8, 105–6, 113
   Locke on, 88
   and public opinion, 106, 111–2

Daoust, Pierre-Yves, 118, 131 (see also *Daoust Report* and also *Daoust2 Report*)
Daoust Report on sealing, 119–21, 124
Daoust2 Report on sealing, 131–3, 144–5, 191–2n
Darwin, Charles, 47
Davidson, Robert, 28
Declaration of Helsinki, 21
deer, *see* hunting and coursing, and Burns Report
DeGrazia, David, 48, 103
Denmark: fur production in, 97
deontological theories
   and experimentation, 156–8
   and hunting, 86
Department of Fisheries and Oceans (DFO), Canada, 119, 124, 130–2, 139, 144, 145

Descartes, René, 45, 80, 174n
differences between animals and humans, 3–4, chap 1 passim, 40
Dillmann, August, 28
Driver, Samuel Rolles, 28
dog-fighting, 82
Dolly (cloned sheep), 64, 177n
dolphins, 26
Dunstan, G. R., 158

equal consideration of interests (*see also* Singer, Peter), 37, 152
Erskine, Lord, 105, 186n
Esau, 108
Europe
   Amsterdam Treaty: protocol on animal welfare, 140–1, 146, 149
   European Commission and animal welfare, 110–111, 114
   European Union (EU) proposed ban on seal imports, 5
   EU ban on leghold traps, 125–6
   EU ban on seal products (1983), 127–9, 134, 147, 194n
   EU regulations re fur farming, 99
   EU Scientific Committee on Animal Health and Animal Welfare, 102
   humane education in, 67
   hunting with dogs in, 75–6, 155
   meat replacement products in, 67
   production of fur in, 97–8, 113
   proposed ban on fur farming, 112
   public morality ground for EU members states to ban fur farming, 98, 141
   standards of humane killing, 142
   university courses on animals, 6
European Convention on Human Rights, 88
experiments on animals (vivisection), 21, 27, 33, 61, 64, 69–70, 156–7, 166, 171n, 177n, 197n

factory farming, *see* intensive farming
Fairfax, Thomas, 75
Farm Animal Welfare Advisory Committee of the RSPCA (*see also* RSPCA), 52

Farm Animal Welfare Council (FAWC) of the UK government, 83, 101–2, 126, 180n
Farm Livestock Advisory Committee of the RSPCA, 52
Federal Bureau of Investigation, 106
Finland, mink fur production in, 97
Flew, Anthony, 156–7
Foster, Michael, 77
foxes, see hunting and coursing, Burns Report, and chp 4 passim
France, hunting with dogs in, 75–6
French Association of Hunting Packs, 76
Fur Commission USA, 97
fur farming, 4–5, chp 4 passim
    fur production worldwide, 97–8, 155, 182n
    legislation against, 99–100, 182–3n
    methods of killing, 98, 182n
    public opposition to, 112, 114, 188n
    typical conditions, 98
    veterinary objections to, 98–99, 113
fur trapping, 97, 106, 112, 124, 135, 182n

GATT (General Agreement on Tariffs and Trade), 141–4, 146, 147, 149
Genesis, Book of:
    divine covenant in, 14
    divine image in, 28–9
    dominion in, 14, 29, 33
    fall in, 14
    vegetarian diet in, 14
George, Henry, 142
Germany, hunting with dogs in, 75
Godlovitch, Ros, 158–9, 163
Gompertz, Lewis, 109
Grandin, Temple, 126
Great Ape Project, 48
grey squirrels, 68, 178n
Greenland: seal hunting in, 115, 147
Griffin, Donald R., 48
Gross, Heinrich, 28
Gulf of St Lawrence, 116, 117, 130, 135, 139 (see also sealing)
Gunkel, Hermann, 28

Hansard, 78
hares, see hunting and Burns Report

Harrison, Ruth, 56, 176–7n
hedgehogs, 68, 178n
Herder, Johann G., 80
higher-order thought (HOT), 54 (see also rationality)
Hobbes, Thomas, 18–20, 80
Holloway, Richard, 109
Humane Society of the United States (HSUS), 133
Humanitarian League, 105
humanitarian movement of the nineteenth-century, 79, 105, 152, 160, 166
Hume, David, 80
hunting and coursing (see also Burns Report)
    as anti-social behaviour, 87–8, 96
    Aristotle on, 3
    attempt at licensing, 92–4, 96 chp 3 passim
    in comparison with bear-baiting, 110
    with dogs worldwide, 75, 155
    illegal coursing, 86
    Jewish perspective on, 108
    as a means of control, 88–2, 96
    as offending two moral principles, 83–4, 95–6
    preservation of foxes and hares for hunting, 85, 96, 181n
    and public opinion, 112
    UK Hunting Act 2004, 76

Ian, Robinson, 126
Iceland, fur production in, 97
image of God, 5, 28–9, 33, 173n
Image of God, The, 28
India, hunting with dogs in, 75
institutionalisation
    of animal abuse, 4, 43, 57–70, 71, 92–3, 96, 103, 106, 151, 155–8, 166
    of critical awareness, 60–1, 65–8, 72
    of ethical vision, 68–70
intensive farming, 52–3, 68, 69, 103, 106, 112, 184n
International Association for the Study of Pain, 47
International Fund for Animal Welfare (IFAW), 48, 118, 120, 131, 133

Internet, 65
Ireland, hunting in, 76
Irish Masters of Foxhounds Association, 76
Isaiah, Book of, 38
Islam, 108–9, 114, 187n (*see also* Qu'ran)
Institute of Biology, 69
Italy, 75, 99, 113

Janzen, Waldmar, 28
Jones, Alwyn Rice, 109
Jónsson, Guunlaugur A., 28
Jordan Report on sealing, 118
Judaism, 108–9, 114, 174n, 187n

Kant, Immanuel, 80, 86
   on animals as ends and means, 104, 137
   on universal community, 195n
Kenya, hunting with dogs in, 75
killing of animals (*see also* institutiona-
      lisation, and vegetarianism)
   definition of "humane killing," 121
   in Aquinas, 13
   in Augustine, 16
   in fur farming, 98, 100
   in hunting, 81–4, 88–92
   of innocents, 153–4
   morality of, 100, 104, 158–6, 166
   of seals and humane slaughter, 121–7,
      142, 190n
Köhler, Ludwig, 28

Labrador, sealing in, 135, 193n
Landau, Ezekiel, 108
la venerie à cheval, 76
Lavigne, David, 119, 134
Law of Nature and Nations, 72
Leahy, Michael P. T., 19, 187n
Leibniz, G. W., 80
Lewis, C. S., 14, 23, 27, 33
licensing of hunting, 4, 92–4, 96 (*see also*
      Burns Report, and hunting and
      coursing)
Locke, John, 80, 88
Lorenz, Konrad, 47, 53

Macaulay, Thomas Babington, 94

Mallalieu, Baroness, 85
Manichaeans, 16
Marine Mammal Act (US), 141
Marine Mammal Regulations (MMRs),
      117, 120, 127, 129–30, 132, 144, 189n
Martin, Richard, 110, 188n
Mascall, E. L., 25
Masters of Foxhounds Association of
      America (MFHA), 75–6
McFall, John, 77
McLeod, George, 50
McNamara, Kevin, 77
Mead, Lucia Ames, 143
media
   and animal issues, 63–4, 72
   portrayal of animal advocates, 48
metempsychosis, 22
Michael, Alun, 92
Mill, J. S., 62, 80, 86–7
Minister of fisheries and oceans
      (Canada), 116, 121, 129, 139–40, 147
      see also, Department of Fisheries
      and Oceans (DFO)
mink, *see* chp 4 passim
Moltmann, Jürgen, 164
Morley, Elliot, 99, 107
Muhammad, The Prophet, 108
Muskerry Hunt, 76

Nagel, Thomas, 50
Namibia, seal hunting in, 115, 147
Napier, John, 52
Newfoundland, sealing in, 130, 135–6,
Newman, John Henry, 38–40, 173–4n
New Zealand, hunting with dogs in, 75
Nietzsche, Friedrich, 80
Nimon, A. J., 102, 185n
Nimrod, 108
Nöldeke, Theodor, 28
North, Richard D., 107, 184n
Norway (see also *Oslo Fur Auctions*)
   fur production in, 97
   seal hunting in, 115
Nuremberg Code, 21

Ontario Veterinary Medical Association,
      Animal Care Committee of, 133

Orwell, George, 59
Oslo Fur Auctions, 97
Our Dumb Friends' League, 45
Oxford, 1, 5, 38, 45, 56
Oxford Centre for Animal Ethics, 6

pain in animals, *see* sentience, and
    suffering of animals
Paxman, Jeremy, 48
Pediatrics, 153
PETA (People for the Ethical Treatment
    of Animals), 53
Plato, 80
Poland, fur production in, 97–8
Potter, Beatrix, 51
Port Royalists, 46
Portugal, hunting with dogs in, 75
pre-Socratic philosophers, 80, 179n
Primatt, Humphry, 10–11, 13, 15
Proverbs, 14
Psalms, 13, 14
Pufendorf, Samuel, 22–3
Puritans, 94
Putman, Rory, 91

Quebec, sealing in, 135
Qu'ran, 108, 142 (*see also* Islam)

Rachels, James, 87
rationality
    animals as non-rational, 16–8
    animals subject to rational control, 13–6
    in humans compared with animals, 54–5
    lack of, in animal debate, 2–3
    scientific evidence of rationality in
        animals, 165
Raven, Charles, 46
reason, *see* rationality
Regan, Tom, 21, 56
religious slaughter, 93, 180n
Richardson, Mary, 133
Rickaby, Joseph, 46
Ricoeur, Paul, 60
Ridley, Jane, 94
Ringgren, Helmer, 28
Roberts, Peter, 50

Robinson, Neal, 108
Rollin, Bernard, 47, 174n
Rousseau, Jean-Jacques, 80
Royal Commission on Seals and Sealing
    (Canada), 117, 125, 127, 128, 129 (*see
    also* Sealing)
Royal Society for the Prevention of
    Cruelty to Animals (RSPCA,
    formerly SPCA), 52, 80, 86, 108, 109,
    160, 187n
ruddy ducks, 68, 178n
Russia
    fur farming in, 5
    fur production in, 97–8, 113, 155
    invasion of Afghanistan, 63
    seal hunting in, 115

Salt, Henry, 105
Scandinavia, production of fox fur in, 97
Schopenhauer, Artur, 80
Schweitzer, Albert, 36–7
Scotland
    ban on fur farming by Scottish parlia-
        ment, 99–100, 113, 141
    killing of seals in, 116
Scott Henderson Inquiry, 77, 81, 95
sealing, 5, *see also* chp 5 passim, Canada,
    Marine Mammal regulations (MMRs),
    and Royal Commission on Seals and
    Sealing
    by aboriginal peoples, 135–6, 193n
    estimates of seals killed world-wide,
        115, 155
    estimates of seals killed in Canada, 116,
        189n
    humaneness of seal hunt, 117–127,
        147–8, 192n
    killing of seal pups, 127–9, 148
    polling evidence on, 195n
    regulation of hunt, 129–134, 148, 189n
    sealing for survival, 134–6, 148, 192–3n
    seals as economic commodities,
        136–9, 148
    trade embargoes on seal products,
        141–4, 146–7, 149, 194n
sentience of animals (see also *suffering of
    animals*), 9–11, 47–8, 55, 70, 137–8,
    165, 169n

Amsterdam protocol on animals as
sentient beings, 140–1
Simpson Report on sealing, 118
Singer, Peter, 5, 20, 62, 87, 152–5, 156, 158,
163, 166, 173n, 186n, 196n
speciesism, 155
Spedding, C. R. W., 101
South Africa, hunting with dogs in, 75
State Veterinary Service, 50
Straw, Jack, 77
suffering of animals (*see also* animals,
institutionalisation, sentience):
in Burns Report, 81–3, 95
in captivity, 17–8
and children, 32–37, 40
Christ-like suffering, 38–40
compared with human suffering, 9
denied by Cartesianism, 45–6
definition of, 9–10
evidence for sentiency, 47–8
in fur farming, 100–3, 107
in sealing, 117–27, 144, 148–9
minimised by intellectual mechanisms, chp 2 *passim*
philosophical agnosticism about, 50, 53–5
rejection of institutionalised, 155–8, 166
scientific scepticism about, 47, 51–3, 71
uncomprehending, 17–8
undeserving, 24
utilitarian calculations of, 162–3
utilitarian emphasis on, 154–5
Sweden
fur production in, 97
new regulations for mink, 99, 113, 183n

The Animals Issue, 54
The Netherlands (Holland)
ban on fox farming, 99, 113
fur production in, 97–8, 183n
hunting with dogs in, 75
theology (*see also* Christology)
God as the basis of rights, 108, 161–2
objections to fur farming based on, 108–9
theological arguments of the book, 164
theos-rights of animals, 161–2
*The Welfare of Animals Kept for Fur
Production,* 102
Torah, the, 108, *see also* Genesis, book of,
and Judaism

torture, 21
and utilitarian arguments for, 156–8
tsaar baalei hayyim, 108
Tudge, Colin, 52
Turner, Denys, 44
Turner, Jacky, 69

UN Convention on the Rights of the
Child, 32, 58
United Kingdom
ban on bull-baiting, 100
ban on cosmetics experiments, 69
ban on fur farming by Westminster
parliament, 99–100, 113, 141
definition of human killing, 121
dog-fighting illegal in, 82
fur farming in, 4
government siding with pharmaceuti-
cals and animal research, 139
history of animal protection in, 66
Home Office, 69
humane education, 67
Hunting Act 2004, 76
hunting with dogs in, 4, 95 (*see also*
Burns Report)
sale of organic produce and meat
substitutes in, 66
thought control in, 59
and UN Convention of the Rights of
the Child, 32
university courses on animals in, 6
United States
attack on Nicaragua, 63
ban on seal imports, 5, 146–7
cattle slaughter in, 126
foreign policy, 59
fur farming in, 4–5
fur production in, 97–8, 113, 155
government support for hunter
harassment legislation, 139
humane education in, 67
hunting with dogs in, 4, 75–6, 95, 155
Marine Mammal Act (US), 141,
145–7
meat replacement products in, 67
poultry slaughter in, 126
thought control in, 59
university courses on animals, 6
and the war in Vietnam, 44, 63

utilitarianism
  anthropocentric calculation of utilities,
    162–3, 167
  calculation of benefits in hunting,
    93–4, and fur farming, 107
  classical and popular, 61–2, 72, and
    hunting for sport, 86–7, 95–6, and
    justifications for experiments,
    156–8, 197n of Peter Singer, 152–5,
    166, and the tests for
    hunting, 92–4

vegetarianism
  Chomsky on, 177n
  as God's original will, 14–5
  meat replacement products,
    66–7, 72
  moral basis of, 159–60
  plant based protein, 70
violence
  of animal activists, 2, 48, 160

  link between animal abuse and human
    violence, 105–6, 113, 154, 186n, 196n
virtue theories, and hunting for
  sport, 86
Vivisection, see experiments
  on animals
von Rad, Gerhard, 28
Vriezen, Theodorus C., 28

Waite, Terry, 17–8, 170n
Westmoreland,
  General William, 44
Whitehouse, Alec, 55
Wilberforce, William, 105
Williams, Rowan, 109
World Medical Assembly, 21
World Trade Organization (WTO), 5,
  141–3, 146–7, 149

zoos, 17, 68